UNIVERSITY OF MISSOURI STUDIES

VOLUME I

SOCIAL SCIENCE SERIES

PUBLISHED BY THE
UNIVERSITY OF MISSOURI
1905

AS
36
.H679
S7
v.1

THE CLOTHING INDUSTRY
IN NEW YORK

139479

Volume I   **SOCIAL SCIENCE SERIES**

UNIVERSITY OF MISSOURI STUDIES

THE CLOTHING INDUSTRY IN NEW YORK

BY

JESSE ELIPHALET POPE
Professor of Economics and Finance

PUBLISHED BY THE
UNIVERSITY OF MISSOURI
September 1905

Copyright, 1905, by
THE UNIVERSITY OF MISSOURI

COLUMBIA, MO.:
E. W. STEPHENS PUBLISHING COMPANY.
1905

PREFACE

The restriction of this study to the production of men's and children's out-side wearing apparel and to women's cloaks is not based wholly on empirical grounds. The work in these branches is of a fairly homogeneous character and the problems involved arise out of the peculiar circumstances and surroundings to be found associated with this industry. There is also justification for restricting the study to New York, only making mention of other centers in so far as they are able to throw light on the conditions in that city. New York was the pioneer in the clothing industry and it occupies to-day a transcendent position in the industry. The conditions in the industry in New York are fairly typical of the rest of the country and social regulation has been worked out to a much fuller extent there. Confining this study to branches forming a well defined group and restricting it to a rather limited field permits of greater detail and gives a definiteness which could not be attained in a wider survey.

In such a study—in which much of the data must be gotten by personal work in the field—the writer has put himself under obligations to many persons, and it is quite beyond his ability to do more than render a general acknowledgment of such obligations. But he cannot refrain from expressing his deep obligation to Mr. Louis Cohen, who has piloted the writer through many scores of workshops in New York and Brooklyn; to Secretary Walter

Chuck, to John A. Dyche, Secretary of the Ladies' Garment Workers Union and to Ex-secretary Henry White, of the United Garment Workers of America, who have never wearied of the many calls which the writer has made upon their time and patience.

To James Thayer Gerould, librarian in the University of Missouri, who has intimate knowledge of conditions on the East Side of New York, the writer wishes to render grateful acknowledgment of his indebtedness for many valuable criticisms and suggestions as the manuscript was in preparation and also to his colleague Professor Isidor Loeb, who has rendered valuable assistance in the same way and has kindly read the proof.

But above all the writer wishes to acknowledge gratefully his indebtedness to Professor Edward R. A. Seligman at whose suggestion the study was undertaken and who has inspired and encouraged the writer at every stage of its progress.

CONTENTS

PART I

PERIOD BEFORE 1880

CHAPTER I

BEGINNINGS OF THE CLOTHING INDUSTRY

PAGE

No clothing industry prior to the close of the eighteenth century—Possibility of procuring cheap raw material the first step towards its development—Creation of demand for the finished product of this material the second step—The production of ready-made clothing a commercial and a technical process—Standardization—The commercial machinery developed by the traffic in second-hand clothing taken over by the clothing industry—Manufacture of liveries and uniforms a contributor to standardization and the technical processes of production—Manufacture of coarse clothing for laborers and sailors an influence along technical lines—Early employment by this trade of factory methods—Supplying of demands for ready-made clothing first attempted by custom trade—Establishments as early as 1840 exclusively for ready-made clothing—Invention of the sewing machine the cause of an enormous increase in the production—Division of labor.................. 1

CHAPTER II

SYSTEMS OF PRODUCTION AND EMPLOYMENT

The custom trade known as the retail, the ready-made as the wholesale trade—The wholesale manufacturer the organizing and centralizing force in production—Warehouses established for preparation of cloth and for marking—Coats made up largely in outside shops not owned by manufacturer—Pants and vests made up in inside shops under manufacturer's supervision—Machine operating and simpler needlework done by: *a*) women at home, *b*) young girls in employer's shop—Early employment of women to make cloaks under inside system—Intervention of contractor between manufacturer and journeymen for the purpose of the employment of cheaper labor—Manufacture from raw material by journeymen of clothing to be sold at retail or to jobbers—Such producers not able to learn the demands of the consumer—Division of labor as to: *a*) product, 1) each part of suit made by a distinct class of workmen, 2) higher grade of garments made by some manufacturers, cheaper lines by others, women's garments by others; *b*) technical processes of manufacture, 1) in warehouses, work divided among foremen, designers, cutters, trimmers, 2) in outside shops, among operators, finishers, pressers, 3) in inside shops, among operators, basters, finishers, pressers—The introduction of machinery essential to the development of the industry....... 14

CHAPTER III

Wages and Conditions of Employment

Movement of Wages—By 1880 cutting process controlled by Irish, the other technical processes by Germans, commercial processes by English, a few Irish, and the Jews—Operating, button-hole making, felling, and basting, the principal functions of female labor—Pitiable condition of women who made garments at home—Condition improved when they confined their efforts to finishing—A few children employed to pull bastings, sew on buttons, etc., a very few as operators, and many to run errands—Level of money wages slightly higher in 1880 than in 1860—Taking into account: *a*) a decline in prices of food products, *b*) a rise in rents from 1860 to 1872, then a decline by 1878, level of real wages in 1872 was somewhat higher, and in 1878 decidedly higher, than in 1860—*Hours of Labor*—Number of hours worked each week in ready-made clothing trade approximately the same as in custom trade but work more evenly distributed through week—Decided degree of variation from season to season in both—Long hours in ill-ventilated rooms wrought a terrible hardship—*Sanitary Conditions*—Ready-made clothing manufactured principally in poorest homes of city by low type of people—The providing of proper sanitation and regulation not attempted by the city—Conditions became still worse when: *a*) introduction of machine increased size of working unit, *b*) tenement houses appeared—Outrageous conditions from 1870 to 1880—In inside shop conditions somewhat better—Strength of women operators and pressers overtaxed—*Conclusion*—During this period the number of manufacturing establishments for ready-made and custom made clothing had more than doubled—Their capitalization had nearly quadrupled—Laborers employed in 1880 more than twice as many as in 1860 and more than three times as much money received in wages—Factory product in the period shows an increase of about six hundred per cent...... 27

PART II

PERIOD FROM 1880 TO THE PRESENT

CHAPTER I

Personnel of the Workers: Nationality, Sex, and Age

Enormous numbers of Jewish immigrants into New York early in this period—A large proportion of these, young men—Majority of newcomers absorbed by clothing industry because: *a*) Jewish employers restricted to this, *b*) immigrants lacked capital and physical strength but were dexterous, *c*) the occupation did not interfere with their religious customs—Growth of contract system due to Jewish preference and necessity—Jewish contractors had immediate supervision over the work of the immigrants—Jews crowded the Irish into upper ranks of the industry, the Germans into other occupations—Introduction about 1890 of Italians because they were not in trade unions and represented a cheaper grade of labor than the Jews—At first, only women who did finishing in their homes—Later, operators and pressers in shops—A few Lithuanians in large shops—Decrease in number of women workers since 1888 due to: a) Jewish custom, b) decline of large outside shop and family system, c) cheap immigrant labor—Decrease checked of late years by growth of the larger shop and division of labor—Prejudice of the Jews was against child labor—From 1880 to 1890 increase of child labor in German shop owing to Jewish competition, but child labor practically absent from the clothing industry........................ 45

CHAPTER II

Systems of Production and Employment

Manufacturer in charge of commercial processes and of cutting—Contractor responsible for manufacture, closely supervising workers and working with them—Small contract system able to: a) produce large product in a unit of time, b) adjust itself to a highly fluctuating demand—Up to 1895 coats manufactured under team system with its superior division of labor—For sake of cheaper labor team system modified by introduction of "second" operators, etc., for production of medium and low grade goods—Team unity, section work, supplanted by shop unity—Better grades made under Boston system where each worker learned one minute process—Division of labor not minute in cloak manufacture—For pants and vests division of labor still remains simple—Section system used for children's jackets—Efficiency of machinery improved greatly since 1880, more by perfecting of machines then in use than by introduction of new machines.............. 61

CHAPTER III

Movement of Wages

Decline in nominal wages from 1873 and succeeding rebound up to 1880 practically paralleled by movement in prices of standard commodities—In family system wages lower but family income maintained by increasing work of women and children—Since the eighties a pronounced movement in the direction of more steady employment and higher wages except possibly among cloakmakers—Pressure brought by labor unions to equalize length of workingday and so lengthen season of production—Through a widely extended market manufacturers enabled to make up goods for different sections of country at different times—Dull season still important, varying from two to five months—Large immigration has not glutted labor market in clothing industry because of: *a*) rapid growth of demand for ready-made clothing, *b*) Jewish use of this industry as stepping-stone to something higher, *c*) growing capacity of employer to pay higher wages which was made effective by trade unions and state regulation—This capacity due to superior organization of industry and to an increase in product in a unit of time on account of improved: *a*) machinery, *b*) division of labor, *c*) skill of laborer—Compensation of contractor not unduly high—Tendency of competition among contractors to force down wages—This evil mitigated by: *a*) contractors becoming persons of larger responsibility, *b*) assuming by manufacturers of such responsibilities as guaranteeing payment of wages—In same grade of work wages the same in outside as in inside shop—Tendency of the decentralized method of production, the contract system, towards non-organized conditions among workers—Sensitiveness of market in clothing industry an important factor in counteracting this tendency—Union demands as to wages impossible of fulfilment in dull season—Hence, manufacturers' manifesto declaring for the open shop 79

CHAPTER IV

Systems of Wage Payment

Under the piece system of estimating, amount received in constant adjustment with product turned out—Under time system wages in a unit of time unchanged, though there be slight changes in product—Either system distinct from the other seldom found—Piece wages most applicable to those industries where there is regularity in processes—This preferred by employers and by skilled laborers—Attitude of all but most advanced trade unions usually hostile to this system—Since 1901 only a minimum set by trade unions in time system so this system has now greater favor with employers than formerly—The "task system" combines piece system and time system: weekly wages paid, but a certain "task" must be performed each day—This is not necessarily connected with team system—Persistent opposition by trade unions on the grounds that lower wages, greater intensity, and longer hours prevail—But, in dull season, workers under task system have more to eat and wear than those under time and piece systems—Long hours not forced on workers by task system—To-day tasks only nominally large.......... 122

CHAPTER V

Conditions of Employment: Hours and Sanitation

Hours—Working day excessively long in outside shops until early nineties—Shorter and more regular hours brought about by: *a*) general betterment, *b*) trade unions—Sanitation—A twofold interest in conditions under which workers live, first, as regards worker himself; second, as regards the industry—Growing density of population in early eighties—Three types of buildings—The small shanties the most unsanitary —These rapidly disappeared after 1880—Conditions in remodeled houses worse than in other tenements—

THE CLOTHING INDUSTRY IN NEW YORK   XV

Many of the abuses corrected after 1887—Early tenements erected without regard to sanitation—Conditions improved by legislation—Conditions of manufacture bad up to 1892—First regulation, the Board of Health Act of 1892—Work in home restricted to immediate members of family—Permits for such work granted after inspection—All clothing so manufactured to be tagged—The Factory Acts of 1892 applied these same regulations as to permits and tagging also to tenement house shops and rear shops—Great decrease in tenement work after 1892—In 1897 tenement house work restricted to immediate members of family—Since then tenement house work not an important factor—Buildings behind tenements still used—Manufacturers made more cautious in giving out work by public lists of contractors and places in which work was done—Law of 1899 provided for the inspection and licensing of home workers but permitted the employment of outside workers—Despite more thorough inspection and higher standards a decreasing number of licenses revoked—Present danger from contagion insignificant—Law of 1904 re-established prohibition of employment of others than members of the family in home—This law made entire building the unit of inspection—Improved conditions in small contract shops outside of tenements since 1897 due to: *a*) better enforcement of existing laws, *b*) general advance of the industry—Carelessness of workers often responsible for such evils as poor ventilation—This and poor lighting offset by decrease in hours—Better conditions in large contractors' shops and inside shop.................. 138

CHAPTER VI

Income and Expenditures

The minimum as compared with the maximum yearly income—Earnings of wife and children important—Table of expenditures for families with minimum income in New York and in the United States—Rent burdensome to East Side workers—Exodus to Brooklyn—Gain in rent and surroundings offset by carfare and loss of time—In winter advantages in items of fuel and lighting with the New York workers—Their expenditure for clothing smaller, for food, larger—Smaller per cent of their income left for miscellaneous expenses—Access to free hospitals, amusements, etc.—Few deposits for old age—Recent increase in old line insurance—Insurance side of trade unions in its infancy—Leading form of insurance fraternal—Bond of union either religious or local—Recent formation of societies with other bonds—A typical life history—Irregularity of employment causes: *a*) reduced yearly income, *b*) demoralization of workmen, *c*) suffering during the dull season 172

CHAPTER VII

Regulation

A national committee appointed in 1892 to investigate conditions—National regulation recommended—Refusal of congress to pass a law of regulation—Massachusetts provided that garments brought into that state for sale be inspected during manufacture and tagged if infected—Consequent decrease in amount of clothing made up in New York tenements—New York forced to regulate such manufacture—Impossible to determine condition of clothing bought ready-made from merchants outside of state—Arguments for national regulation: *a*) danger of infection, *b*) lack of uniformity—Danger of infection practically stamped out by state and local authorities—Uniform conditions can come only through voluntary state cooperation and the creation of a saner public opinion—Manufacturers of to-day establish a high minimum of conditions—The trade union label a particular phase of regulation on the part of labor—It appeals to the consumer on the ground of: *a*) self-interest in conditions of

THE CLOTHING INDUSTRY IN NEW YORK   xvii

manufacture, *b*) social interest, *c*) direct interest in the class that is pushing the label—Failure of executive officers to enforce union demand that label be granted only to firms which have inside shops, give out no work to be done in the home, and do no jobbing—Label stands for a union shop and usually, but not always, such a shop is superior to a non-union one—The influence of the label not important nor enduring—Regulation due to the gradual evolution of social forces—The label of the Consumers' League a phase of regulation on the part of the public—The activity of this league is: *a*) to bring about the enforcement of existing laws, *b*) to suggest new laws and agitate for their enactment, *c*) to investigate work places and establish a standard known as a fair house............ 189

CHAPTER VIII

Trade Unions

No trade union activity except among the cutters in the early years of the clothing industry—Trade union growth hindered by: *a*) large mass of unskilled labor, *b*) lack of development of the industry, *c*) decentralization of the workers, *d*) their attitude towards the trade union idea, *e*) seasonal character of the industry, *f*) furnishing of numerous accessories of manufacture by the workers, *g*) immigration—Trade union growth helped by: *a*) homogeneity of the workers, *b*) their comparatively high order of intelligence, *c*) sympathetic and fair attitude, on the whole, of the employers, *d*) contract system—Steps of organization: *a*) local unions, *b*) organizations comprising the various divisions of a given branch, *c*) district councils, *d*) Knights of Labor until United Garment Workers of America was organized and gained control over the industry—The small local the unit in early times—Uniformity in the trade grew with the centralizing of authority—Now the consent of the General Executive Board necessary for any large strike—Liberal policy

ii.

in regard to entrance to the trade—Difficulties in the way of regulating overtime: *a*) irregularity in the trade, *b*) peculiar economic position of the worker, *c*) decentralization—Employers forced by unions to furnish the accessories of manufacture—No consistent policy regarding the system of work—Of late less opposition to the piece system—Many strikes caused by attempts to adjust wages at the beginning of the busy seasons—Usually successful and the cause of small loss in the industry—Frequent failure of strikes against piece work and contract system—Union has sought to hold contractors for damages in case of breach of contract—Legality of such contracts not yet determined by the courts—Recent universal agitation for an eight hour day—The Rochester strike—The question of the open shop—The Philadelphia strike—Proposed labor bureau of the Manufacturers' Association—Resolutions adopted by the Association against: *a*) the closed shop, *b*) limiting apprentices, *c*) restriction of output—Deep resentment on the part of the union caused by: *a*) posting of these resolutions, *b*) card of the labor bureau—Inability of labor and capital to come to an agreement—A strike was called—Cutters and tailors act in cooperation—Numbers engaged in the strike—Strike a failure—*Analysis of These Facts*—Return to earlier conditions not desired by manufacturers—Economic and social pressure would not permit it—The New York Association opposed not to the union but to the abuses of the union—The hope of the union found in: *a*) public opinion, *b*) attitude of the Clothiers' Association of New York City—The referendum vote the greatest handicap under which trade unions labor—Formerly the activity of the union largely confined to the development and education of its members—Its policy now becoming more militant................ 211

CHAPTER IX

The Sweating System

Clothing industry and sweating closely associated—Modern use of the term due largely to Kingsley—Origin of the term sweating—Causes offered by Kingsley are superficial—Other writers have followed his footsteps—Charles Booth the first writer to get at the real causes—The conditions which constitute sweating are well defined—Society on the basis of development and adjustment falls into well defined classes: *a*) the defective—those lacking power to maintain a normal standard of living, *b*) those who are developed but out of adjustment, *c*) those retarded in development and incapable of perfect adjustment, *d*) those who are developed and in adjustment—The causes which are responsible for such classes—Our chief concern is with the third class—Analysis applied to the clothing industry—Workers in the early years of the industry belonged to the first class—These were succeeded by the Jews who fall in the third class—From 1880 to 1890 conditions in the clothing industry were frightful—Since 1890 movement has been toward better conditions—The growing power of society to cope with bad conditions precludes a return to them—Sweating evils to some extent due to cosmic forces and therefore beyond control of society—Causes, within the control of society—The characteristic features of modern industry: *a*) the world market, *b*) capitalistic production, *c*) centralized direction of industry, *d*) industrial classes giving rise to the industrial community—Not all these characteristics peculiar to modern industry—Wherever these features are present we have the factory system—May have the factory system without the factory—Definition of a factory—Clothing industry is carried on under the factory system—Factory system socializes industry but factory permits of further socialization—Work outside the factory gives opportunity for certain abuses—Home workers are at a disadvantge when competing with superior systems of production—Home work in city makes for more unfavorable conditions than in smaller centers—Abuses more likely where home work is primary source of income—Contractor said to be responsible for many abuses known as sweating—Abuses due to small employer rather than to the contractor—Passion for cheapness and sweating—No necessary connection between price of the commodity and the conditions under which it is made—Conclusion..................... 256

CHAPTER X

Conclusion

New York City the chief center for the manufacture of the better grades of clothing because it is: *a*) the center of fashion, *b*) able to secure labor, *c*) an important port of entry for the raw material, *d*) a great manufacturing center, *e*) a depot for vast quantities of merchandise—New York City's great disadvantage is the item of rent—Decline of clothing manufacture in New England due to: *a*) changed conditions of manufacture, *b*) demands of the labor unions—Small towns usually manufacture cheaper grades—Differences between American and European clothing decreasing—Foreign competition in cloaks important—Growing intimacy between the lower branch of the custom trade and the upper branch of the clothing industry—Attempted mapping out by the unions of the respective fields of the two branches—Jews deserve most credit for the development of the industry—The commercial processes will probably remain in their hands—What the industry has done for the workers in it and for the masses 288

BIBLIOGRAPHY OF THE SOURCES CITED.................. 295

APPENDIXES.

APPENDIX A. Statistics of clothing industry in chief centers 303
APPENDIX B. Circulars sent out by trade unions........ 304
APPENDIX C. Miscellaneous notices 307
APPENDIX D. Agreements 308
APPENDIX E. Scale of Prices 318
INDEX 323

THE CLOTHING INDUSTRY IN NEW YORK

PART I

PERIOD BEFORE 1880

CHAPTER I

Beginnings of the Clothing Industry

Prior to the close of the eighteenth century, when the great inventions wrought a revolution in the manufacture of textiles, the procuring of the raw material for clothing was a slow and comparatively costly process. Only the favored few were enabled to satisfy the requirements of comfort and decency, while for the masses clothing sufficient even for an approach to comfort was often out of the question.

Despite the fact that the introduction of machinery made it possible to supply an abundance of raw material at a cost that would bring it practically within the reach of all, half a century went by before its fruits began to be realized in so far as outer wearing apparel was concerned, and the industry of furnishing such apparel did not become of great importance till almost an entire century had elapsed.

While the ability to procure a cheap raw material was of prime importance and was the first great step toward the development of the clothing industry,[1] other obstacles had to be removed before advantage could be taken of it. There was, it is true, an enormous increase in the demand for textile products, but the increased consumption was not so much in raw material for clothing, as it was in the lighter textiles, women's dress-goods, linen fabrics, etc. The product of the textile mill also took the place of homespun, and cotton was substituted for wool. While these changes all made for better standards of comfort and decency no radical change took place in the variety and quality of clothing consumed.[2] The reasons for this tardy development are social rather than economic. For the expansion of the demand for clothing, cheapness was of first importance, and this depends on a wide consumption. At the time of the industrial revolution, there was little demand for ready-made clothing; the masses regarded other than everyday working clothes as articles of luxury. The expensive suit of the custom tailor was worn only on holidays and special occasions, and one such suit often did service for a lifetime. The two great classes in society were the well-to-do upper class, who of course patronized the custom tailor, and the great mass of manual wage earners whose chief demand was, as we have indicated above, for coarse working clothes. Between these classes was a comparatively small number of persons engaged as servants, attaches, etc., of the upper classes, who usually wore livery, the

[1] The term "clothing industry" will be used throughout this study to mean, manufacture of ready-made outside wearing apparel, other than costumes for laborers.

[2] The beginning of the manufacture of material for clothing on a large scale dates from about 1850.

product of the custom tailor or of the tailor regularly employed by the master[3]; but who also, were sometimes clothed in the discarded garments of their superiors.

The last twenty-five years of the eighteenth century and the first fifty of the nineteenth, are characterized politically by the growth of democracy, and industrially by a growth and wide extension of wealth which made possible a corresponding expansion of wants. To minister to these new wants there was gradually formed a new class, distinct from the manual wage earning class, possessing a higher standard of living and engaged in what are considered to be more polite occupations. The vast army of public school teachers, the clerks and persons engaged in the multifarious details of transportation and commerce, are examples of people who constitute this class. Their income is not greatly above that of manual laborers, but their vocation requires better clothing. They differ from the manual laborers in that a neat and tasty dress is a requisite of their calling, and are yet similar to that class in that their incomes will not permit them to patronize the expensive custom tailors. Cheapness, and at the same time a certain elegance, are to them prime requirments. Accordingly with the appearance of this class, the clothing industry entered upon a second phase of development.

The consumption of ready-made clothing has gradually extended downward to the manual laboring class, as well as upward into the professional and capitalistic classes, going not only where it has created a new demand, but also rivaling and supplanting the custom branch. The mechanical triumphs of

[3] In the olden time the custom was to have tailors in every retinue. Galton, The tailoring trade, p. 44.

the industrial revolution made possible a cheap raw material; its social and economic triumphs created a demand for the finished products of this material. With these two conditions, time only was needed for the satisfaction of the demand and the extension of the industry.

Production as a whole, the processes involved in furnishing the consumer a finished product, falls into two well defined divisions, the technical processes and the commercial processes. Under the former, are included the mechanical operations of fabrication through which the raw material passes before it assumes its final form. Under the latter are included such operations as buying the raw material and placing the finished product on the market, and also of adjusting production both as to quality and quantity to meet the demands of the consumer.

The relative importance of the technical and commercial processes varies with the nature of the product. Where commodities appeal to individual tastes or idiosyncracies or where they undergo no change in the hands of the consumer, the commercial processes become of very great importance; manufacturers of the raw material must be informed as to what particular style the consumer is going to demand and in what quantity; the manufacturers who make up this raw material must be acquainted with the particular style which will be in vogue, and since each unit of the product must meet such peculiar requirements of individuals as to form, size, etc., it is necessary that they possess intimate and detailed information of what in general terms is known as the market.

The production of ready-made clothing is an excellent example of an industry possessing the characteristics enumerated above —— an industry, in which the commercial processes are very important.

If, however, each individual consumer demanded a separate style, or if no two consumers were approximately of the same form and size, the task of anticipating the demand would be impossible, and order production would be the rule. As a matter of fact a few determine the style for the many and while individuals possess peculiar characteristics as to form and size, they fall nevertheless into well defined classes which conform to certain types. Of course, the more minute the classification and the greater the number of ascertained types, the more perfectly does the product conform to the demands of each individual. The determination of these classes and the establishment of corresponding types is known as the process of standardization. It is at once evident that this problem of standardization in the clothing industry is all important. In so far as it has to do with ascertaining the nature of the wants of the consumer, it belongs to the commercial processes, but in so far as it involves the application of ascertained data in such a way that the product shall conform to them, it is in the realm of the technical division of production.

The high degree of perfection which obtains to-day in the various processes involved in the production of clothing has not been attained without experimentation. Many of the problems were peculiar to the industry and had to be solved as they arose independently of outside aid, but the industry has taken over much knowledge and experience which had been acquired in the manufacture of outside wearing apparel in general, from the traffic in second-hand or cast off clothing, from the manufacture of liveries and uniforms for servants and soldiers, from the manufacture of coarse clothing for workingmen and sailors, and finally, from the custom or order trade. What these contributions were and to what extent each of these branches contributed, we shall now attempt to point out.

The traffic in second-hand clothing is an old one. Previous to the industrial revolution, when material was scarce and costly and before the clothing industry, as we now know it, had developed, such clothing found a ready market and was a decided boon to a large class of society. Depots for the renovation and distribution of such clothing existed in all parts of Europe in the eighteenth century, and its importance at a later time is indicated by Senior's statement, made in 1836 that "In this Country the poor are, to a great extent, clothed with garments originally provided for their superiors."[4] He considered this fact of so much importance that he shaped the theory of expenditure which he put forth, by reference to it. Under modern conditions the relative importance of this industry has declined, and the use of this class of clothing now falls to a more indigent and less respectable part of society. Those who carry on the traffic in it are also, perhaps, of a lower order than the average merchant and the extent and importance of the business may be underestimated; but to-day large quantities of this class of clothing are still shipped from the larger cities, and find a ready market in the West and South. In New York City many men, immigrants, who are too old to find employment in the higher branches, are engaged in repairing and renovating such clothing preparatory to its shipment. Certain streets in the lower part of the city are almost entirely given over to its sale at retail.

In the United States, prior to the Civil War, the trade in second-hand clothing was perhaps more important than that in

[4] Treatise on political economy, London, 1850, p. 172.

ready-made. The product was consumed largely in the West and South, the greater part finding its way to the plantation. Advertisements for such clothing are frequent in the daily metropolitan press; in the New York Herald of May, 1863, twenty such advertisements appear. The majority of these advertisements are for clothing destined for the Southern and Western markets, but a number of them offer it for sale in New York at retail.

The traffic in second-hand clothing has always been an object of ridicule and contempt, and it is therefore, not strange that it should be included among the few industries in which the Christians permitted the Jews to engage. In the advertisements just alluded to, it is significant that all the advertisers but two have Jewish names, but what is of more importance is the fact that many of these dealers advertise that they also handle new ready-made clothing.[5] This new clothing which was sold in connection with the second-hand was a cheap—a "slop" product, thrown on the market by jobbers,[6] and its direct bearing on the development of the clothing industry was not important. Its indirect bearing, however, was of significance; for in this way the Jews, the race which later dominated the industry, gained a foothold, and afterwards exerted an influence out of all proportion to their numbers on the well-being of large numbers

[5] In a New York Herald during the spring of 1863, there is a want advertisement calling for $8,000.00 worth of new and cast-off clothing for the Western trade; during the same time there are advertisements in the same paper of twenty-five firms who are handling both second-hand and ready-made clothing.

[6] The sentiment against this class of clothing was shown as early as 1846. At that time Western dealers were careful to state that their goods were not the product of jobbers. Advertisement of St. Louis firm in Jefferson Inquirer, March 25, 1846.

of immigrants of their own stock. On the market side the influence of the traffic in second-hand clothing was direct and important. The commercial machinery thus developed was, when the time arrived, taken over by the clothing industry, and many who had received experience and training in its working passed over with it into the clothing industry.

As second-hand clothing was placed on the market practically in the same form in which it came into the hands of the dealer, it contributed little or nothing to the technical processes of production. It is also evident that it threw no light upon the problem of standardization.

When the modern state began to depend upon the standing army, it was forced to furnish clothing for its soldiers, and for this purpose government workshops were founded. This early manufacture of uniforms has little or no direct bearing upon the clothing industry as that industry had not yet appeared. But at a later date, when the clothing industry was in its infancy, such manufacture must have exerted a very important influence. The first and most important contribution was to the solution of the problem of standardization. The thousands of measurements which were accumulated in meeting the demands of the soldiers, furnished data for meeting similar demands of consumers of ready-made clothing.

The government also introduced a more minute division of labor into its workshops, employing labor that had not served a regular apprenticeship, and in general introducing factory methods. This was true even of the early workshops; it was very markedly true of those workshops which existed at the time the clothing industry took its rise. When the demand for government orders slackened, these factories often turned their attention to the manufacture of clothing for civilians; thus it is seen that the manufacture of soldiers' uniforms contributed largely to the technical processes of production.

The influence of the American Civil War upon the clothing industry deserves particular attention. The sudden demand for uniforms brought into existence a large industry, solely given over to their manufacture. In New York the manufacture of such clothing during the war was probably of more importance than the manufacture of ready-made clothing for civilians. Despite this fact, however, a large amount of army clothing was bought in Prague and Vienna. The knowledge and experience gained from the manufacture of this clothing, particularly along technical lines and in the problem of standardization, gave an immense impetus to the industry, and the years immediately following the war were marked by its rapid expansion and growth. Previous to the war, the industry had steadily, though slowly, expanded.

The manufacture of coarse working clothes involves no great difficulty, and the industry of making clothes for laborers soon came to be important after the production of cheap raw material became possible. In France this industry dates from the early years of the last century. A. Picard states that one of the earliest of these establishments was known as La Belle Jardinière, which was founded in Paris by M. Parrisot, in 1826.[7] Such establishments were founded in other large centers in France. In the United States, as the masses of the population were engaged in agriculture, the demand for such clothing was not large. Establishments, however, grew up in the early part

[7] Picard, A., Rapport général de l' exposition universelle de 1889 à Paris. Paris, 1891-92, V. p. 554.

of the century which made clothing for sailors and for negroes on the Southern plantations. A. Picard states that M. Parrisot after the first eight years improved his product and began to make clothing which deserves to be classed with ready-made clothing proper. In England this transition from the manufacture of working clothes to that of ready-made clothing was common; in the United States we have been unable to discover any account of manufacturers of laborers' clothing eventually turning their attention to the higher product. Since the making of ready-made garments in this country was largely influenced by tailors from England, the influence which the making of laborers' clothes had upon the industry came from English sources. Such influence was largely along technical lines for as in the case of military clothing, factory methods were employed at an early date in the establishments engaged in making laborers' clothes.

The development of the clothing industry is most intimately associated with the custom trade. At a very early date, master tailors began to make clothing for unknown consumers, although by so doing they incurred the hostility of the journeymen, who felt that the increased use of such clothing would make it more difficult for them to become masters. A champion of the journeymen, writing in 1681, says:

"Concerning taylers and others being salesmen. This is another thing that doth add to the great number of shop-keepers, *which was never wont to be formerly*; for although a merchant tayler is a very ancient trade, yet it is supposed that either they themselves did transport those garments that they made, for which reason they were called merchants as well as taylers; or else they sold many garments together by wholesale to them that did transport them; *but not one single garment at a time as now our salesmen do; for if so, then there would have been many of this trade in London, long before the memory of man now living, but it's otherwise, for many remember when there were no new garments sold in London as now there are, only old garments at second-hand."* *

The times were not ripe for the growth of the consumption of ready-made clothing, and its manufacture remained of comparatively small importance. But when the demand for ready-made clothing made its appearance, it was the custom trade that was the first to attempt to supply it.

The disadvantages under which the custom tailor labored, in furnishing a cheap product, are apparent. The division of labor was such that it precluded the employment of the cheaper grades, and therefore the cost of his was high. He was at a marked disadvantage in buying. He could use only small quantities of suiting and it was necessary that he should keep a large variety. His season was a short one [8] and this fact tended to keep wages high and made it essential that he should receive large profits during the working period. When the custom tailor discovered that there was a demand for cheaper clothing, he began to employ his journeymen during the dull season in making up left-over suiting. Gradually he extended his operations, and soon began to purchase raw material which was to be worked up during the slack season, and this line of his business soon became quite as important as the regular order trade. The master was content with smaller profits and the journeymen with lower wages. The garments themselves

* Galton, The tailoring trade, p. xvii.

[8] The third annual report of the Massachusetts bureau of labor, 1871-2, p. 83, gives the period of work in the custom trade as twenty-four weeks in the year, but states that in many cases the period was even shorter.

were inferior in workmanship to those of the order trade, and therefore, it was possible to place them on the market at a greatly reduced price. This close association of the custom trade and the clothing industry during its early period is shown in the advertisements of ready-made clothing. In an advertisement in the New York Herald, December 28, 1842, the announcement is made that J. H. Sikes, 35 Maiden Lane, sells ready-made clothing and keeps a special cutter for orders.

By the year 1840 the clothing industry had become firmly established and while it was usually carried on in connection with the custom trade, establishments were appearing which gave their entire attention to it. Large quantities of clothing began to be distributed throughout the chief cities,[9] St. Louis being the chief distributing center for the West, and New Orleans for the South.

The invention of the sewing machine in 1846 revolutionized the methods of manufacture, and the production of all classes of ready-made wearing apparel began to increase at an enormous rate. The custom trade itself was attempting to meet the changing conditions by introducing cheaper labor. There had been little division of labor and therefore a high degree of skill was required, which demanded a long apprenticeship on the part of the journeymen. In other industries, apprenticeship had broken down and the same tendency was at work in the cloth-

---

[9] Spring and summer clothing manufactured in New York was offered for sale in St. Louis as early as 1842. Jefferson Inquirer, May 5, 1842.

In the same paper for March 25, 1846, the firm of C. & T. Lewis advertised that they were selling clothing both at wholesale and retail; they also stated that their clothing was made in New York and that they kept two thousand hands constantly employed.

ing industry. The tailor began to take his work to his home, where he was assisted by his wife and daughters in those processes requiring little skill. At first, this female labor belonged inside the ranks of the craft, but later women were employed who formerly had had no connection with it. Thus, as the work on waistcoats and trousers was for the most part unskilled, nearly the whole of it came to be done by women sewing in their homes.[10]

Before the clothing industry became differentiated from the custom trade, the introduction of unskilled labor had reached such a stage that three distinct grades of clothing, based on the manner in which the manufacture was carried on, were recognized. The best was that made in the inside shop where the tailor worked on the master's premises. A second grade was made by the tailor who took the work from the shop of the master and made it up at home with the assistance of his wife and children. The third grade was given to contractors, who in turn either let it out to be done at the home of the worker, or had it made up in their own workshops. This last grade represents, of course, a long step toward the use of cheaper labor. And as the clothing industry developed and became of more relative importance it fell more and more into the hands of the makers of the second and third grades of clothing.

---

[10] Galton, The tailoring trade, pp. 103, 191, notes the appearance of women in the custom trade. Galton, quoting from the London Times, 1834, says: "Women have long made trousers and waist-coats, but were now being employed to make coats also." Ibid., p. lxxxvii.

CHAPTER II

Systems of Production and Employment

In the custom tailoring trade, as far back as the early years of the eighteenth century, large numbers of journeymen had become permanent wage workers. The industry was centralized in the hands of the master tailors who possessed large capital and had become accustomed to production on a large scale. With the growth of the clothing industry in the nineteenth century many of the master tailors turned their attention to it, and in time the product of the new industry surpassed that of the old. Even though the same individual conducted both lines, there soon came about a complete differentiation between them. The custom trade was known as the retail, the ready-made as the wholesale trade, and the master tailors in the new industry soon became known as wholesale manufacturers. As the clothing industry increased in importance, there appeared wholesale manufacturers who gave their entire attention to it, having given up the custom trade or never having been engaged in it.

The wholesale manufacturer provided the capital and brains of the business, and was the organizing and centralizing force in production in both the technical and the commercial processes. He sold at wholesale either to middlemen or jobbers, or throughout the country by means of his own agents. He also sold at retail, establishing shops in the large centers immediately under his own supervision. In the custom trade the preparation of the cloth and cutting were done in the shop furnished by the master tailor, the journeyman taking the material to his home or shop to make it up. The same methods of work were employed in the wholesale industry. Large accommodations were necessary and the warehouse was established. To it the workers went for the material already cut and marked for putting together.

On completion of the work the garments were returned to the warehouse, and if the work met the approval of the foreman the price agreed upon was paid. This system, where the tailor worked in his home, in a room rented in coöperation with fellow tailors, or in a contractor's shop, the two latter places being known as outside shops, was known as the outside system. In some cases, however, the master tailor employed workmen in his own shop and when he became a wholesaler the custom was often continued. Such shops were known as inside shops.

As we have pointed out, the real cause for the appearance of the outside shop in the custom trade was the pressure for cheaper labor, particularly, the labor of the journeyman's family. The invention of the sewing machine at this time merely accentuated the division of labor which had already appeared. In the custom trade it increased the relative number of outside shops as the work of operating[1] was done more and more by the wives and daughters of the tailors. Only the higher grades of the order trade were manufactured without the aid of the machine, the cheaper grades being made under conditions identical with those of the clothing industry, at least, so far as coats were concerned. The central figure in both branches was the skilled tailor who was responsible for all the

---

[1] By "operating" is meant, sewing on the machine. The person who does the sewing is known as the operator.

work on the garment and who did all the work except the easier operating and simpler needlework which, as we have said, were done by the members of the family. We have called attention to the fact that trousers and waistcoats[2] were mostly made by women; first, by women inside the tailors' family, and afterwards by those outside the ranks of the tailors' craft. The machine was at once widely used by women for the manufacture of these garments, and the work fell almost exclusively to them. These women workers may be divided into two classes. First, those having household duties, widows, and unfortunates of one sort or another; and, second, young women. The former had sewed by hand before the introduction of the machine, and now, where it was possible, they purchased machines and continued working at home. The young women, however, not being able to purchase machines, went to work in the workshop of the employer, who furnished the machines.[3] In some cases, it is true, even the other class of women, where they could leave their homes, worked in the shop of the employer, and there were cases where girls owning their machines, carried on the work in the shop of the employer.

It appears that in the making of coats the outside system prevailed, while pants and vests were largely made up under the inside system. Previous to the invention of the sewing machine many women had found employment in their homes making

[2] Pants and vests are terms used in the clothing industry, and correspond to trousers and waistcoats in the custom trade.

[3] In the New York Herald for 1863 there are a number of advertisements for operators, some with and some without machines. Aug. 1, 1863; "Wanted fifty first-class operators, with or without machines." Aug. 3, "Wanted operators for Wheeler and Wilson machines, operators to have their own machines."

articles of wearing apparel such as undergarments, men's shirts, women's skirts, etc. The invention of the machine gave an immense impetus to this manufacture, and many large inside shops sprang up in which the workers were almost exclusively female. Cloaks had been largely imported from France and it was not until just previous to the Civil War that their manufacture began to be of importance in this country. The traditions behind men's clothing in the custom trade favored the skilled male workman, and the chief influence was English. In women's garments the tradition was that of the woman tailoress, and the chief influence was French. In the early years of the cloak industry the retailer employed a French tailoress to do the cutting and to have general supervision over the workers,[4] who were largely women. The employer usually furnished the workplace. With the expansion of the cloak trade many establishments, that before had been engaged in making the wearing apparel to which we have already alluded, extended their operations to include cloaks, and many workers in these lines shifted to the better paying and more skilled field. The fact that the cloak industry had behind it a tradition of unskilled female labor, unprejudiced against the factory, coupled with the fact that many of the workers were young women who could not easily furnish their own workplace, accounts very largely for the making of cloaks in inside shops. In the coat industry no such reason existed for the employers furnishing either work-

---

[4] Wanted:—A first-class cutter to take entire charge of a work room for cloaks and mantillas. S. Jones, 310 Canal Street. NewYork Herald, Aug. 1863.

Wanted:—A lady who thoroughly understands cutting and trimming cloaks and mantillas, a French woman preferred. George A. Hearn, 425 Broadway. New York Herald, Aug. 22, 1860.

place or machines, and the more skilled workers with the old handicraft tradition behind them clung to their old condition of employment.

In the making of pants and vests we find both systems striving for mastery, the victory finally resting with the inside shop. We do not mean to imply that no coats were made up on the inside, but merely that the prevailing systems of employment were as we have indicated. We have called attention above to the fact that in the cheapest grade of the custom trade the master tailor did not give the goods directly to the journeymen, but to a middleman[5] who became responsible for their manufacture. This middleman became known as the contractor. He gave the work out to the journeyman who became responsible to him, or he employed labor himself, either in a shop or in his home, and directly superintended the manufacture.

The cause of the introduction of this middleman was that he was able to make use of a cheaper grade of labor than the master tailor. He employed journeymen with whom the master tailor would have nothing to do, those who were broken down, dissipated, or untrustworthy for one cause or another. In cases where he employed labor to work under his immediate supervision, a still cheaper form could be made use of— labor that had not served its apprenticeship, and casual workers of one kind or another.[6] It is readily seen that this plan made the handicraft system more elastic, and that it was an attempt to make it conform to modern conditions. This method

[5] Men in 1844 refused to accept a reduction in wages, and Nicoll, a large London custom tailor, dismissed them, and let out the work to Jew middlemen. Speech of Henry Mayhew, Esq., London, 1850, p. 8.

[6] A vivid, though perhaps overdrawn picture of this form of employment is portrayed in certain chapters of Kingsley's Alton Locke.

with slight modification was carried over into the making of the ready-made product for reasons similar to those noted above. On receiving the material from the warehouse, the isolated worker was obliged to make a deposit for security against damage to or loss of the goods.[7] Many of the poorer workers were unable to furnish this deposit and were glad to pay the contractor a commission for procuring the goods for them. Again, many women with household cares could not afford to buy a machine, and were forced to rent one from the contractor who would also agree to furnish work. Often the contractor passed the goods on to other contractors who became responsible for their manufacture. These latter were known as subcontractors and the system as subcontracting. In New York during the period under consideration, this system did not become of much importance. Conditions were not favorable for its development. At a later date it became the predominant system, and we shall defer a more detailed discussion of it. We might add that during its early development in New York it was not confined to any one branch of the clothing industry but was prevalent to some extent in all.

While the wholesale manufacturer was the prevailing type of producer, there was still another form of production that was of sufficient importance to demand attention. With the expansion of the clothing industry many journeymen tailors, who had been unable to maintain themselves in the custom trade,

[7] This practice of demanding security led to grave abuses. Often as much as five pounds was demanded on deposit, and these deposits for which the employer paid no interest, often furnished the capital to carry on the business. In cases where the employing firms failed, the workers lost the money which they had thus deposited. Alton Locke, London, 1889, p. xvii.

or who found the clothing industry more profitable, began the manufacture of ready-made clothing.

The tailor bought his raw material, sponged and cut it, and worked it up into the finished product in his own home, with his own labor or with the help of his family, placing his product on the market either by retailing it himself or selling it to the jobbers. During the early part of the period this form of production was relatively important. The industry itself was unorganized, and as long as the product was crude this form of production was possible. As the industry developed, changed conditions made it impossible for the small master to maintain himself. Gradually, the more successful, those who were able to carry on business on a larger scale, began to employ labor to increase their business, and later passed into the ranks of the wholesale manufacturers. Many who were not thus able to take a higher position dropped into the ranks of wage workers in the wholesale industry; others continued to hold on and to drag out a miserable and precarious existence. So far as New York is concerned, this class has practically disappeared.

An important factor in this form of production was the jobber through whom the product was placed on the market. The position of this dealer is peculiar in that he dealt only in the lowest grade of the ready-made product and was entirely out of touch with market conditions. In the custom trade the form which the product shall take is determined by the demands of particular consumers. In the clothing industry the connection between production and consumption is not so intimate; yet the demand of the consumers is thoroughly studied by the large

---

[8] Often workers were brought in from outside the family. The custom also prevailed for two tailors to form a partnership, and work in cooperation.

dealers, and has a decided influence in determining the direction of production. In the case, however, of the product of the small master, put on the market either by himself or through the jobber, there is no direct way of ascertaining whether the product is meeting market conditions or not. The small master in the clothing industry is an excellent example of the blind producer. His product is ill-adjusted, both as to quantity and quality, to the demands of the consumer, and his profits are uncertain and fluctuating.

The division of labor in the clothing industry takes on a variety of forms. We may distinguish a division as to product, coats, pants, etc., and division as to the technical processes of production. Early in the custom trade we find a well-defined division of labor as to product, that is, certain tailors gave their attention to the making of coats while others gave their attention to the making of trousers, and still others to the making of waistcoats.[9] This division as to product very naturally came about on account of the different kinds of work which the making of each garment required. Each tailor by confining himself to a particular garment would become more adept, and therefore in the large custom shops certain tailors made only coats while others made trousers and still others waistcoats. At first, all would possess the same degree of skill. It was not long, however, before the pressure for cheaper labor forced out the skilled tailors engaged in making waistcoats and trousers, and workmen of a distinctly lower grade were substituted. Thus the manufacture of these classes of goods became completely separated

---

[9] Before the war the work "was divided among vest-makers, pants-makers, and coat-makers." Report of the committee of the senate on education and labor, 1885, I. p. 414.

from that of coats. In the clothing industry this division of labor was accentuated, each part of the suit being made by a distinct class of workmen, to be finally assembled at the warehouse. The making of women's garments has always fallen to a distinct class of manufacturers. While certain manufacturers make only garments of the higher grade, others confine themselves to the cheaper line.

Such division is due partly to the demand for different degrees of skill, and partly to the fact that the adjustment of production to consumption in the clothing industry is so complex that a high degree of specialization is necessary. In the larger custom tailoring shops there was a division of labor between the preparation of the cloth, including sponging and cutting, and the other processes of manufacture. The greatest skill was required of the cutter,[10] who took the customer's measure, cut the goods, superintended the "try-on" and acted as foreman, usually dealing directly with the journeymen. The cutter also did the designing. These functions required marked ability and the cutter became differentiated from the mass of journeymen, and indeed often rose to the position of the large master. With the rise of the wholesale manufacture there appeared at once a differentiation of functions; the old cutters became the foremen and had general charge of the manufacture, and in their place grew up a new class of cutters who did nothing but the cutting, and a class who gave their attention to designing. As differentiation went on, the position of the cutter became of less importance, since a large part of his functions had been taken

[10] "Every cutter is supposed to be a tailor, but that is not the fact at the present day. Previous to 1864 it was so; previous to the introduction of cutting machinery." Report of the committee of the senate on education and labor, 1885, I. p. 747.

over by other individuals. His importance was further diminished by the introduction of standard patterns which were placed on the goods by the marker, whose chief skill lay in securing from a given piece of goods the maximum number of suits, a former function of the cutter. To-day the operation of cutting is divided into cutting proper and trimming. Those who do the former are the more skilled; they lay the patterns on the goods and mark out the suits.[11] Both in the custom and the wholesale trade, the cutters from the very nature of their work have been employed on the premises of the employer.

After the goods had gone through the hands of the cutter they passed to the workmen either in the inside or the outside shop. The introduction of the sewing machine increased the quantity of work that could be done in the outside shop, as a great amount of the simpler operating could be carried on by the members of the tailor's family. This was of course merely the beginning of division of labor but in the inside custom shop even such an elementary form of division of labor was impossible.

During the early period of the clothing industry, practically the same division of labor existed in it as in the custom trade. After the introduction of the machine, however, operating, finishing, and pressing, became more or less distinct processes, and classes were developed that gave their entire attention to one or the other of them. In the outside work the central factor of production was the skilled tailor, and the unit of production was the family. This system came to be known as the family sys-

[11]The best cutters to-day are those who have a good knowledge of tailoring. Manufacturers have tried in vain to introduce workmen of less skill and experience, but such attempts have usually ended in costly failures.

tem. The head of the family performed the more difficult processes, whether operating or needle work, while the easier kinds of work were left to his wife and daughters. Later, however, there are numerous instances of a sharp division between hand and machine work, the wife and daughter taking over the work done on the machine, and the husband that done with the needle. This family system under the domination of the Germans later became the predominant system of production. Certain writers have held that the Germans were responsible for its introduction,[12] but it is not characteristic of any particular country and was in use in New York before the arrival of the Germans, and although its great prominence is largely due to their control of the industry, they cannot be said to have originated it.

The inside shop during this period was in general engaged in the manufacture of pants and vests, although there were some few manufacturers who made, under their own supervision, coats as well. In the shops of the wholesale manufacturer, so far as the manufacture of coats was concerned, division of labor was not radically different from that under the family system. The tendency was, however, for each process to be more clearly defined and allotted to a more definite class than under that system. The following classes began to be differentiated, operators, basters, finishers, and pressers. In pants and vests the division of labor is simple. With the introduction of machines a class who did nothing but operate them was almost immediately developed, pressing, basting, and finishing falling to other classes. In the manufacture of coats a skilled tailor capable of making the entire garment was present as in the family system, while in the

[12] Willett, Mabel Hurd, Employment of women in the clothing trade, 1902, p. 34.

manufacture of pants and vests the skilled tailor was eliminated. In the manufacture of cloaks the chief work lies in operating, pressing, and finishing, and in the very infancy of the industry, namely, just before the American Civil War, distinct classes arose to perform this work, and up to 1880 no radical change in the division of labor had taken place.

We have already spoken of the importance of the invention of the sewing machine. It worked a veritable revolution in the manufacture of all classes of clothing, and without it any great development of the clothing industry would have been impossible. The machine as a piece of mechanism was not brought to a high degree of perfection for years. It was cumbersome and difficult to operate, and the amount of work that could be turned out on it was much below that of to-day. It was usually operated by foot power, though in England steam power was used as early as 1865.

As soon as it became possible to cut more than one garment at a time, shears gave way to cutting machines. Such machines were introduced about 1875. The one most commonly used at that time, was a large knife, used somewhat like a saw, which worked up and down through a form cut in the table. Another kind of machine consisted of a rapidly revolving circular disc attached to an arm. This machine was considered dangerous and was not in favor with the workmen.

Button-sewing machines, button-hole machines and pressing machines were not introduced during this period. The methods employed in carrying on these processes were the same as they were in the custom trade.

The importance which machinery plays in the clothing industry is shown by the following comparisons made by the United States Commissioner of Labor [13] in 1898, between hand and machine production.

Cutting machines, cutting sixteen thicknesses, would cut in four hours thirty-two and five-tenths minutes, as compared with thirty-three hours and twenty minutes work by hand. For 100 vests the cutting, which if done by hand would take eleven hours and forty minutes, occupies one hour and thirty-four minutes. For cutting 100 pairs of pants, the time under hand production was sixteen hours and forty minutes; under machine production two hours and fifty-eight minutes. To cut button holes for 100 coats required under hand production three hours and twenty minutes; under machine production, seventeen and five-tenths minutes. On vests the reduction was from three hours and twenty minutes to twenty-one and three-tenths minutes. While it took 1000 hours to sew the seams on the coats under hand production, the sewing machine consumed only sixty six hours and forty minutes; on pants the time neecssary under hand production was four hundred and thirty-three hours and twenty minutes, while with the machine the same work could be done in sixty-four hours seventeen and one-tenth minutes; on vests, the respective times required are four hundred and sixteen hours and forty minutes, and sixty-four hours and thirty-five minutes.

---

[13] Report of the United States commissioner of labor, 1898, I. p. 198 et seq.

CHAPTER III

WAGES AND CONDITIONS OF EMPLOYMENT

In its early period the custom trade of New York was in the hands of English, Irish, and German tailors. From the custom trade the English and Irish passed into the higher branches of the clothing industry, in other words they became the manufacturers, the cutters, and foremen who directed the industry. About 1850 there was an increase in the number of Irish engaged in the trade. They became cutters and foremen—the directors of the industry next in rank to the manufacturer. There was also a large number of immigrant German tailors, who with their families performed the greater part of the labor involved in putting the garments together, thus taking over a large portion of the work formerly performed by the native American and Irish women, who were on this account forced into a lower grade of work. From the time of the introduction of machinery an increased number of American girls were given employment in the large inside shops, particularly those manufacturing pants, vests, and cloaks. Beginning with 1870 the Jews made their appearance in the clothing industry, both in the upper and the lower ranks, but in 1880 the technical processes of manufacture were still controlled almost entirely by the Germans, with the exception of the cutting process, which was controlled by the Irish. The commercial processes were in the hands of the English, a few Irish, and the Jews.

In the early days of the custom trade the workers were almost all men. With the appearance of the outside shops the employment of women began, and as we have seen, they soon controlled the making of waistcoats and trousers. The introduction of the sewing machine gave a great impetus to the employment of women. In the clothing industry women were from the start an important factor. In the inside shops, especially in the manufacture of pants, vests, and cloaks they were employed almost exclusively. In 1860 out of a total of 397 persons employed in New York and Brooklyn in the manufacture of cloaks and mantillas, 379 were women[1] and in Boston out of a total of 285 employed 273 were women.[2] Not only did the inside shop prove favorable to the increased employment of women, but the outside shop, owing to the family system, offered larger and larger opportunities for the employment of female labor. The fact also that the family system was so largely controlled by the Germans was a stimulus to female labor, for the Germans had no prejudice against the employment of women in the manual labor of manufacture. The percentage of women in the inside shops manufacturing pants, vests, and cloaks, however, was higher than in the family system. In the early period of the industry women were often employed as cutters, in the manufacture of both men's and women's clothing, being principally engaged in the cutting of cloaks. With the later development of the industry, however, the employment of women cutters rapidly declined till at the close of the period now under consideration they had completely disappeared. Operating and the less skilled tailoring work, such as button-hole making, felling and basting came to be the principal functions of female labor.

[1] Bishop, A history of american manufactures, 1864, II. p. 583.
[2] Ibid., p. 658.

There is still to be noticed the isolated woman worker who received her goods from the warehouse or from the contractor and made them up into the finished product in her own home. The number of these women up to 1880 was relatively large. By far the greater number of them made the entire garment, though there was already arising a class of women who worked in their homes on the one process of finishing. The economic and social condition of the isolated woman was pitiable indeed. She was usually unfitted for the burden thrown upon her and her labor was of a low grade of efficiency. She bargained with the foreman at the warehouse, and this again often worked against her. Her hours were frightfully long and her earnings meager, and these were often further reduced as she was obliged to buy her needles, thread, trimmings, etc. Hood's immortal lines are no exaggeration. She literally toiled

"In poverty, hunger, and dirt."

As this class of workers gave up attempting to make the entire garment and confined their efforts to the single process of finishing, they became more efficient and their condition has decidedly improved.

The number of children employed in the clothing industry has never been great. The work that children can do being limited to pulling bastings, sewing on buttons, and the like, and as these operations are but a very small part of the entire manufacture, it is evident that no great number of children could be employed. In rare cases children were employed as operators. Many were hired for such tasks as carrying "bundles" to and from the warehouse, and this, combined with the fact that the relative amount of basting work was larger during this period than in more recent years, makes it true that the number of children employed, while never large, was relatively greater about 1880 than at any other time.[3] Moreover, the majority of those engaged in the industry at this time were not opposed to child labor.

The difficulties which beset the discussion of wages during this period are many. The workers often furnished their own machines, some rented them from their employers and still others worked on machines furnished them. They also furnished numerous accessories of manufacture, trimmings, thread, buttons, silk twist, etc., and fuel for heating the irons. The greater number of such accessories were furnished by the workers in the outside shops, but even in the inside shops workers often furnished their own machines and fuel for heating the irons; and of course, such items as needles, thread, etc., were also furnished by this class of workers. The industry during the greater part of this period was unorganized, and in general crude methods prevailed. A study of the advertisements for labor during this period shows that rates of wages were generally uniform whether the workers used their own machines or those of their employers. It is evident, however, that at this time the worker owning a machine possessed an advantage over those who did not, as he was given the preference in employment, and also workers of slightly inferior ability, owning their machines received the same wages as those of superior ability who did not possess them.

---

[3] The number of children employed has been greatly overestimated by sympathetic visitors, who, having seen a few children engaged in pulling bastings, have at once jumped to the conclusion that large numbers of small children were being worked to their mental and physical injury.

The rates of wages quoted below represent a gross sum including the many items of expenditure on the part of the worker, and of which no account was taken, and of which moreover it is impossible to make even an approximate estimate.

Outside workers were paid a piece rate and it is difficult to determine just what weekly wages these rates yielded. When time wages are given the unit is often the family, the composition of which is uncertain. In the inside shops the custom prevailed of taking work home to be completed after the regular working hours. It is not always clear how much allowance should be made for such work. Finally the disturbance in the currency caused by the Civil War places almost insuperable difficulties in the way of determining the relation of real to money wages.

The above mentioned factors combined complicate the all too scanty information which we possess, and in the discussion of wages for this period these limitations should be borne in mind. In the manufacture of coats, wages just preceding the Civil War ranged from $8 to $10 a week for a man and his wife.[4] In this wage, was included payment for the use of his machine, fuel for heating his irons, thread, buttons, etc., and light, which was of course an important item in winter. From the close of the Civil War to 1873 the period of inflation, the wages for this same grade of work ranged from $20 to $25 a week,[5] but following that date, until the early eighties, there was a steady fall in wages. From about 1876 to 1880, after the

---

[4] Report of the committee of the senate on education and labor, 1885, I. p. 414.

[5] Ibid., pp. 414, 748.

introduction of the team[6] system in the manufacture of coats, during the busy season the operator, who was a skilled mechanic, received $3 a day or $18 a week; the baster $16 a week and the girl finisher, $7 to $9 a week. A tailor who worked during this time states that the period for which such wages were paid was very short. During the dull season, operators received from $12 to $15, basters from $10 to $13, and finishers, $5 to $7, a week. As we have already seen, the outside shop was principally engaged in the manufacture of coats, so the wages paid to the coatmakers represents fairly well the income of the workers in that class of shops.

There is little information in regard to wages paid in the inside shops during this period, but the compilation made by the Massachusetts Bureau of Labor[7] represents fairly well the wage movement in that state, and since the movement in New York was in the same direction as in Massachusetts, we may derive a general notion as to the conditions existing in that center from a study of the following tables:

Cutters' wages averaged as follows:

1860	$13.92 a week
1872	19.85 a week
1878	16.00 a week

[6] The team system was introduced about 1876, and though a comparatively small amount of clothing at this time was made under it, it affords a fair criterion for wages of workers on coats. The team consisted of operator, baster, and finisher. At this time, the operators and basters were men, while the finishers were girls. The wages quoted above are often cited. They seem to have no other basis than the tradition of the trade, except the statements of tailors who are still living and who worked under this system at this time in New York. The figures have been verified by the statements of such tailors.

[7] Tenth annual report, 1879, p. 70.

Pressers' wages.

 1860 ....$ 9.17 a week
 1872 .... 16.05 a week
 1878 .... 10.28 a week

Basters' (women) wages.

 1860 ....$ 6.32 a week
 1872 .... 7.77 a week
 1878 .... 6.46 a week

Operators' (women) wages.

 1860 ....$ 5.53 a week
 1872 .... 10.81 a week
 1878 .... 5.92 a week

Finishers' (women) wages.

 1860 ....$ 4.56 a week
 1872 .... 4.74 a week
 1878 .... 4.58 a week

In 1872 an investigation was made by the Massachusetts Bureau of Labor which showed the following conditions existing in Boston.[8]

Pants basters 1015 or 77 per cent received $4.00 to $6.00 a week.
Pants finishers 1022 or 66 per cent received 3.75 to 7.00 a week.
Vest basters 1049 or 62 per cent received 4.00 to 7.00 a week.
Vest finishers 1125 or 77 per cent received 4.00 to 7.50 a week.
Operators 525 or 94 per cent received 6.00 to 10.00 a week.
Press women 30 or 56 per cent received 8.00 to 10.00 a week.

Wages were about their maximum eight years after the Civil War. According to a report published by the Massachusetts Bureau of Labor[9] the average weekly wage in gold of first

[8] Third annual report, 1871-2, p. 86.
[9] Fifth annual report, 1874, p. 72.

grade pressers was $23.11, of first grade women basters, $10.67, first grade women operators, $15.11, and of first grade finishers, $6.22.

As it was the custom in many cases for the workers to take work home at night, their wages represent not only the labor put in during the regular working hours, but also in part their earnings at home. This was especially true in the manufacture of cloaks.[10]

In speaking of wages in this industry at this time Bishop says, "Sewing machines are largely used in this manufacture, the operatives being paid about six dollars per week, and handsewers four dollars." [11]

From the facts presented it is evident that money wages in the clothing industry had at least suffered no diminution in the twenty years from 1860 to 1880. But in order to arrive at any conclusion as to the real well being of the workers, we have still to consider what changes, if any, had taken place in the cost of living.

In general the season in the clothing industry was longer than in the custom trade. In Massachusetts in 1872 the busy season in the manufacture of ready-made clothing is given as thirty-two weeks a year, while that of the custom trade was twenty-four or less.[12]

---

[10] The mantilla and cloak trade was of considerable importance in New York at the beginning of the civil war, the annual production being about $3,000,000. Bishop, A history of american manufactures, 1864, II. p. 614.

[11] Ibid., p. 614.

[12] Third annual report of the Massachusetts bureau of labor, 1871-2, p. 83.

While the season is longer than in the custom trade, yet evidently even here a nominally higher wage would be required to furnish a fair yearly income.[13]

Estimated on a basis of eight months employment during the year, the yearly income of the various classes enumerated on the preceding pages would be as follows:*

Cutters   Yearly income
  1860 .... $445.44
  1872 .... 635.20
  1878 .... 512.00

Pressers
  1860 .... $293.44
  1872 .... 513.60
  1878 .... 328.96

Basters (women)
  1860 .... $202.24
  1872 .... 248.64
  1878 .... 206.72

Operators (women)
  1860 .... $171.20
  1872 .... 151.68
  1878 .... 146.56

Finishers (women)
  1860 .... $145.92
  1872 .... 151.68
  1878 .... 146.56

[13] "The great complaint of employees in this department as in most others, is, that, in the season of slack or no work, thousands are thrown out of employment, and that generally in the worst season of the year." Ibid., p. 73.

*Supra, pp. 32, 33.

The cost of living during this period was subject to wide fluctuations. The following table, taken from the Aldrich Report,[14] indicates the movement of wholesale prices from 1840 to 1880.

Year	General average price
1840	116.8
1850	102.3
1860	100.0
1872	127.2
1878	99.9
1880	106.9

Considering the wages paid in 1860 as having standard purchasing power, the relative wages of the laborers reported by the Massachusetts Bureau of Labor and given above, are as follows:*

Cutters	Relative wages
1860	100.0
1872	115.4
1878	115.0

Pressers	
1860	100.0
1872	147.8
1878	112.2

Basters (women)	
1860	100.0
1872	95.7
1878	102.3

[14] Aldrich, Wholesale prices, wages, and transportation, 52 Cong. 2 sess. S. R. 1394, 1893, part 1. p. 100.

*Supra, pp. 32, 33.

Operators (women)   Relative wages

   1860 .... 100.0
   1872 .... 174.8
   1878 .... 110.7

Finishers (women)

   1860 .... 100.0
   1872 .... 76.7
   1878 .... 100.5

These prices are wholesale and therefore do not actually reflect the purchasing power of daily wages. F. B. Thurber of New York, writing in 1878, says, "There has been a large decline in the prices of all food-products, both at wholesale and retail, during the last ten years, and especially during the last two years. In some cases I do not think the full decline has yet been realized by the retailer, and it is probable that retail prices will in some cases further decline.

The prospects for the future are, that there will be a very low range in the price of all food products, . . . in some measure a recompense for the great decline in wages which has taken place."[15]

The above table shows real wages to be higher in 1872 in all cases except in that of basters, which shows a decline over 1860 of nearly 5 per cent, and of women finishers, which shows a decided decline of 23.3 per cent. The variation in these cases may be explained on the ground that both basters and finishers represent a low grade of female labor, and their wages would therefore tend to respond less quickly. In comparing 1878 with 1860 the above table shows an increase in all cases.

[15] Consular reports, 1879, p. 323.

Carroll D. Wright made a careful investigation of wages and retail prices of Massachusetts in 1879, and came to the following conclusions: The *"average weekly wages, on a gold basis, were twenty-four and four-tenths per cent higher in 1878 than they were in 1860."* In regard to the "cost of living we find that *the average price was fourteen and a half per cent higher in 1878 than it was in 1860."*

"To sum up, the result of our investigation as regards wages and prices in 1860 and 1878 may be stated as follows: *That the average weekly wages of working men in manufacturing and mechanical industries in Massachusetts, allowing for the advance in the cost of living, were ten per cent higher in 1878 than they were in 1860, no account being made of the fact that the wages in 1878 were paid for fewer hours of labor per week, in many industries, than were required in 1860."*[16]

Up to this point we have taken no account of rent, a very important item in the budget of the working man. Accurate information in regard to the movement of rents in New York is not available. From the report of the select committee appointed to examine into the condition of tenant houses of New York and Brooklyn in 1857, we know that rents for the class of buildings in which the garment workers lived were quite as high as they were in 1880, if not higher.[17]

---

[16] Tenth annual report of the Massachusetts bureau of labor, 1879, pp. 80, 82, 90.

[17] At 80 and 90 Willet street, the committee examined a tenement house which consisted of a building six stories high, and occupied by twenty-six families, aggregating one hundred and twenty-three persons; a room and bed room renting for $4, $6, and as high as $9 per month. . . . At 34 Baxter street there is a tenement house containing

Witnesses before the Senate Committee in 1885 were unanimous in their testimony that following the war a decided rise had taken place in rents, and that after 1874 there had been a decided decline.[18]

It is probable that the movement of rents in the Eastern states was at this time in the same general direction as the movement in New York. Carroll D. Wright came to the conclusion that rents in Massachusetts were 156 per cent higher in 1872 than in 1860, and only 25 per cent higher in 1878 than in 1860.[19]

It is therefore evident that when the item of rent is taken into account the purchasing power of wages in 1872 as compared with their purchasing power in 1860 is little if any higher, while the fall which had taken place in rents by 1878, together with the fall in prices, gives a decidedly higher real wage for this year than for 1860.

Exceedingly long hours and uncertainty of employment have always been notorious in the custom trade. For certain periods during the year there would be no work for the tailor and at other times he would be rushed to excess, being compelled to put in frightfully long hours in order to complete the work on

one hundred and one families, called a "model house," where a room thirteen feet by eight feet two inches is let for $7.00 per month. . . . "Rotten Row" consists of fourteen houses, front and rear; forty-eight apartments in the front and one hundred and twenty-eight in the rear. There is not a single room the wood work of which is not decayed, and half the plaster rotted from the walls. The stairways are all dark, broken and filthy. Rent for a single room from $3 to $9 per month. Report of the select committee, pp. 24, 28.

[18] Report of the committee of the senate on education and labor, 1885, I. p. 421 et seq.

[19] Tenth annual report of the Massachusetts bureau of labor, 1879, p. 82.

time. During these periods of feverish activity, little or no time would be taken out for rest, the worker often being employed twenty or more hours on a stretch. The dilatoriness of the consuming public was largely to blame for the existence of these conditions, customers being in the habit of delaying till the last minute to put in their orders, and then insisting that they be filled in an unreasonably short time. Moreover, the custom trade was subject to unexpected demands that had to be met at once, as for example if a season of mourning was declared the custom tailor would be greatly rushed to supply this demand. Often the bad conditions could be traced to the shop of the master. When the tailor came for the goods on which he was to work he frequently found that they were not ready for him; moreover, owing to favoritism on the part of the foreman, goods were given out to certain tailors and withheld from others until the immediate completion of the work became necessary, thus causing the disfavored laborer to work excessively long hours.

With the introduction of the sewing machine, hours were somewhat shorter, although fifteen to eighteen hours were the day's work in many homes. One of the causes leading to shorter hours at this time was the fact that the noise of the sewing machine if operated late at night, aroused complaints among persons sleeping in the same apartments or buildings.

It is evident from the very nature of the clothing industry that the causes which operated in the custom trade toward great extremes in the working hours could not exist to the same extent in it, although it is true that under both systems the number of working hours a week was approximately the same, yet in the clothing industry the work was more evenly distributed, and instead of the tailor working twenty hours one day and two hours the next, it was possible for him to work the same number of hours each day. It is to be noticed, however, that the clothing industry was subject to one of the causes that operated under the custom trade toward variations in hours, namely, the fact that it also was a seasonal trade, and hence, to that extent was still subject to a decided degree of variation from season to season.[20]

From 1870 to 1880 there was no striking change in the hours of labor, the tailor working during the busy season as many hours as his physical endurance would permit. In the outside work, hours were from fifteen to eighteen a day; in the inside shops the working period was from ten to eleven hours, but the day was often lengthened from two to four hours, by performing at home those portions of the work that could be done outside of the shop. In Boston, where conditions were better than in New York it was the general rule, in 1872, for women to work in all from twelve to fifteen hours a day.[21]

These long hours in close, ill-ventilated workrooms, or in the living room of the workers themselves, wrought a terrible hardship, and it is difficult to exaggerate the evils growing out of such conditions. But a partial mitigation is found in the fact that the work was carried on at a leisurely pace with frequent interruptions for lunches, and there was much opportunity for gossip and talk.

Throughout the greater part of this period the manufacture of ready-made clothing was carried on principally in the homes

[20] To some extent the abuse of favoritism in the giving out of work still existed.

[21] Third annual report of the Massachusetts bureau of labor, 1871-2, p. 84.

of workers living in the poorest parts of the city. Those engaged in the manufacture were of the lowest rank of American women, the lowest grade of Irish immigrants, and a rather low type of German immigrants. No attempt was made on the part of the city to provide for proper sanitation and regulation. The workers themselves were unaccustomed to sanitary surroundings, and were indifferent to bettering their condition in this respect. These people lived in tumble-down shacks or in damp cellars.[22]

The living room was generally used as a work room but, as little help was employed outside of the family, overcrowding was not so serious an evil as it became later. Conditions became worse in consequence of the introduction of the machine, since it tended to increase the size of the working unit, and its noise disturbed the rest both of the family and of the neighbors.[23] But the machine and the bulky pressing table were advantageous in that they demanded a certain amount of room and therefore provided more air space. The considerable amount of artificial light used and the gas and heat arising from the crude stove used for heating the irons vitiated the air and during the summer made the heat almost unendurable. Insufficient light, both natural and artificial, caused eye diseases to be common among those who worked in the home shop.[24]

[22] John H. Griscom, Sanitary condition of the laboring population of New York, 1845, p. 9.

[23] To-day ladies' tailors find it difficult to rent apartments in the better part of the city because of the noise of their sewing machines.

[24] In a document presented to the house of commons, Jan. 28, 1752, and quoted by Galton, The tailoring trade, p. 53, this statement appears; "Nature is wearied out and their health and sight are soon impaired; insomuch that many, in the prime of their years, are become

With the appearance of the tenement house in the early sixties overcrowding became worse and general sanitary conditions deteriorated, and we have the beginning of the notorious conditions culminating in the period from 1870 to 1880. A tailor, speaking of these times, says: "Living conditions in New York were a by-word. The tenement houses in Mulberry, Mott and Baxter streets were worse than anything we have to-day. From 1875 to 1880 these were inhabited largely by Jews engaged in making clothing. Each family employed from one to two hands, all living and working in the same rooms. There was no water in the building, and toilets were situated in the back yard."

In the inside shops sanitary conditions were, in general, somewhat better, though even here conditions were far from good. These shops were generally located in buildings unfitted for such uses, and lighting, ventilation and general sanitary arrangements were very defective.

One of the most serious evils common to both inside and outside work grew out of the fact that the mass of operators during this period were girls and women. The machines were driven by foot power, and as they were heavy and cumbersome, the strength of the operators was overtaxed. Pressing when done by the hand iron requires great physical exertion, and is unfitted for women, but the practice was common throughout this period for women to do much of this work.

despised by their masters, by reason their sight is decayed and they cannot see to work so well as others."

The strain on the eyes in the custom trade, in general is much greater than in the clothing industry. The invention of the sewing machine has greatly mitigated this evil, as the operator is not obliged to give the same minute attention as did the old hand sewer.

At the close of this period the clothing industry in New York was no longer in its infancy. The number of manufacturing establishments had grown from 303 in 1860 to 736 in 1880.[25] The capitalization of these establishments had in the same twenty years nearly quadrupled, being in 1880 $22,396,893 as compared with $5,645,800 in 1860. In 1880 $40,209,340 were expended in purchasing raw material as against $9,970,297 used for the same purpose in 1860. In 1880 47,647 laborers as against 21,568 in 1860, received in wages $14,012,805 as compared with $4,338,396 in 1860. In 1880 the product was valued at $60,798,697 as compared with $17,011,370 in 1860.[26] These figures, however, include custom made products which in the United States in 1865 it is estimated comprised about 75 per cent, and in 1880, 60 per cent of the combined product.[27]

Estimated, then, on the very conservative basis that the factory product in 1860 was 20 per cent, and in 1880, 40 per cent of the total, the factory product for 1860 in New York City would be $3,402,274, and that of 1880, $24,319,478, showing an increase of about 600 per cent in twenty years.[28]

---

[25] Census, 1860, manufactures, p. 380. Census, 1880, manufactures p. 417.

[26] Censuses, 1860 and 1880.

[27] Report of the committee on manufactures on the sweating system, 52 Cong. 2 sess. H. R. 2309, 1893, p. iv.

[28] It is to be noticed that the actual product at both of these times was probably larger in New York than would appear from these figures, owing to the predominating place which New York held in the clothing industry, but still these figures give a fairly accurate statement of the percentage increase in production during the twenty years.

PART II

PERIOD FROM 1880 TO THE PRESENT

CHAPTER I

PERSONNEL OF THE WORKERS: NATIONALITY, SEX AND AGE

The chief interest in our study of the clothing industry lies in its history since 1880, for at that time began the great influx of the people who control the industry at the present day, and to whom must be given the credit for its splendid development, namely the Jews. Those Jews who came to this country prior to 1880 had almost all been engaged in commercial pursuits. As previously indicated, they first appeared in the clothing trade in the marketing of second-hand goods, passing next into the jobbing of ready-made garments, and a few ultimately into wholesale manufacture. It was also true that in a small way the Jews were becoming employers of labor, in the capacity of subcontractors, and in 1880 we find a few of them engaged in the technical processes of production. In the manufacture of cloaks the German Jews were in control; moreover, at this time, some Jewish tailors who had learned and practised their trade in England had found their way to New York by way of Boston and were employed in the manufacture of coats. The influence of these Jews was to prove out of all proportion to their number.

The Jews had been the object of persecution in every

country of Europe. During the past century persecutions have been most frequent and persistent in Russia. The assassination of Czar Alexander II in 1881 furnished an excuse for one of these outbreaks, the crime being charged to the Jews. As a part of the reactionary policy of the new Czar the enforcement of the old laws relating to the Jews, which for some time had been lax, was made very rigorous and the persecution became so violent that a wholesale exodus of the Jews began. The vast majority of the emigrants found their way to England and America, many of those who landed in England immediately continuing their voyage to America. The magnitude of the emigration is seen from the fact that while the total immigration of Russians from 1820 to 1880 had been less than 40,000,[1] the number landing on our shores[2] in the five years succeeding 1882 was 89,097. The vast majority of these immigrants were of the Jewish race. From 1887 to 1900 the immigration continued at an average rate of 48,000 per annum, and in 1902 the enormous number of 107,347 Russians entered this country. A large proportion of the early immigrants were men between the ages of twenty and forty, the women and children having been left at home until enough money could be earned to pay for their passage. By 1890 whole sections of the city which had formerly been populated almost entirely by Germans and Irish had become almost exclusively Jewish.[3]

[1] Compiled from the Statesman's year-books, from 1870 to 1880.

[2] Tables showing arrivals of alien passengers and immigrants, prepared by the U. S. bureau of statistics, 1889, p. 8.

[3] Dr. Annie S. Daniel, in 1892, says: "The character of the population has changed between Grand and Houston streets. Formerly, almost entirely either Germans, or Irish, or American-speaking people,

In Russia the Jews had for generations been herded in the smallest and meanest quarters of the towns. They were not permitted to hold land or engage in any industry out of which Christians saw fit to keep them. They had little opportunity to acquire property, and were too often despoiled of it when acquired. Their chief occupations were those of petty money lending, small retailing, peddling, and such minor industries as those of junk dealing and handling of cast-off clothing. In so far as the clothing industry had developed, the Jew was the chief factor in it.[4] They were deprived of the opportunities for education, except in the practice and tradition of their religion. Persecuted and oppressed, and dwelling apart, they had become timid, conservative, cowering and exclusive. They had become physically weakened through long periods of privation and starvation, and had grown accustomed to a low standard of living. They were unused to orderly industry, untrained in the crafts, and violently attached to a religion and to customs out of all adjustment to those of their new home. They belonged to a race subject to contempt and persecution, and in this case they had been suddenly forced to emigrate in large numbers. Accordingly, the Russian Jews of the early eighties were the most helpless and inefficient immigrants that have ever entered this country.

American born, this population is changed to Jews, Russians, Germans, Roumanian Jews, entirely, . . . in Ridge street . . . there is not a family, scarcely, that is not a Jewish family . . . east of the Bowery it is again Jews." Eight out of every ten persons in the section below Houston street, north of Chatham Square and east of the Bowery are Jews. Before this time the population had been German, Irish, and American. Report of the committee on manufactures on the sweating system, p. 182.

[4] Consular reports, 1884, p. 1471.

There are, however, certain points in their favor. While they possessed little capital [5] they were thrifty, temperate in all things, and determined to succeed at any cost. Their standard of living was low, but this was not of their own choice, and if they were given a fair chance it was certain to be raised. While unsuited to heavier manual labor, they were gifted with a singular dexterity necessary to many forms of lighter work. Moreover, while physically small, they possessed great power of endurance and a remarkable freedom from disease.[6]

While untaught so far as modern knowledge is concerned, they had mental acuteness and a shrewdness that made them in this respect, far superior to the mass of our immigrants.

There were serious objections in the mind of every Jew against exchanging city and town life for that of the country. He was utterly lacking in all instinct for farming, being urban

[5] The fact of their poverty is shown by the organization of the Jewish Colonization Society, whose purpose was the furnishing of financial aid to prospective Jewish immigrants. Baron de Hirsch gave $50,000,000 toward the carrying out of this aim. Pop. Science Monthly, LXII. p. 336.

[6] Their immunity from disease is shown by the low death rate in the wards populated by them, notwithstanding the fact that these wards are in the center of the tenement house district. In 1894 the general death rate for all New York City was 23.5 per thousand (Report of New York tenement house committee, 1894, p. 259) while in the seventh ward (Jewish) it was only 22.36 (Ibid., p. 28) and in the tenth ward (Jewish) 17.14 per thousand. In the fourteenth ward (Italian) the rate was 35.12 per thousand. The committee says: "The low death-rates of the seventh and tenth wards are largely accounted for by the fact previously mentioned, that they are populated largely by Russian Jews." (Ibid., p. 29.)

In the term "Russian Jews" we include those coming from Russian Poland.

by descent and choice and if any line of work could be found in the city he would choose it without hesitation. The further objections of the Jew to taking up rural life were: that he would have to go into a world of strangers with whom he could not converse; that he would have to give up his synagogue; and finally that in the rural districts he would be unable to procure articles of food prepared in conformity with his religious customs, a very important consideration with the orthodox Jew. He had no friends in the rural districts to assist him in getting a start, and the obstacles in the way to taking up agriculture even had he been so disposed were more than he was able to overcome.

What line of work in a city could the Jew follow? He was physically unfit for the heavier forms of manual labor, and his natural inclination toward business could not be gratified, owing to the fact that commerce requires capital. His lack of skill, moreover, made his labor so inefficient that it could not be employed with profit in those industries requiring a large amount of capital.

The clothing industry was, previous to 1882, practically the only one in which Jews were engaged as employers of labor. It was but natural that the new arrivals should seek employment in it. And it is also probable that large numbers of immigrants had had more or less intimate connection with some one of the branches of the clothing industry. A Consular Report says: "Nearly all the smaller ones (tailor stores) belong to Jews, and the ready-made clothing without exception are owned by the latter (Jews). The hands are also nearly all Jews and Jewesses."[7] Such employers would understand

[7] Consular reports, 1884, II. p. 1471.

their peculiar characteristics and would be willing to adjust the industry to meet their needs. The industry itself was peculiarly fitted for the employment of the grade of labor which they could furnish. It suited their lack of capital and physical strength, yet it offered excellent opportunity for the exercise of the dexterity which has been mentioned as one of their prominent characteristics. Furthermore, it did not interfere with their peculiar religious customs. It is not surprising, therefore, that the clothing industry absorbed the great majority of the newcomers.

As we have indicated above, clothing was manufactured in New York under the following systems: isolated home work, the family system, inside shop work and the contract system. The newly arrived immigrant was entirely unsuited for isolated home production by reason of the fact that he was without experience in the work and lacked the necessary knowledge of conditions and of the English language. He lacked, too, a room in which to work, for in most cases he was a boarder rather than a householder. In general these disqualifications kept the Jew out of isolated home work, yet a few who were possessed of sufficient means, and had brought over their families did engage in this mode of production. The family system also was unsuitable, because it had for its basis the skilled tailor assisted by members of his family. The Jew was in general disqualified for this form of work, for he was not a skilled tailor and had not brought over his family. Even though his family had accompanied him, it is doubtful whether the women of the family would have been permitted to engage in the work owing to the prejudice of the Jews against the labor of women. Neither was the inside system adapted to his needs. While a very small percentage of the immigrants were capable of working under factory conditions and indeed had done so in Russia, yet by far the greater part of them had been engaged in decentralized forms of industry, and their natural inclinations were toward it. But the determining factor against their employment in the inside shop was their need of a direct, personal supervision which that system could not give them.

The system of manufacture which seems to have most attracted the Jews and for which they seemed best fitted was that known as the contract system, which had been growing up alongside of the old family system, and which by 1880 was a well recognized form of manufacture. As the volume of the clothing industry increased, the family system under which much time was lost by the worker in going to and from the warehouses, became highly unsatisfactory.[8]

Hence, there sprang up as early as 1875 an intermediary between the home worker and the employer who took the work from the warehouse at a certain piece rate and became responsible for its manufacture. He in turn distributed the "bundles" among those who performed the actual processes of manufacture.[9]

[8] In the great strike in Berlin in 1896 complaint was generally made by the strikers against the time lost and the abuses arising from going to the warehouse for work. A great abuse existed in the giving out and receiving work. There are cases where workers have stood five or six hours and then many times have had to go home and come back later. Vorwärts, Jan. 18, 1896.

[9] "His part of the business is to save the time necessarily taken in going to and returning from the shops in getting the work." Testimony of Albert Hochstadter, a wholesale manufacturer. Report of the committee on manufactures on the sweating system, p. 16.

This early middleman was not a tailor, and neither did he perform nor superintend the processes of manufacture.[10]

It gradually came to be the custom for the contractor to turn over the bundles to a subcontractor, who in turn distributed them among those who worked under his immediate supervision. It was not long before the subcontractor began to deal directly with the employer, thus removing the irresponsible middleman.

It is under this type of contractor many of whom had occupied the position of subcontractor, and who generally were Jews, that we find the newly arrived immigrant employed, and it is under this system that the immigrant Jew came to be the dominating element in the manufacture of clothing.[11] The contract system was especially adapted to meet the peculiar characteristics of the Jew. It permitted the observance of his social and religious customs to which he so tenaciously clung, and what is perhaps of still greater importance, it made possible that close, personal and direct supervision which he could not have obtained under any other method of manufacture.

The better class of the Irish and Germans were pushed up rather than supplanted by the Jews.[12] Displacement was fol-

[10] The feeling against this type of middleman in the Berlin strike of 1896 was very strong. A writer in Vorwärts, Feb. 13, 1896, says: The vast majority of the middlemen are not of the trade. Among their numbers are found cabdrivers, druggists, gardeners, menservants, etc.

[11] In 1897 the factory inspector says that of the 66,500 workers in the clothing industry in the county and city of New York, 75 per cent are Jews. Twelfth annual report of the New York factory inspector, 1897, p. 45.

[12] Mayo-Smith says: It is not always true that displaced labor is pushed up higher. "Where the immigration is large in amount the displacement may occur without any corresponding 'placement'." Emigration and immigration, 1901, p. 127.

lowed by a corresponding placement. The Irish found a place in the upper ranks of the industry while the Germans went into other lines. But it must be noted that this displacement owing to the enormous expansion of the industry,[13] extended over a considerable period of time. In 1892, ten years after the beginning of the influx of the Jews, many Germans were still found engaged in the clothing industry on Manhattan Island. From this time on, however, they rapidly disappeared, those who remained in the trade moved to Brooklyn, where they still are an important factor in the manufacture of pants and vests, and a few are also engaged on the fringe of the coat manufacture.

The Italians began to enter the clothing industry about 1890. At first the workers of this nationality were chiefly women, who did finishing in their homes, but in 1891 the Italians had become sufficiently important to attract the attention of the Factory Inspector, who remarks in his report of that year that the Italians were commencing to bid against the Russian Jews for the privilege of making clothing, and that while in 1889 there was scarcely an Italian shop in the city, there were then hundreds.[14] After 1894 Italian male workers began

[13] In 1880 the total product of clothing in New York was, as we have seen, $60,798,697. Of this slightly over $24,000,000, or about 40 per cent was factory made. Census, 1880, manufactures, p. 417. See supra, p. 44. In 1890 the census gives the product of factory made clothing alone as $68,796,435, and the cost of the raw materials as $31,522,892. Census, 1890, manufactures, part ii. p. 397.

Thus it is evident that the industry had expanded from 1880 to 1890 over 75 per cent. During the same time the production of women's clothing had increased from $18,930,553 to $42,121,271. In the first figures are included the custom product, an increase of over 123 per cent.

[14] Sixth annual report of the New York factory inspectors, 1891 p. 40.

to be employed in those shops where a minute subdivision had been adopted. They were usually operators or pressers. The immediate cause for the introduction of Italian labor was the attempt on the part of the employers to escape trade union demands, as the Italians at this time were unorganized, but since 1898 large numbers have been employed owing to the fact that they represent a cheaper grade of labor than the Jew, who is being drawn off into higher forms of industry. If this movement continues, we have every reason to expect the Italians in their turn to become the dominant race in the industry. In 1900 the percentage of workers in the clothing industry who were Italians is given by the census as slightly over 12 per cent.[15] This growing importance of the Italians in the industry is strikingly shown by the fact that in the official bulletin of the clothing workers the proceedings of the recent strike (1904) were printed in three languages, English, Yiddish, and Italian. No great prejudice exists among the Italians to the work of married women. Many are found at work outside the home, but the greatest number are employed at their homes as finishers. In many respects the Italian is very similar to the Jewish laborer. While mentally he is not as alert, he is sober, industrious and dexterous. His lower standard of living, his unsanitary habits, and improper food, make his susceptibility to disease higher, and his power of endurance lower than that of the Jew. While he is an apt worker, his productive efficiency is decidedly lower.

[15] Census, 1900, occupations, p. 653. "10 to 15 per cent of all the workers in the cloak trade are Italians. This influx of Italians is the primary cause for the comparative inferiority of trade unions in cloaks." J. A. Dyche, secretary of international ladies' garment workers union.

Within the past few years, a few Lithuanians have drifted into the industry. They are principally confined to a few large shops in Brooklyn, but owing to labor disturbances, have been introduced as pressers and operators in some of the better class shops in New York. While their standard of living is quite as low as that of the Italians, they are exceptionally strong physically and it would seem that they are much better adapted to other forms of industry, but so far as their aptitude for the clothing industry is concerned, they are far behind the Italians. Their number in the trade is small, and we should not expect them to become an important element. However, the Lithuanians have become a factor of so much importance that an attempt is now being made to organize them. At the recent convention of the garment workers, $200 was voted to enable them to establish a trade paper in Brooklyn.[16]

While we have no actual statistics as to the exact proportion existing between the sexes in the clothing industry in New York City previous to 1880, we have every reason to suppose that the percentage of female workers was higher than of male. In the inside shops comparatively few males were employed. In the family system there was a large opportunity for female labor, and isolated home work also offered employment to large numbers of women.

With the influx of the Jews the absolute number of male workers increased but no radical change in the relative proportions of male and female workers took place until about 1890. The Jewish immigrants were largely males, and their customs

---

[16] Proceedings of the thirteenth annual convention of the united garment workers of America, p. 24. See also resolutions, 26 and 94, Ibid., p. 53.

were opposed to the work of women, hence in general the influence of the race which was fast dominating the trade was exerted toward male labor. It was true, however, that some of that small class who were acquainted with the industry sufficiently to carry on production without personal direction, and who had brought over their families did, owing to the pressure of necessity, permit the female members of the family to work by their side. Again, the large outside shop, which had formerly employed many women, was, owing to its inability to compete with the contractor, gradually disappearing. The decline of the family system was a further cause of the decrease of women's labor, and after 1892, as previously noted, the decay of this system was very rapid. With the influx of cheap immigrant labor, the German and American girls found themselves confronted by sharp competition for employment. Instead of accepting the lower wage necessary to exclude the immigrant, they passed into other lines of work which were found to be more pleasant and quite as remunerative. Work in department stores and offices claimed a large proportion of this class.[17]

[17] That they would have been forced to meet the competition of the cheap male immigrant, had not these other lines of employment been open, is shown by the fact that in the smaller centers, such as Rochester and Utica, where no such opportunities for other employment existed, they have held their former position in the clothing industry, and in these smaller places a far greater percentage of the workers are female than in New York. The following table compiled from the factory inspectors' reports, shows the comparative proportion of women employed in New York, Rochester and Utica.

Year	Pants New York	Pants Rochester Utica	Coats New York	Coats Rochester Utica	Vests New York	Vests Rochester Utica
1888	62.4 per cent	79.1 per cent	28.3 per cent	42.9 per cent	63.6 per cent	
1891	54.8	72.3	19.1	55.9	55.4	
1896	25.0	70.4	20.6	51.4	42.8	71.3 per cent
1900	23.8	61.8	22.7	55.1	43.2	74.7

1902 Workers in Men's and Boys' Clothing New York City, 27.8 per cent.
" " " " " " Rochester and Utica, 53.9 per cent.

The tenement and factory laws of 1892 and succeeding years have also been effective in bringing about a decrease in female labor, by forcing the Jewish contractors to rent shops outside their homes, thus destroying the opportunity for the Jewish women to work. In the shops connected with, but technically separate from, living rooms the percentage of women workers remained high.[18]

This decline has been checked during the last few years by the growth of the larger shop, bringing with it an increase in the number of women employed, owing to the attempts of employers to avoid trade union demands, and to the further fact that the growing division of labor makes the employment of women more profitable.

From the rather incomplete returns of the Factory Inspector the decline since 1888 is evident, although it is impossible to give exact figures for the entire industry. In the shops manufacturing pants, vests, coats, and cloaks inspected, the percentage of women to the total number employed was, in 1888, 40.7 per cent; in 1891, 27.5 per cent; in 1896, 26 per cent; and in 1900, 25.3 per cent. The following table shows the results of the Factory Inspector's investigations, as to the percentage of women employed in the manufacture of cloaks, pants, coats, and vests respectively in New York City:

---

[18] A condition is thus brought about just opposite to that which we should expect, namely that the smaller the shop the higher the percentage of women. Charles F. Reichers, secretary of the united garment workers, stated in 1892 before the investigating committee, that in the large shops only one-third of the employees were women, while in this particular kind of small shop one-half of the workers were women. Report of the committee on manufactures on the sweating system, 1893, p. 221.

Year	Cloaks	Pants	Coats	Vests
1888	45.5	62.4	28.3	63.6
1891	39.1	54.8	19.1	55.4
1896	29.0	25.0	20.6	42.8
1900	23.6	23.8	22.7	43.2

1902—In men's and boys' clothing 27.8 per cent.

In the investigation made by Mrs. Willett, it was found that, after deducting the German family shops, which are not typical, the percentage of women in the 40 shops visited was as follows: coat shops, 26 per cent; vest shops, 38 per cent; and pants shops, 52 per cent.[19] These women were for the most part engaged in the minor operations of manufacture.

We have already called attention to the fact that the opportunity for child labor in the clothing industry is not great, and that if we take into account the magnitude of the industry it has been singularly free from this abuse. From 1880 to 1890 child labor increased in the German shop, owing to Jewish competition. The prejudice of the Jew was against child labor, but as in the case of the labor of women, the small home shop offered an easy opportunity to overcome this prejudice. Many children were employed in carrying garments to and from the warehouse, but it is easy to exaggerate the evils of this kind of work. Clothing is bulky rather than heavy, and the bundles of clothing therefore, would not in general weigh enough to overtax the strength of the child. Better conditions in general in the trade coupled with better regulation and inspection have restricted child labor. The work formerly done by children has either been done away with by the invention of machinery, or has been turned over to the cheap Italian home workers. In

[19] Willett, Employment of women in the clothing trade, p. 57 et seq.

the census of 1890 only forty-three children are given as being engaged in the manufacture of men's factory product.[20] In the testimony before the Committee on Manufactures on the Sweating System in 1892 the child labor problem in the clothing industry receives very little attention.

Chas. F. Reichers, the Secretary of the United Garment Workers of America says there are generally not more than three or four children in a shop of fifty or sixty people, although in the smaller shops the percentage of children to adults is much larger.[23] Dr. Daniel in her report of thirty-one families engaged in making clothing,[22] working under the very lowest conditions, finds that twelve only employed child workers, the total number of children being fourteen.[23]

Hon. John DeWitt Warner, in his report, says, in speaking of the small tenement house shop workers, "The women are

[20] Census, 1890, manufactures, part ii. p. 396.

[21] Report of committee on manufactures on the sweating system, 1893, p. 220.

[22] Ibid., p. 187.

[23] Much has been written regarding the abuses of child labor, but although the writer has visited during the last six years, scores of shops of all classes in all parts of New York City, he has not recorded one instance of flagrant abuse of children. A few instances, where boys who seemed to be under fourteen were operating by foot power in a pants shop, one instance where two boys about ten or twelve years were pulling bastings in their father's shop, a few instances where children about ten in Brooklyn were pulling bastings after school hours, were the only cases of the employment of child labor which the writer saw. Miss Hannah H. Sewell's recent investigation in regard to child labor bears out the statement that there is practically no child labor in the clothing industry, only two instances of the employment of children being encountered in New York City. Bulletin of the U. S. bureau of labor, May, 1904.

more numerous than the men, and the children are as numerous as either. . . . Children are worked to death by the side of their parents." [24] The evidence presented before the Committee does not seem to warrant Mr. Warner's statement. In a personal interview with the writer in 1902, Mr. Warner said, "The conditions in New York to-day, are not comparable with those existing at the time this report was made. There has been a great change for the better."

[24] Report of committee on manufactures on the sweating system, p. viii.

CHAPTER II

SYSTEMS OF PRODUCTION AND EMPLOYMENT

There is under the contract system an almost complete differentiation between the commercial and technical processes of manufacture. The wholesale manufacturer has entire charge of the commercial side including the work of designing, while of the technical processes he has charge of only one, namely the cutting of the cloth, which is still done on his premises.[1] After the goods have been prepared and cut they pass directly to the contractor, who takes them at so much a piece, and becomes entirely responsible for their manufacture. He furnishes all the capital necessary for carrying on the work, workplace and necessary machinery.[2] He determines the rate of wages and becomes responsible for their payment. He exerts close personal supervision over the workers and at the same

---

[1] This was beyond the capabilities of the contractor in the early part of the period. As we shall see later the contractor, as he develops in efficiency, has in some few cases taken over this work also. In the case of designing discretion and judgment, are required as well as an intimate knowledge of market conditions, and it would seem that this function must remain under the direct supervision of the manufacturer, who by the nature of things, is the only person in a position to have the requisite knowledge.

[2] In exceptional cases the worker furnishes workplace and machinery.

time works along with them.³ During the early part of the period under consideration the average contractor possessed little more capital than the men who worked under him. He was, however, superior in other ways, and was able to buy his machinery on the instalment plan, although for the payment of wages he was forced to rely upon the money received from the wholesale manufacturer during the week.⁴

A great advantage of the contract system is that owing to the close personal supervision it permits the use of a grade of labor that could not be utilized in any other way. The superintendence that can be given by the foreman to the individual unskilled laborer in the large inside shop is not sufficient to insure a satisfactory product. As the system developed, less and less time was given to instruction, and more to care that no time was lost through lack of organization or through voluntary idleness on the part of the workers. In general the close touch coupled with the personal interest of the contractor insures a larger product in a unit of time than does the foreman system.⁵

---

[3] This necessity for close supervision and the equally strong necessity for the contractor to make use of his own labor does not permit a large number of people to be employed in one shop. During the early period the average number of people employed was nine or ten. While the shop has increased in size, most contractor's shops are still relatively small.

[4] This lack of capital on the part of the early contractor is strikingly shown by the fact that as he paid wages at the close of the week and often could not get his pay from the manufacturer until the following Monday, he was obliged to resort to the pawn shop to secure a loan to tide him over.

[5] The fact that a system in which the supervisor has a direct interest in the amount of product turned out results in a larger product in

Another great advantage which this system possesses over the others is that it permits of great elasticity and can adjust itself to the uncertain and fluctuating demand which is characteristic of the clothing industry. The manufacturer is not obliged to maintain a large factory and to keep workmen constantly on his payroll. The contractor employing a few men in an inexpensive workshop is able to call his men together for a few hours' work; while the manufacturer would have to meet the expenses of rent, and wages of foremen simply to fill such orders and could not afford to take the work under these conditions.[6]

When the contractors' shop passes beyond a certain size it loses this advantage to a considerable extent, but since the large contractor always works for a number of manufacturers he can still carry on his work when orders from one source cease by

---

a unit of time is recognized in other industries as well. In the textile industry the so called 'inside contract system' is common. In order to gain a closer supervision the manufacturer says to the foreman of the room; "I will give you a certain gross sum for a certain amount of work to be performed in your room. Make what you can with your workmen; I will pay their wages and your profit will be the difference between the amount paid in wages and the gross sum offered." Report of Connecticut bureau of labor, 1885, p. 72. The Baldwin Locomotive Works resort to a form of contract where foremen are given certain jobs by the piece and in turn employ labor to do the work. This system results in a larger product in a unit of time with the same labor, and the same product with a cheaper grade of labor. In a fanning mill in Montreal where the contract system was introduced employers testify to a much larger product in a unit of time. This custom seems to be on the increase.

[6] In cloaks the small contractors' shops work nine months in the year, while the large shops work only about six. What is true in cloaks is also true to a greater or less extent in other branches of manufacture.

taking work from other manufacturers, perhaps in other cities. Moreover, as work slackens every manufacturer gives the large contractor preference over the smaller, and turns all extra work, such as the making of samples, to him. The fact that he is favored in these ways enables the large contractor to exist.

The immense superiority which the small shop possesses over the larger is well shown by the conditions existing in the cloak industry to-day. Formerly this industry in New York was in the hands of large firms employing their help directly in inside shops. The manufacture of cloaks being highly seasonal, and the large shops being subject to the disadvantages which have been pointed out, the large firms have been forced out of business by the small manufacturer [7] who possesses all the characteristics of the small contractor, except that he works for himself. At the present time there are about 1300 employers in the industry, employing approximately 30,000 workers, an average of 23 to the shop. The larger cloak shops are compelled to resort to the employment of the small contractors during the rush season, showing the greater comparative power of the small shop to adjust itself to changes in demand.[8]

Two striking advantages, then, are possessed by the small contract system, first, its power to produce a large product while

[7] In a recent letter from John A. Dyche, secretary of the international ladies' garment workers union, the following statement is made: "There is a marked tendency toward decentralization in our trade. Quite a number of the large manufacturers have gone out of business this last season, but the amount of cloaks manufactured in New York is constantly on the increase."

[8] Secretary Dyche says: "The large manufacturer employs a small portion of his workpeople on his premises. The great bulk of the work goes to the outside contractor."

employing a low grade of labor;[9] and second, the power of the system to adjust itself to a highly fluctuating demand.

Considerable attention has been given of late to the growth of the inside shop in the manufacture of men's garments. This tendency is more apparent than real, and the ability of these shops to maintain themselves against the competition of the contractor is easily overestimated. It is true that their numbers have increased since 1897, but they are usually engaged in the making of cheaper garments which are not so much subject to a fluctuating demand, and where the necessity for careful work is not so great.[10] The inside shop by resorting to an increased division of labor employs that of a lower grade, and this in part compensates for the disadvantages of the foreman system. It is still more significant that the manufacturer in the inside shop also employs outside contractors, thus gaining the important elastic element. This also enables him during the dull season to throw work to his own shop and have his samples made up there. When these facts are borne in mind, it is quite evident that the inside shop has not as yet proved its ability to drive out its smaller rival.

With the development of the contract system came changes in the division of labor, and what was known as the "team

[9] To remedy the evils of poor supervision many of the large inside cloak shops resort to what is known as "the inside contract system." Garments are turned over to certain men in the shop who become responsible for their manufacture under exactly the same conditions as in the case of the outside contractor, with the exception that they are working on the premises of the wholesale manufacturer and are using his machinery.

[10] Secretary Dyche states this fact as follows: "It is well known that the more artistic the make the more chance for the small manufacturer."

system" was introduced. The work formerly done by one tailor was divided as follows: the machine work was given to one man, known as the operator; the needle work was divided between a baster and a finisher; while minor work, such as the sewing on of buttons, the making of button-holes, felling, and pressing was usually done by other workers. The first three workers constituted a team, and at the beginning were skilled tailors. This system had been introduced into New York about 1875 by English Jews, and with the great immigration of Jews in the early eighties, it became the dominant method in the manufacture of coats. Up to 1895 practically all the coats made up in the contractor's shop were the product of team work, but since that date there has been a decline until at the present it is estimated that only about 25 per cent of the coat manufacture is carried on in this manner. The great gain of the system was the superior division of labor. By confining their labor to one process the workers became more adept. The dexterity of the Jew made it possible for one who had never formerly worked in the trade to work in a team after serving a short apprenticeship. If we compare the Jewish team worker with the custom tailor we should say he is unskilled, but if we compare him with the workers in the other systems in vogue in the clothing industry we should call him skilled. Where the contractor employed only one team he was often a member of it and performed a large part of the minor work, in addition to his work as a member of the team. The characteristic shop, however, employed two teams, since it requires the work of two teams to keep one presser busy. The contractor dealt with the warehouse, prepared the work for the operator, trimmed the linings, arranged the parts, marked the button holes and saw that the work advanced as a unit, giving his assistance wherever needed. The workplace was formerly either the home of the contractor or a small shop furnished by him. After 1892 the home shop became illegal and disappeared. In the most economically arranged shops there were to be found two machines, a pressing table, an appliance of some kind for heating the irons, and about ten workers, including the contractor, the two teams, the presser and one or two low grade workers used for such minor processes as sewing on buttons.

While the team system was a marked advance over the family system, yet there was a still cheaper grade of labor which could not be used under it. With the impetus toward an increased size of the shop brought about by the Tenement House Act of 1892[11] which forbade contractors to carry on manufacture in homes, the demand for cheaper labor became more pressing, and some modification of the team system became imperative. This modification was brought about by the introduction of so-called "second" operators, "second" basters, and "second" finishers, who took over the less difficult processes. For example, while the first operator did the sewing on the edges of the coat, the making of the pockets, etc., the second operator did the machine work on the linings and the less difficult seams on the body of the coat.[12]

[11] New York state laws, 1892, chap. 655.

[12] Following is the list of workers given in a price list of the brotherhood of tailors. It exhibits the division of labor under the modified team system. Operator, first assistant operator, second assistant operator, baster, assistant baster, finisher, assistant finisher, first grade presser, second grade presser, edge presser, under presser, fitter, and busheler.

One of the characteristics of the old team system was that each team worked as a unit; the absence of one of the three workers threw the whole team out of work. When only three men were thus employed together, it was not difficult to arrange that they should be present at the same time. When the team became expanded by the introduction of these "second" workers, each necessary to the completion of the process, it is evident that it was much more difficult to preserve its unity, and much time was constantly lost by the failure of one or more of the members to appear. Even when all were present, it was much more difficult to keep the work moving together, in other words to arrange that a given operator should just keep pace with a given baster, and he in turn with a given finisher. In coat making this attempt to maintain team unity was soon given up, and the whole shop became the unit, the attempt then being made to arrange that the whole body of operators should just keep pace with the whole body of finishers, etc. In the making of children's jackets this team unity, known as section work, is still maintained, but there are frequent complaints on the part of the workers that time is lost by the absence of individuals or their failure to keep up with the rest of the section.[13]

[13] Much of the opposition to section work as well as team work seems to rest on tradition. Among the trade union leaders themselves, the opposition to these forms of work has been largely withdrawn. The following occurs in the report of the general president of the united garment-workers of America. In speaking of a strike against the team system, he said: "The local was under the impression that team work was not allowed, while the firm was operating a team system, the same as used in many of our clothing centres. When I heard the cause of the trouble I told the local union of the conditions in other cities, and told them that the firm had a perfect right to make their coats in that manner; in fact, that there was no clothing centre in the

In the modified form of the team system which developed in the coat manufacture the majority of the laborers were men, women being employed only in the minor work of finishing. This is due to the fact that the modification exists only in the manufacture of the cheaper grade of coats, where practically all the work is of the low grade machine type where cheap Jewish male labor can successfully compete with female labor.[14]

There is a constant tendency in industry to make use of cheaper labor where it is possible. In England the custom grew up of subdividing the work, not alone in the manner of the team system, but further, so that one worker did the operating on one part of the coat, another operator that on another part; a given baster the basting on one part of the coat, another, that on another part. This division of labor completely eliminated the skilled tailor, as each person simply had to learn one minute process. The work that had formerly been done by the male baster and the male finisher passed to women and girls. This sys-

---

country where that system was not used. On being informed of this fact, the local decided that there would be no further controversy about the team system. Fair prices were being paid for the making of the garments.'' Proceedings of the thirteenth annual convention of the united garment workers of America.

[14] The system of section work is found in both the inside and outside shops. The following resolution, which was concurred in by the convention shows the attitude of the workers in overalls towards this system: "WHEREAS, The system of section work which some of the clothing manufacturers have inaugurated in their factories is detrimental to, and at the same time obliterates the mechanic; be it *Resolved*, That this thirteenth annual convention of the U. G. W. of A. devise some ways and means whereby the section work system be done away with.'' Introduced by delegate of labor union 105, St. Louis, Mo. Ibid., p. 53.

tem was introduced into the United States by English tailors who settled in Boston, and was used extensively in that city. From Boston it was introduced into New York about 1895, and became known as the "Boston system." The immediate cause of its introduction into New York was the attempt on the part of certain contractors to escape the demands of the labor unions by the employment of persons, particularly women and girls, who were outside the unions. Male labor was still largely retained to do the operating work, but the greater subdivision made it possible to employ a lower grade of that labor, not controlled by the union. The Boston system is chiefly used in the manufacture of the better grade of coats.

The principle of this system has been widely adopted but the extent to which the division of labor has been carried varies greatly. The extreme of this division is seen in one of the leading contractor's shops in New York City, where thirty-nine different processes, carried on by the same number of people, are represented in the manufacture of a coat.[15]

[15] This shop turns out a very high grade of work, and two-thirds of its employees are women. Those who carry on the processes of manufacture spoken of above are as follows: (1.) The fitter, who also cuts the linings, marks the pockets, and puts on tickets, (2.) pocket maker, (3.) canvas baster, (4.) padder of lapel, (5.) bar tacker (on pockets), (6.) seam presser, (7.) lining maker, (8.) lining operator, (9.) sleeve maker, (10.) lining presser, (11.) sleeve presser, (12.) collar padder, (13.) shaper, (14.) baster and fuller of stay tape, (15.) lining baster, prepares for machine, (16.) operator, (17.) presser, (18.) edge cutter, (19.) edge baster, (20.) lining baster for shoulders, (21.) operator for shoulders, (22.) sleeve baster around edge, (23.) collar and sleeve baster, prepares for operator, (24.) presser on sleeve, (25.) joiner of collar to lapel, (26.) arm-hole baster, (27.) operator who sews in sleeves, (28.) garment examiner, (29.) collar finisher, (30.) lining finisher, around arm-hole, (31.) basting puller, (32.) edge presser, (33.) button-

It is necessary at this point to specify in greater detail the improvements which have taken place in the quality of the manufactured product and also to point out under which system of production these improvements have come about. Broadly speaking, there are two classes of coats on the market, those made up on the "open" plan, and those manufactured on the "closed" plan. In the closed coat the lining and outer material are made up separately, laid together, stitched by the machine around the edges, and then turned like a bag. Little padding and stiffening material are used. The coat is put into shape largely by pressing. This is known as the "balloon" coat.[16]

This class of coats was formerly made up under the team system; later it was taken over by the modified team system. It was the prevailing type of coat manufactured in New York previous to 1880, and with certain improvements, for example the introduction of more padding and more needle work, it has continued to be manufactured in large quantities up to the present, the bulk of the medium grade output being of this character. The medium clothing of this class to-day is as good as the best grade in the period preceding 1880.

In the "open-work," linings and outside material are built up together, the former being fitted and adjusted to the outside material piece by piece. The result is a garment equal in every

---

hole cutter, (34.) button-hole maker, (35.) general busheler and hanger sewer, (36.) presser of entire coat, (37.) button marker, (38.) button sewer, (39.) busheler. With the single exception of the pocket maker, a highly skilled mechanic, every one of these workers can become proficient in his line within a few months.

[16] It has been excellently described by Miss Potter, now Mrs. Sidney Webb. Booth, Labour and life of the people, I. East London, p. 211.

way to that turned out by the custom tailor. Mrs. Webb calls attention to the fact that in rare cases this class of garment was made in London by Jewish contractors.[17]

The manufacture of this class of garments has been carried to its highest perfection in this country. If such garments are to be made by cheap labor a very minute subdivision is required in order that the processes may be brought within the skill of the workers. Accordingly it is not strange that the Boston system is usually employed on this class of goods. In the manufacture of other grades sufficient skill can be acquired without this minute subdivision; in fact for the cheaper grade of work the division under the Boston system has proved disadvantageous.[18]

Experience has shown that division of labor under the old team system was not efficient. It exists to-day only in a very few shops. It is not with this antiquated method that the Boston system must be compared, but it is with that which we have termed the modified team system, employing a greater division of labor than the older one, that comparisons must be made. In what measure division of labor is to be employed depends upon the grade of labor used and the quality of product desired. If a manufacturer produces high grade goods and wishes to employ a low grade of labor, a division of labor typified by the Boston system must be employed. The cheap worker is not capable of producing any large portion of a garment, and must confine his attention to a repetition of very simple processes. That this degree of subdivision is sufficient to bring the work

---

[17] Ibid., 215.

[18] Contractors making this class of goods have often been compelled to abandon it and return to the other system.

within his skill is shown by the fact that he frequently becomes so skilled that the need for basting with its consequent expense is largely eliminated.

The modified team system, where division of labor is not carried to this extent, will be employed by the manufacturer engaged in the production of a medium or low grade of goods, who desires to use cheap labor. This results from the fact that the work is so simple that the comparatively unskilled man can perform several processes, and the division of labor, so minute as under the Boston system, does not increase his skill sufficiently to overbalance the necessary cumbersomeness of that method of work. Moreover, the opportunity that exists for saving in the manufacture of high grade goods, does not exist in so great a degree in the production of this class; for example, there is very little basting done in cheap garments and the saving in that respect which would result from the employment of the Boston system would be small.[19]

In the manufacture of cloaks, division of labor is not carried so far as in coat manufacture. Two classes of cloaks may be distinguished, lined and unlined. In the manufacture of unlined cloaks there is little chance for minute division. This is true because the number of processes in the making of a cloak is less than in the making of a coat, there being for example no padding, lining, or materials for stiffening; and as each cloak must possess individuality, the reduction of the processes to routine is therefore impossible. In the highest grade of work a skilled tailor actually makes the whole garment. In most

[19] From the above it is evident that it is not the size of the shop that determines which system of work shall be used but rather the grade of goods manufactured and the class of labor employed.

cases, however, the work is divided among the operator, the tailor, who does the needle work, and the presser. All these are skilled mechanics and receive high wages. It is to be noticed that the presser occupies a much more important position in cloak manufacture than in that of coats or pants; the cloak receiving its shape, not from the padding and other materials used in a coat, but from the pressing which it receives over a "form," and it requires skillful workers to do this properly. The cheaper workers, introduced as helpers and apprentices and employed on the less difficult processes of the work, are under the direct supervision of the chief worker in each line, and are engaged and paid by him. The greater number of these assistants are engaged in finishing and pressing. When the dull season comes on, most of them are discharged.

In the manufacture of the cheaper grade of lined cloaks a more complete division of labor is possible. The processes of operating, finishing, and pressing are broken up into various divisions similar to that of the modified team system in the manufacture of coats, thus making possible the use of a cheaper grade of labor. The workers of the lower grade form a permanent part of the force, and are hired and paid by the employer.

In the manufacture of pants and vests the division of labor still remains simple. In pants the work is divided into operating, and pressing; the finishing, which consists in the comparatively simple process of felling the seams, stitching in the lining and turning up the bottoms, is usually done by cheap female help. In vests and knee pants there is very little finishing.[20]

[20] A common form of work in vests is "section work" resembling the team system. The ordinary shop employs three operators, three basters, one presser and one finisher.

On practically all the cheaper grades of men's clothing the button-holes are made by people who do nothing else. They own their machines and represent a distinct division of the trade. Since no one shop can furnish sufficient work for a button-hole machine, a single operator is employed by a number of contractors. Women and girls usually sew on the buttons, machines for this purpose not being in general use except in the manufacture of the cheaper grade of goods in the large inside shops.

We have already called attention to the fact that children's jackets are manufactured under the section system, the division of labor being that of the modified team system. In the two classes of the work, "basted" and "unbasted" the division of labor is slightly different. In basted work, the operators are divided into head operators, and lining makers, basters into head basters and basters' helpers, pressers into head and under pressers. Finishers and bushelers complete the list. In the unbasted work there are operators for sleeves and "coat stitchers," pocket tackers and trimming makers. Fitters and bushelers do not appear.[21]

The efficiency of the machinery has improved greatly since 1880 more by the perfecting of the machines then in use than by the introduction of new machines. The sewing machine has been made much lighter, less noisy, and more perfect in mechanism, so that there is less loss from the breakage of needles and thread. There has been a great gain in the speed as shown by the increased number of stitches per minute.[22] Greater

---

[21] Taken from scale of prices issued by locals nos. 10 and 155. Appendix E.

[22] This progressive speeding up of the machine is shown by a statement of the Singer Manufacturing Co., as follows: "Stitching

speed and ease of production are also gained by the multiplication of appliances such as self-winding bobbins, gauges, and guides to enable the operator to make a straighter stitch, devices for turning under the cloth, etc. Gain has also been made in the manner of applying foot power, through the introduction of the swinging treadle, thereby enabling the operator to attain a high speed with much less effort than formerly. Old tailors in the trade estimate that the sewing machine of to-day will turn out 50 per cent more product with the same effort than would the machine in use previous to 1880. In England machines were driven by steam power as early as 1865. Steam power has, however, been superseded by the gas or gasoline engine which occupies much less space and requires much less attention than the steam engine. Moreover the gas or gasoline engine can be set up in the work room, and the fuel is of such a nature and the mechanism so simple that the contractor is not compelled to employ a special engineer to manage it. , Despite these advantages the use of this form of power is only possible in shops larger than the average and then the heat and smell of the engine when in the same room with the workers is very annoying

machines were first operated in the clothing trade by foot power at a speed of 800 or 900 stitches per minute. The construction was clumsy and hard to operate. Gradually machines were built with less motion and friction in the parts and were able to attain greater number of stitches per minute with less labor, but still operated by foot power . . . . Machines on mechanical power were able to be operated on a speed of about 1200 to 1500 stitches per minute," and finally to 1800. Later machines with a speed of 2000 stitches per minute came into general use. In 1895 a machine was put on the market permitting a speed of 2800 stitches per minute, and finally in 1900 first class results were obtained on a machine with a speed of 4000 stitches. "During all these changes the desire has been to get as little motion in the machine and confine the mechanism to as few parts as possible."

and unsanitary.[23] The latest improvement of power is the application of electricity.* Each machine has its own motor and it is evident that it can be economically applied in a shop of any size.

Attention has already been called to the two forms of cutting machines in vogue before 1880, namely the long knife and the circular disc. The best machine of to-day is the "reciprocal" cutter, the principle of which is a blade having a rapid vertical movement. Each machine is operated by electricity and furnished with its own motor. While this form of machine is used by many of the larger firms, knife cutting is still very extensively employed.

The common form of pressing is by the use of a large iron, or "goose" which is heated on a stove or furnace and applied directly to the goods without mechanical aid. The heating of these irons has been improved by providing a heating apparatus for each individual iron, the heat being obtained by the use of ordinary illuminating gas. The great bulk of the pressing is still done in this way. Much physical exertion on the part of the presser has been saved by attaching the goose to a crane or movable arm. The apparatus is not expensive, and combines all the advantages of hand pressing as far as perfection of work is concerned. The greatest innovation in pressing has been the introduction of the coat pressing machine in the less complex parts of the work. It is estimated that with it one man can turn out as much work as seven men using only hand methods.[24]

---

[23] The economical use of this form of power demands the use of at least twenty machines.

[24] Twelfth annual report of the New York bureau of labor, 1894, p. 284.

*This costs from one to three cents a day for each machine.

In the manufacture of all but the highest grade clothing the making of button-holes has been taken over by the machine. So perfect has this work become that it takes an expert to tell whether a button-hole is made by a machine or by a skilled tailor. By hand methods a skilled tailor could make one hundred button-holes a day;[25] with the latest machine a girl can make over 3000.

Machines for sewing on buttons have not been extensively used. The earlier machines were unsatisfactory because they did not knot the thread after it passed through the cloth, and if the end became unfastened the button came off. A new machine which tied the knot and did away with this drawback was introduced about 1898, but it is not widely used, as it is suited only for the cheapest grade of goods. Many other appliances have also been introduced which increase the productiveness of the worker without a corresponding increase in effort on his part. Double needle double shuttle machines and machines for barring the corners of pockets and the ends of button-holes and a serging machine for over-edging raw edges of seams are examples of these appliances.

---

[25] Ibid., 1894, p. 283.

CHAPTER III

Movement of Wages

From the time of the Civil War, and during the time of currency inflation the wages of a tailor working under the family system had been from $20 to $25 a week.[1]

From 1872 to 1878, as we have previously seen, there was a considerable fall in wages, as is evidenced by the statistics of the Massachusetts Bureau above cited,[2] which show a decline in all lines except the wages of overseers. This decline was most marked in the case of pressers, women operators, and cutters. From 1878 to 1880 the wages paid weekly under the team system were on the average as follows: Operator, $18; baster, $16; presser, $12; finisher, $11; and low grade girl helper, $4.50.[3]

In 1881 the statistics compiled by the Massachusetts Bureau show that a considerable decline had taken place in the wages of trimmers, but that advances had occurred in all other lines since 1878. As compared with 1872, wages in Massachusetts were higher in the case of overseers, trimmers, women basters, and finishers who worked inside the shop; in the case of cutters, pressers, and operators, however, there had been a decline since 1872, and in the case of the two last mentioned it had been of considerable im-

[1] Report of the committee of the senate on education and labor, 1885, I. p. 414.

[2] Supra, p. 32.

[3] Where girls were employed as regular members of the team they received $7 to $9 a week.

portance, the average paid to pressers being $1.35 a week less than that paid in 1872, and that paid to operators being $1.34 less. The following table exhibits the actual amounts paid in 1878 and 1881.[4]

	1878	1881
Overseers	$24.82	$28.33
Cutters	16.00	19.81
Trimmers	14.31	13.69
Pressers	10.28	14.70
Women basters	6.46	8.00
Women operators	5.92	9.47
Finishers in shops	4.58	4.95

In 1883 the wages of low grade cutters were given by a witness before the Senate Committee as $15 a week, or $640 per annum.[5]

The Secretary of the Independent Clothing Cutters (high grade) gave the highest wages of cutters in 1883 as $20 a week, and the lowest as $17.[6]

Wages of pressers averaged $12 to $14 a week, of bushelmen $10 to $18, and of operators $15.[7]

It is evident that while no great change had taken place in the wages of this class of workmen after 1880, a comparison with the figures given above for 1883 probably indicates a slight fall.[8]

[4] Twenty-eighth annual report of the Massachusetts bureau of labor, 1897, p. 5. These wages, as indicated above, were for the busy season. The skill of this class of workers was higher at that time than to-day.

[5] Report of the committee of the senate on education and labor, 1885, I. p. 748.

[6] Sixth annual report of the New York bureau of labor, 1888, p. 497.

[7] Ibid., p. 501. Coat tailors received an average of $12 to $14. Ibid., p. 500, while cloakmakers in 1882 averaged $15 a week.

[8] The apparent fall of three dollars a week in the wages of operators was, however, not so great as would appear from those figures,

In 1883 the wages earned under the family system seem to have been considerably lower than in the period prior to 1873, $15 to $20 a week being the average earnings of a man and family working very long hours.[9]

Witnesses before the Senate Committee agreed on the fact that since 1874 their wages had fallen very decidedly.

From 1873 to 1880 there had been a general decline in wages throughout the country, and it is well to compare the movement in the clothing trade with the general one. The following table exhibits this decline. The base 100 represents the average wages in all industries in 1860.[10]

Year	Average wages	Year	Average wages	Year	Average wages
1873	167.1	1877	144.9	1881	146.5
1874	161.5	1878	142.5	1882	149.9
1875	158.4	1879	139.9	1883	152.7
1876	152.5	1880	141.5		

The reasons for the steady decline in the general level of wages up to 1880 are complex, but although the Aldrich report[11] states that "the effect of currency depreciation and the disturbed state of affairs was much more marked on prices than on wages," the unstable state of the currency undoubtedly had a very considerable effect on the latter.

Wage statistics in the clothing industry up to the year 1883 are so indefinite and meager that it is possible to make only general statements concerning the conditions then existing. According to the Aldrich report the wage move-

owing to the fact that the wages quoted as $18 were computed, on a basis of $3 a day. Under the task system the size of the task was so great that it could not ordinarily be performed in a day, and the $18 therefore often represented seven days' work and six days' wages.

[9] Report of the committee of the senate on education and labor, 1885, I. pp. 421, 751.

[10] Wholesale prices, wages, and transportation, 1893, p. 176.

[11] Ibid., p. 177.

ment was downward until 1879, and after this date there was a gradual upward movement. From the statistics cited and from statements made by men who worked through this period, it would seem that in the clothing industry, so far as New York City is concerned, the movement of wages was about the same as in other industries. Beginning with 1876, the large immigration of workers who went into the clothing industry tended to depress wages, but as the industry was rapidly expanding, creating a demand for new workers, a depression in wages was prevented. Moreover, the system under which a part of the clothing was manufactured permitted a lengthening of the hours of work in lieu of a reduction of wages. This was particularly true under the so-called "task system." In the family system hours could not easily be made longer, but the family income was maintained by increasing the work on the part of the women and children. The decline in nominal wages which has been pointed out as having taken place from 1873 to 1880 in the clothing industry, as well as in the general industry of the country, and the succeeding rebound up to 1883 were practically paralleled by the movement of prices of standard commodities, so that the decline was not so injurious nor the advance so beneficial to the laborer as would appear from casual examination of his nominal wages. The Aldrich report[12] gives the movement of wholesale prices of commodities weighted according to their importance as follows:

1873	127.2	1878	99.9
1874	119.4	1879	99.6
1875	113.4	1880	106.9
1876	104.8	1881	105.7
1877	104.4	1882	108.5
		1883	106.0

[12] Wholesale prices, wages, and transportation, 1893, p. 100.

As rent is such an important item in the expense account of the clothing worker, it is important to repeat that rents had fallen largely from the level of 1873 and 1874,[13] and in 1884 the average rent for a room paid by workers in the clothing industry was $3.58 a month, the average size of the apartment being three and four rooms.[14]

All in all, it would appear that the material well being of the workers in the clothing industry, with the possible exception of the workers under the family system, was little if any below that of ten years before, and even in the case of the latter the income was maintained by long hours of labor.

The wage problem in the clothing industry is exceedingly complex, and it is not strange that there is and has been a great deal of dispute as to what wages actually were, and what the movement has been. The sources for a discussion of wages are: (1) the reports of various bureaus and committees of investigation; (2) statements of wages in trade union agreements; (3) personal interviews and observations.

It is well to point out the elements of error that must be taken into account in making use of these sources. Statistics collected by bureaus represent only a small part of the industry. These statistics are derived from statements of trade union officials and cover only the wages of trade union labor, or they are made up from wage schedules of employers in the larger shops. It is evident then, that in the one case, returns from only the better grade of workers in the industry would be secured, and in the other case from shops that are not typical of the entire industry. On

---

[13] Testimony of S. Carl in Report of the committee of the senate on education and labor, 1885, I. p. 421.

[14] Third annual report of New York bureau of labor, 1885, p. 77.

the other hand statistics of the bureaus consulted have great merit in that they have taken into account the consideration of seasonal employment and that of overtime work[15]; and the wage statistics collected by them are given by quarters, and the earnings for those quarters represent not only the nominal weekly wage but the additional amounts earned in overtime.

The scales in union agreements are open to the objection that they are made up at the beginning of the busy season and are not usually maintained throughout the year. Moreover, even in the busy season, the union scale does not represent actual wages paid, for employers often find it impossible to fill orders if the union scale is enforced, and therefore a comparatively large percentage of the workers do not receive the wages stated in agreements. The union scales compared from year to year do possess a positive merit in spite of the defects just mentioned, in that they show the general trend of the wage movement. If in a given year the union scale declares that wages of operators shall be $18, and the next year it states that they shall be $20, and the year following $22, the presumption is at least in favor of the conclusion that wage conditions are becoming better. Moreover, the union scale does give us an idea of the average wages paid to given classes, for although it is true that, as pointed out above, by no means all of the workers receive these scheduled wages, and hence union schedules do not give us extremes, yet the greatest number of the workers in the industry receive wages approximating the union scale.

---

[15] This is especially true of those of New York since 1897.

The personal interview, while not general in its nature, acts as a corrective to the too rigid data collected from bureaus of statistics and trade union agreements.

We shall now proceed to take up the wage movement of the various branches of the industry in detail.

Cutters—The following tables are based on statements of trade union officials or trade union organizations, and are compiled from the reports of the New York Bureau of Labor and of the Board of Arbitration and Mediation.

Year	Range of weekly wages	Year	Range of weekly wages
1883	$17 to $20	1888	$16 to $18
1884	14 to 20	1889	15 to 18
1885	16 to 20	1892	19 to 21
1886	18 to 21	1893	18 to 21
1887	18 to 22	1894	16 to 19
		1895	18 to 21

Up to 1892 there is no distinction made between knife and shear cutters. The following table shows the movement of wages for knife cutters from 1892:

Year	Range of weekly wages	Year	Range of weekly wages
1892	$22 to $25	1894	$19 to $22
1893	21 to 24	1895	21 to 24

Combining the first table[16] with the statistics compiled from the New York Labor Bureau's reports since 1897, we arrive at the following as the course of yearly wages of cutters from 1883 to 1902.[17]

---

[16] Up to 1896 these figures are compiled on a basis of ten months' work per annum (Twelfth annual report of the New York bureau of labor, 1894, p. 69); after that date they are based on actual figures given by trade unions as the sum of quarterly earnings.

[17] Total number in the industry about 5000.

Number reported	Year	Yearly wages
	1883	$680 to $800
	1884	560 to 800
	1885	640 to 800
	1886	720 to 840
	1887	720 to 880
	1888	640 to 720
	1889	600 to 720
	1892	760 to 840
	1893	720 to 840
	1894	640 to 720
	1895	720 to 840
	1896	720 to 840
1832[18]	1897	820.75
1640	1898	845.33
1299	1899	863.02
1447	1900	775.02
1896	1901	849.68
2498	1902	938.38

Coatmakers—Figured on an eight months' basis[19] the yearly wages of all coat tailors from 1883 to 1887 were as follows:

1883	$384 to $448		1885	$480 to $512
1884	384 to 448		1886	480 to 512
			1887	384 to 448

The yearly wages of each separate class of coatmakers is not obtainable from 1883 to 1887, but from 1889 to 1904 such data are obtainable and the following table gives the range, figured on an eight months' basis.

	Operators			Assistant Operators	
Year	Weekly wages	Yearly wages	Year.	Weekly wages	Yearly wages
1889	$13	$416			
1892[20]	16 to 17	512 to 544			
1894	15	480			
1895	15 to 18	480 to 576			
1896	18	576			
1897	18	576	1897	$ 9	$288
1901	16	512	1901	16	512
1902	18	576	1902	16	512
1904	18	576	1904	16	512

[18] Since all grades are included the average appears low.
[19] Ibid., p. 69.
[20] Report of committee on manufactures on the sweating system, 1893, p. 703.

THE CLOTHING INDUSTRY IN NEW YORK

Year	Basters		Year	Assistant Basters	
1894	$13 to $16[21]	$416 to $512	1894	$10 to 13	$320 to 416
1895	13	416	1895		
1896	15	480	1896	10	320
1897	16	512	1897	12	384
1901	15	480	1901		
1902	17	544			
1904	17	544			

	Pressers			Tailors or Finishers	
Year	Weekly	Yearly	Year	Weekly	Yearly
1889	$6 to $11	$192 to $352	1891	$17	$544
1891	12	384	1894	10 to 12	320 to 384
1894	10 to 12	320 to 384	1895	10	320
1895	10	320	1897	12 to 15	384 to 480
1897	12 to 15	384 to 480			

From 1897 we have the combined average wages of coatmakers engaged in all branches of the trade, as stated by union officials, in the following table:

Year	Number		Yearly wages	
	Males	Females	Males	Females
1897	1216	38	$349.23	$207.16
1898	790	129	344.80	164.58
1899	2618	512	484.85	239.65
1900	3022	256	608.88	257.40
1901	834	284	443.34	240.26
1902	5710	315	531.96	344.06

The following tables compiled from trade union agreements show the general trend of weekly wages:

Year	Operators	Assistant Operators	Basters	Assistant Basters	Pressers	Finishers	Bushelers
1894	$15		$13		$10	$9	
1896	18		15	$10	12	11	$12
1897	18		16	12	12 to 15	10 to 12	
1901	16		15		13	12	11
1902	18	$16	17		15 to 18	14	11
1904	18	16	17		15 to 18	14	11

[21] On authority of international tailors' union. Twelfth annual report of the New York bureau of labor, 1894, p. 70.

Vestmakers (operators)

Year	Number reported Males	Females	Yearly wages Males	Females
1894			$384 to $480	
1895			416 to 512	
1897	297	182	375.85	$143.79
1898	315	205	260.45	154.49
1899	152	118	545.97	193.73
1900	464	341	402.66	251.04
1901	668	470	400.72	221.52
1902	965	736	645.48	389.60

Pantsmakers

Year.	Pressers yearly wages	Operators yearly wages	Year	Pressers yearly wages	Operators yearly wages
1888	$320	$288	1890	$320	$256
1889	256	192	1891	320	256

Average wages of all engaged in the pantsmaking industry.

Year	Number reported Males	Females	Average yearly wages Males	Females
1898	1214	236	$366.05	$324.64
1899	2623	141	364.38	328.49
1900	2559	105	376.78	225.14
1901	2348	427	424.18	240.84
1902	1827	16	533.14	366.44

Pressers in all lines

Year	Number reported	Average yearly wages
1888		$320
1889		256
1890		320
1891		320 to 384
1893		352
1894		320 to 384
1895		368 to 448
1897	1076	375.50
1898	635	317.36
1899	470	474.30
1901	1007	420.00[22]
1902		487.74

[22] Twentieth annual report of the New York bureau of labor, 1902, p. 980. This is estimated from the statement on that page.

Jacketmakers

Year	Number reported Males	Number reported Females	Average yearly wages Males	Average yearly wages Females
1894				$216 to $288
1895				360 to 432
1897	2334	334	$339.39	176.39
1898	1095	150	361.01	283.19
1899	100		412.32	
1900				
1901	698	38	335.10	218.52
1902	2851	134	477.42	364.04

The following table compiled from trade union agreements exhibits the movement of wages in the two classes and the different branches of jacketmakers work:

BASTED WORK

Year	Operators	Assistant Operators	Basters	Assistant Basters	Pressers	Under Pressers	Bushelers
1895	$13 to 16	$6 to 12	$10 to 12	$6 to 8		$6 to 10	
1901	16	10	15	11	$13	10	$12
1902	17		16	11	14	11	13

UNBASTED WORK

Year	Operators	Assistant Operators	Under Pressers	Pressers	Pocket Tackers	Sleevemakers	Coat-Stitchers
1895	$10 to 14	$6 to 7	$6 to 7	$8 to 12			
1901	16		10	13	$13	$7	$12
1902	17		11	14	14	8	13

Cloakmakers—In 1882 the average wages of cloak makers is stated to have been about $15 a week,[23] but by 1885 a considerable decrease had taken place, owing to the introduction of cheap labor, so that at this time the average for male workers was from $7 to $10, and for women from $3 to $6 a week. From 1885 to 1890, however, a large portion of the loss had been made up, and in 1888 the average weekly wage for males was $12.[24]

---

[23] Third annual report of the New York bureau of labor, 1885, p. 289.

[24] Sixth annual report of the New York bureau of labor, 1888, p. 483.

From 1890 to 1895 we are able to give statistics showing the movement in the various branches of cloakmaking. They are as follows:

Year	Operators	Tailors	Pressers	Finishers
1890[25]	$18	$16	$14	$ 8
1891[26]	18	15	13	8
1893	18	15	13	
1894[27]	15 to 22	15 to 22	14 to 18	9 to 15
1895[28]	17 to 25	17 to 25	16 to 21	10.50 to 17[29]

The following table shows the average yearly wages of all the workers in the industry from 1897 to 1902:

Year	Number reported		Average yearly wages	
	Male	Female	Male	Female
1897	4006		$585.57	
1898	6431	900	377.94	$200.05
1899	8634	1749	606.15	335.15
1900	6000	1400	360.28	202.16
1901	4400	687	484.40	282.36
1902	5250	1425	443.06	243.36[30]

Having pointed out the course of nominal wages it becomes necessary, before drawing any conclusions as to the comparative well-being of the workers now and in the past, to consider the movement of prices.

The following table exhibits the movement of wholesale prices from 1880 to 1902, and is compiled from the Aldrich report of 1893 and the Bulletin of the United States Department of Labor for 1902. The wholesale prices are based on the prices existing in 1860, the average

---

[25] Ninth annual report of the New York bureau of labor, 1891, part i. p. 132.

[26] Seventh annual report New York board of mediation and arbitration, 1893, p. 55.

[27] Twelfth annual report New York bureau of labor, 1894, p. 70.

[28] Ninth annual report New York board of mediation and arbitration, 1895, p. 162.

[29] Compiled from trade union agreements.

[30] Compiled from reports of New York bureau of labor.

at that date being 100, and all variations in the years noted being from that figure.

Year	Average wholesale prices	Year	Average wholesale prices
1880	106.9	1892	87.5
1881	105.7	1893	87.1
1882	108.5	1894	79.3
1883	106.0	1895	77.2
1884	99.4	1896	74.6
1885	93.0	1897	74.0
1886	91.9	1898	77.0
1887	92.6	1899	83.9
1888	94.2	1900	91.2
1889	94.2	1901	89.5
1890	92.3	1902	93.1[31]
1891	92.2		

From this table it is evident that from 1882 until 1897 prices underwent an almost continuous decline, but from that date to 1902 rapid advances were made, the average level in the latter year being almost the same as in 1885. It is true, however, that these figures do not represent exactly the movement in retail prices. The New York labor report for 1902 says on this point: "Retail prices are ad-

[31] It will be noticed that in the above table the index numbers for the years 1890 and 1902, vary by eight-tenths of one per cent, while the department of labor gives the same index for these years. The basis of this table is the index number of the Aldrich report, but as this report does not come down further than 1891, the department of labor index is used from that year. These two separate sources were reduced to the same basis by multiplying the index number given in the department of labor by .834, the ratio which the 1891 index of the Aldrich report bears to that of the department of labor. The difference of eight-tenths of one per cent alluded to above arises from the fact that the Aldrich report and the statement of the department of labor do not exactly agree as to the course of prices between 1890 and 1891. Hence, taking the index numbers of each authority for 1891 as being equal, there is a difference in them for 1890.

mittedly subject to less violent fluctuations than wholesale prices."[32] The Massachusetts Bureau of Statistics of Labor has lately investigated retail prices and found an advance since 1897 of 15.37 per cent.[33]

The advance shown in the above table in the same time was about 26 per cent. But while it is true that retail prices, on which the cost of living of the laborer is based, have not advanced so markedly since 1897, it is also true that they had not declined so markedly in the previous period. Accordingly over the entire period the statistics for wholesale prices give us a fair if not an exact estimate of the movement of retail prices, and we may at least closely approximate the changes in the laborer's cost of living. Bearing this in mind we may come to a consideration of the real wages of the workers whose nominal wages we have just traced. It may be objected that the figures of the United States Department of Labor are for the whole country, and local conditions in New York may vitiate any comparisons made. In this connection it is only necessary to point to the fact that the chief way in which such vitiation could occur would be through a wide variation of rents in New York City as compared with the rest of the country, since the course of prices of articles of food, clothing, etc., is the same in that center as it is in the whole country. Furthermore, it can be shown conclusively that rents in New York in the past twenty years have varied but very little, and hence deductions drawn from the Department of Labor's table can be relied upon to reflect the actual course of the real wages of those engaged in the clothing industry,

---

[32] Twentieth annual report of the New York bureau of labor, 1902, p. 406.

[33] Thirty-second annual report, 1902, p. 310.

since only in the items covered in that table has there been a wide variation.

The following table shows the rentals for one, two and three room apartments in typical tenement houses in New York City for the year 1885:

	One room Monthly	Two rooms Monthly average for each room monthly		Three rooms Monthly average for each room monthly	
Six story buildings	$5.75	$7.13	$3.56	$10.59	$3.53
Five story buildings	5.29	7.67	3.83	11.24	3.74
Four story buildings	6.42	8.03	4.01	10.07	3.36
Three story buildings	5.72	7.81	3.90	11.09	3.69[34]

In 1894 in testimony before the New York Tenemen House Committee, A. S. Woolfolk reported the results of an investigation of 600 families, in which he found the average rents for the same grade of houses investigated in 1880, to be as follows:[35]

		Average for each room
For one room monthly	$4.24	
For two rooms monthly	8.08	$4.04
For three rooms monthly	10.75	3.58
For four rooms monthly	14.46	3.61
For five rooms monthly	19.66	3.93

Before the same committee Robert Graham, Secretary of the Church Temperance Society, testified that from an investigation of 19,191 German, Jewish, and Italian families he had found the following to be the average rents paid:[36]

		Average for each room
For one room monthly	$5.04	
For two rooms monthly	7.85	$3.93
For three rooms monthly	11.12	3.70
For four rooms monthly	15.38	3.84
For five rooms monthly	21.39	4.27

[34] Report of the New York tenement house commission, 1884, p. 68.
[35] Report of the tenement house committee, 1895, p. 434.
[36] Ibid., p. 423.

E. R. L. Gould, in his investigation made under the authority of the act creating the Tenement House Commission of 1900, found the following to be the average rentals in twenty-five tenement houses visited:

For three room apartments the range was from $2.33 to $5.00 for each room monthly, the average being $3.63.

For four room apartments, the range was from $2.25 to $6.25 for each room monthly, the average being $3.93.[37]

The Tenement House Commission made a careful study of rents on Forsyth, Canal, Chrystie, and Bayard streets in New York, and the following table shows the results of their investigation:

Number of rooms	Average monthly	Average for each room monthly	Number reported
Two rooms	$7.42	$3.71	253
Three rooms	11.03	3.68	174
Four rooms	14.35	3.59	100
Five rooms	21.70	4.34	20[38]

The real estate firm of George J. Kenny & Bro. writing in 1900 gives the following to be the rentals in first class tenement houses which fulfill all the requirements of the Tenement House Laws.[39]

Average for three room apartments, each room, $4.44

Average for four room apartments, each room, $3.92

From these figures it is evident that since 1885 there has been no noticeable increase in rents for the same class of tenements, and that even in the model tenements of much better

---

[37] De Forest and Veillier, The tenement house problem, 1903, I. p. 360.

[38] Ibid., II. Appendix, ix.

[39] Ibid., I. p. 380.

character, rentals are little higher than they were in the early eighties.[40]

In the following comparison of wages and prices it has been impossible to take as a basis the wages in all branches for the same year, and therefore the earliest possible date has been used in each branch respectively. This results in slight confusion, but on the other hand, it avoids the error arising from using as basis of comparison wages reported for a single year.

Cutters—In 1902 cutters were receiving an average yearly wage of $938, as compared with a range of from $680 to $800 in 1883, a nominal increase of from 17 per cent to 38 per cent. Moreover, in 1902 the average price of the commodities was 12.2 per cent lower than in 1883, hence not only was the cutter receiving from $1.17 to $1.38 for every dollar he got in 1883, but each of these dollars had a purchasing power of about one eighth more than at that date.

Coatmakers—In the manufacture of coats, operators in 1902 were receiving an average yearly wage of $576 as compared with $416 in 1889, an advance of 38 per cent, and each dollar had increased in purchasing power approximately one per cent. Since 1894 the yearly wage for basters has advanced from $416 and $512 to $544, an increase of from 5 per cent to 30 per

---

[40] During the past few years it is possible that there has been some advance in rents. Numerous authorities have estimated an advance of from 10 to 15 per cent. That there should be such an advance is not strange. The cost of building has increased greatly, and the demand for housing accomodations has not diminished. So far as the dwellings on the east side are concerned, it is highly probable that the betterment in conditions of the dwellings themselves have at least offset the advance in rents. This being the case, we are justified in eliminating the rent factor from the discussion of the movement of real wages.

cent. Since that time, however, prices have advanced 17.4 per cent, so that their increase in wages is rather nominal than real. The average yearly wages of all coatmakers as shown by the table previously given has increased since 1883 from $384 and $448 to $513, an increase of, from 14 per cent to 33 per cent, and in the same time the purchasing power of their wages has increased approximately one eighth.

Vestmakers—Up to 1901 there seems to have been very little gain in the wages of this class of workers, but in that year an increase came about which placed the level of yearly wages for men at $645, and $389 for women as compared with an average yearly wage for both men and women of from $384 to $480 in 1894. It must be borne in mind, however, that in this period prices of commodities had advanced 17.4 per cent, so that the apparent gain is far greater than the real.

Pantsmakers—While no exact percentages can be given as to the advance in this line, yet it is evident that from 1888 to 1902 there was a considerable upward movement. In 1888 pressers averaged $320 and in 1889 only $256; in 1888 operators averaged $288, and in the next year only $192. In 1901, however, the average yearly wages of women was $240 and in 1902, $366.44, more than was earned by either operators or pressers in 1888. In 1901 the average yearly wages of men was $424.18, and in 1902 $533.44, a great increase over the last years of the eighties. Averaging the yearly wages paid to all workers, male and female, according to their numerical importance we find that in 1901 the result is $395, which is much higher than the income of either presser or operator in 1888 or 1889. Moreover, since 1888 wholesale prices have declined 1.1 per cent, and the present wages are even greater in comparison than would appear from the mere dollars and cents.

Pressers—Since 1888 the average yearly wages of pressers has advanced about 52 per cent, the yearly wages of that year and 1902 being $320 and $487 respectively. The decline in wholesale prices just noted of course contributes to make the advance in economic welfare of the presser even greater than appears from the figures.

Jacketmakers.—Since 1894 there has been an increase in the wages of jacketmakers. From a yearly wage of $216 to $288 they have risen to one of $477 for men and $364 for women. the advance of 17.4 per cent in prices since 1894 lessens the magnitude of the advance in wages, but the increase still remains.

Cloakmakers—If we take 1882 as a starting point the advance in this line seems to be confined exclusively to the women workers, and a positive decline is evident in the case of the men. It is, however, hardly fair to take 1882 as a base owing to the fact that wages were at an abnormal level as compared with the years immediately following. If wages for 1902 be compared with those for 1885 we find that from an average for male labor of $224 to $320 and for female of $96 to $128, an advance has taken place to a point where the average for men and women together is higher than either of these, in fact is a few cents above $400. The nominal wage movement in this case is almost identical with that of real wages, for prices are practically the same in 1902 as in 1885.

In all the above computations it is to be noted that the greater part of the statistics refer to union labor, data for unorganized labor being almost impossible to collect, and it may be true that the conclusions made will have to be somewhat modified for this reason. Since, however, such a large portion of the workers are members of unions and since the movement is so marked in its direction, it can hardly be denied that the conclusions drawn are to a considerable degree applicable to the clothing industry as a whole. In the case of the cloakmakers, however, union statistics leave out of account the majority of the highly skilled workers who draw very high wages, for it is not true that in this branch all the most highly skilled labor is in the union, hence the average earnings as given in our discussion of the cloakmakers is really lower than the actual average. Moreover, since the union, although apparently strong in numbers, has little control over its members, the reports made by the heads of a trade union as to the wages received by its members do not represent accurately the real conditions. The union opposes working over time and has a certain standard of speed at which its members are supposed to work, and returns are given by the officers on that basis; but as a matter of fact work is carried on overtime, and at a higher speed than the union dictates, hence the earnings of its members are higher than would appear from the reports given out by the unions. During the busy season the skilled workers, both in and out of the union, often earn from $30 to $40 a week and even more, and it is safe, therefore, to place the average yearly wages of this highly skilled class at from $600 to $650. Accordingly the averages given in our tables are too low. With this one exception, however, the figures given above may be taken as fairly representative.

We have noted a general marked advance in the wages of labor engaged in the clothing industry since the eighties.

Our conclusions in regard to the wage movement are diametrically opposed to those arrived at by Professor Commons in his investigation for the Industrial Commission. His conclusions do not seem to be based upon the tables which he presented as much as on the statements of workers in the trade or on data from a few shops which are supposed to be typical. For example, it is stated [41] that the weekly wages of male operators and basters on coats in task shops in New York have fallen one sixth, while their hours have increased one fifth. There is a traditional statement among coat tailors that when the team system was introduced the operator earned three dollars a day or eighteen dollars a week. The wages actually received were, as we have seen[42] two or three dollars less than this amount. Moreover, within a few years after the introduction of the system, wages for the more skilled fell below this level even in the busy season. In 1902 the wage of operators was about eighteen dollars a week, and moreover this was an average wage which took into account, not only the highly skilled workmen counted in the early history of the system, but also the medium and low grade operators. Hence, the wages of all classes of operators, averaged together, in 1902 even exceeded those received by the most highly skilled in the early eighties. As the following tables show, this increase in wages manifested itself in two ways, increase in weekly wages and increase in the number of working days a year. A careful study of the entire period since 1882 reveals the fact that the working time has increased almost continuously[43] although it is only since 1897 that sufficient data exist for a detailed proof of the statement.[44]

[41] Report of the industrial commission, 1901, XV. p. 368.
[42] Supra p. 32.
[43] Twelfth annual report of the New York bureau of labor, 1894, p. 69.
[44] This increase in the number of days employed in the stated occupation reflects on actual increase in yearly income, as the earnings in subsidiary employment are so small that it is not necessary to take them into account.

Cutters

Year	Working days[45]	Weekly wages
Previous to 1894	240	$14 to $21
1894	240	16 to 19
1897	261	18.86
1898	266	19.02
1899	270	19.14
1900	260	17.88
1901	274	18.60
1902	298	18.99

Coatmakers

Year	Working days Males	Females	Weekly wages Males	Females
1894[47]	192	216		
1897	224	173	$ 9.36	$7..4
1898	223	127	9.24	7.74
1899	240	269	12.12	6.46
1900[46]	270	286	13.53	5.72
1901[46]	208	242	12.78	5.95
1902[46]	240	284	13.29	7.30

Vestmakers

Year	Males	Females	Males	Females
1894[47]	192			
1897	210	213	$10.86	$6.90
1898	137	133	11.40	6.96
1899	240	236	13.64	4.67
1900[46]	210	218	11.50	6.90
1901[46]	186	180	12.92	7.38
1902[46]	274	268	14.13	8.72

Jacketmakers

Year	Males	Females	Males	Females
Previous to 1894[47]	168	192[47]		
1894[47]	216			
1897	204	144	$ 9.96	$6.54
1898	201	214	10.74	6.96
1899				
1900	180	178	11.17	7.36
1901	224	224	12.78	9.75

[45] Twelfth annual report of the New York bureau of labor, 1894, p. 69. These figures are rough averages and in the figures used hereafter from this report this fact should be borne in mind.

[46] Computed on a basis of two quarters reported.

[47] Twelfth annual report of the New York bureau of labor, 1894, p. 69 et seq.

Pressers

Year	Working days Males	Working days Females	Weekly wages Males	Weekly wages Females
Previous to 1894[47]	168			
1894[47]	216			
1897	202		$11.10	
1898	198		9.60	
1899	281		10.12	
1900				
1901				
1902[46]	240		12.19	

Pantsmakers

Year	Males	Females	Males	Females
1894[47]	192			
1897				
1898	243	248	$ 9.00	$7.80
1899	236	267	9.26	7.38
1900[46]	232	218	9.24	6.19
1901[46]	228	276	11.16	5.23
1902[46]	252	282	12.95	7.79

Cloakmakers

Year	Males	Females	Males	Females
1894[47]	120			
1897	248		$14.16	
1898	181	190	12.52	$6.31
1899	248	247	14.66	8.13
1900[46]	172	162	12.56	7.48
1901[46]	186	174	15.62	9.73
1902[46]	182	178	14.60	8.20

From these tables it is evident that jacketmakers, pressers, vestmakers, coatmakers and male pantsmakers have received both an increase of weekly wages and an increase in employment during the year. Cutters and female pantsmakers have received an increase in the number of days employed, and if the entire period be taken into account, an increase of wages but since 1897 their wages have remained practically stationary. While all cloakmakers have received an increase in weekly

[46] Computed on a basis of two quarters reported.

[47] Twelfth annual report of the New York bureau of labor, 1894, p. 69 et seq.

wages there is a tendency for the number of days employed a year to become less.[48]

It appears then that the movement has been pronounced in the direction of more employment and higher weekly wages, with the possible exception of the cloakmakers. The reasons for this apparent exception are the fact that wages are actually higher than those reported by the unions, and the increasingly seasonal character of the work, due to changing styles, thus making it impossible to carry on a jobbing trade.

Certain inherent influences tend toward irregularity of employment in the clothing industry. Production must be closely adjusted to consumption. The demand for clothing is highly seasonal and is influenced by causes that are beyond control. The expenditure of that portion of a person's income which is necessary to provide him with a new suit of clothes, in place of the old suit which can still be worn, is marginal in its nature, and as a consequence is among the first to respond to a disturbance. Business dullness, a warm winter, or an unusually late spring, are factors which will decrease the normal expenditure for clothing. This being true, it is evident that the demand for clothing is one that cannot be accurately estimated until near the time when that clothing is to be worn; stock production then, is impracticable and seasonal production the rule. Moreover, the greatest care must be taken to conform to the changing styles. The range for class or individual choice is wide and the demand for a particular style of garment cannot long be anticipated. The strength of the clothing industry must

---

[48] If compared with 1894 this last statement would appear untrue, but it must be remembered that in 1894 there occurred a long strike of cloakmakers and a large part of their lack of employment in that year is traceable to that fact.

ultimately depend upon its power to supply the public with the same choice of goods as can be had of a custom tailor.

There are, however, certain modifying influences that have combined to make work less irregular and to give the worker a greater number of days employment during the year. Formerly it was the custom for the workers during the rush season to work excessively long hours; now labor, in its organized capacity, is constantly bringing pressure to equalize the length of the working day, thus forcing the manufacturer to lengthen the season of production. It is at this point that trade unions have exerted the greatest influence for good in the clothing industry. The development of the clothing industry, bringing with it a better organization and concentration of capital, has relieved the manufacturers of the necessity of catering so closely to those unnecessary demands of the public which, in the past, have been responsible for much unnecessary rush during certain seasons of the year. The pressure to keep large amounts of fixed capital employed has not been and is not great in the clothing industry, but the magnitude of the industry to-day is such that expenses go on during all seasons of the year, and sometimes production is stimulated. By resorting to various devices, manufacturers have been able to meet the demands of the clothing industry and at the same time extend the number of days worked in the year. Because of a widely extended market they are enabled to make up goods for the different sections of the country at different times. Cheaper grades of goods are often manufactured during the dull season for the trade of those sections where the so-called "tasteless" consumer predominates. A great part of what is known as the "western trade" is of this character. The question of style does not play so important a role here and greater cheapness is gained by throwing the manufacture into the dull season.

The fact that the retailer orders more frequently and in smaller quantities also enables the manufacturer to extend his period of production. The peculiar elasticity characteristic of the contract system has lengthened the period of work so far as New York is concerned. It makes possible the manufacture of large quantities of goods for other centers during dull seasons, and enables the adjustment of the working force and its wages in such a way as to attract work from other cities. Wages during the dull season range from 15 per cent to 20 per cent lower than during the busy season.

After taking into account all these factors which make for longer periods of employment, the dull season is still an important one, varying from two to five months, the shortest dull season being found in the case of cutters and the longest in workers on cloaks and women's suits. In almost every case the wages of the busy season are increased on account of a higher piece rate and on account of overtime, this being particularly true, so far as overtime is concerned, in cloaks, though the amount of overtime and the variation of wages is much less marked at the present time then a decade ago. As the shops have increased in size they have become more amenable to regulation and the minute division of labor makes it impossible for the worker to take home work after regular hours. Here again women's cloaks, particularly the higher grades, are an exception, for the lack of division of labor makes it possible for workers to take to their homes garments on which they have worked during the day; and during the busy season it is almost the invariable rule for workers in all classes of shops to do this.

It is generally agreed that during the period under consideration the general movement of wages in all industries has been upward. No industry can live to itself and we should expect that the forces which have made themselves felt elsewhere would also have their influence in the clothing industry. But the influences peculiar to the clothing industry are so important that they must be studied in detail.

In the past twenty years immigration to the United States has been of immense proportions. New York, as the greatest port of entrance has had a constant glut of cheap labor. Over 70 per cent of the twenty million foreign immigrants who have entered this country since the establishment of immigration records, have entered that port and the percentage of those who have remained there is indicated by the fact that in 1900, of the 1,469,908 persons engaged in 159 occupations in New York City, 1,171,732 were persons one or both of whose parents were foreign born.[49] The clothing industry has been peculiarly attractive to a large portion of these people, because, as they believed, and as we have pointed out, it was by its very nature suited to them. The fact that a large number of any nationality were in the trade would be an inducement for new arrivals to enter it. The extent to which the Russian Jews entered the trade is shown by the fact that in 1900 out of the 71,163 persons reported by the census as being engaged in the tailoring business, 28,011 or nearly 40 per cent were of Russian descent.[50]

The Italians were also attracted in considerable numbers toward the clothing trade, and in 1900, 8674 of them are given by the census as laborers in that line.[51]

[49] Census, 1900, occupations, p. 635.
[50] Ibid., p. 635 et seq.
[51] Ibid.

The natural inference from the fact that so large a horde of cheap laborers poured into the trade would be that wages would be sharply depressed from year to year as the competition of cheap with cheaper labor became fiercer, but strange to say we find that while wages in some lines are lower than in others, yet the advance is no less striking in the branches entered by the immigrant than in the others.

The demand for ready-made clothing was rapidly growing and hence the demand for labor to manufacture that clothing was likewise on the advance. The great expansion of the clothing industry is evident from the census figures, which show that in New York from 1880[52] to 1900[53] the value of the men's factory product increased from $60,798,697 to $103,220,201. Between the same dates the value of women's factory product increased from $18,930,553 to $102,711,604, or about 440 per cent. With such a demand for labor as must have arisen we can partially understand why the rate of wages did not fall as sharply as would have been expected had the demand remained constant.

Placement plays a very prominent part in preventing a glut of laborers in the clothing industry. The statement has been repeated until it is trite that the Jew considers the industry as a stepping stone to something higher, and in no industry in this country has the upward movement been so pronounced as in this. Every year large numbers desert the clothing industry to go into such occupations as small shopkeepers, insurance agents, and clerks. The importance of this movement is seen by the

---

[52] Census, 1880, manufactures p. 417. For 1880 the figures included the custom trade.

[53] Census, 1900, manufactures, part ii. p. 622.

study of the migration of the Jews into the better residence districts uptown. The Industrial Commission says: "Tailors who have been displaced by green immigrants of the same or other nationalities have found better positions as contractors, manufacturers, or small tradesmen, or have created a new line of product of a better grade."[54] Out of 159 different occupations for men in New York City the census of 1900 states that Russians and Poles engaged in 155, and of 88 occupations engaged in by women, Russian and Polish women were found in 83.[55] Of the 88,827 males, Russians and Poles, 25,674 were engaged in the manufacture of clothing.*

*The following table shows their distribution in other branches of industry:

Laborers (not specified)	4088
Agents	1663
Clerks and copyists	2754
Hucksters and peddlers	4215
Retail merchants	9016
Salesmen	3256
Boot and shoemakers	1554
Carpenters and joiners	1574
Lawyers	217
Hat and capmakers	1543
Manufacturers and officials	2513
Tobacco and cigar operatives	1778
Teachers and professors in colleges	526
Physicians and surgeons	305
Clergymen	298
Dentists	75
Musicians	403
Electricians	135

[54] Report of the industrial commission, 1901, XV. p. 369.

[55] Census, 1900, occupations, p. 640 et seq.

Of the 24,321 Russian and Polish women engaged in gainful occupations, 8545 were engaged in the clothing industry.*

A third influence counteracting the depression of wages caused by the immense immigration is the growing capacity of the employer to pay higher wages, and the ability of the trade union to make this capacity effective. In order that labor may receive a constantly increasing share of a given product, the employer of that labor must be able to make savings along other lines. The fact that the employers of to-day are able to make those savings is traceable to the general advance of the clothing industry. The clothing industry is no longer marginal, employing marginal entrepreneurs. To-day it enlists entrepreneurs noted for their insight and skill, and possessing large capital. In point of wealth and managing ability the directors of the clothing industry compare favorably with those in any other. Along with this change in the upper ranks of the clothing industry came naturally a better organization, eliminating many of the wastes common before. The market is more carefully studied and production and consumption are more nearly in adjustment. No longer is it true that large stocks of clothing remain unsold at the end of the season to be auctioned off at a great sacrifice. The retailer buys in small quantities and at

---

*This table shows their distribution in some other branches of industry.

Servants and waitresses	2878
Saleswomen	1306
Dressmakers	2168
Teachers and professors in colleges	132
Musicians and teachers of music	114
Actresses	37

more frequent intervals thus preventing a glut of clothing on his hands which must be sold at cut rates. Credit associations have largely eliminated the losses from bad debts.

The savings just enumerated may result either in a lessened cost to the consumer, or in greater profits to the producer. In the latter case a fund is created which did not exist before from which the worker may obtain higher wages. It is along the line of securing a portion of this fund that the activities of trade unions have been directed. In those branches of the industry where immigrant labor most strongly competed for employment trade unions from an early time exerted a powerful influence. Unions were formed among workers on knee pants and children's jackets in 1888, among coatmakers in 1890, and among the pantsmakers in 1894.[56] While they have not always been able to make their demands effective, yet their influence has been such that minimum conditions, below which the trade was not permitted to fall have been established. It is to be noticed that the establishment of the minimum prevented those immigrants from entering the clothing industry whose efficiency would not permit of their employment under such requirements. Trade unions have therefore raised the general level of wages by shutting out a mass of low grade labor which no manufacturer could afford to employ if he observed trade union regulations.

Closely allied to this influence of trade unions is that exerted by state regulation, which also set up certain minimum requirements which must be observed, with the result that a considerable portion of the immigrants were debarred from enter-

[56] Twelfth annual report of the New York bureau of labor, 1894, p. 28.

ing the trade. For example, the state made it impossible for production to be carried on profitably under the conditions of isolated home work, and those who were fitted only for this form of employment were forced into some other industry.

Wages have advanced not only on account of the superior organization of the clothing industry, but also on account of an actual increase in product in a unit of time, due to improved machinery, improved division of labor and improved skill of the worker. In the early eighties the proportion of green immigrants to the entire number in the trade was very high and a great many of these were of a very low grade of skill and efficiency. At present those who have remained in the clothing industry for a number of years have acquired a skill that naturally results from continued application, while the immigrants who are entering the trade are of a higher efficiency than were those of twenty years ago. Hence, the average efficiency is greater, and this contributes in no small measure to the steady advance in wages.

The contract system has been charged with having a tendency to depress wages and exploit labor. One of the arguments brought forward to substantiate this statement is that the contractor is not of the trade and receives compensation for services which he does not render, that which is paid to him being just so much deducted from the wages of labor. A writer in the Report of the Ohio Bureau of Labor in 1894,[57] says "the truth is that the price offered by the manufacturers is so low that the intervention of the middleman is impossible." As we have already indicated, the modern contractor has been confused with the old type of middleman, against whom this charge

[57] Nineteenth annual report, 1896, p. 59.

was well founded. From 1882 to 1895 the prevalent system of subcontracting made it possible for the middleman to receive an undue share of the price paid by the manufacturer. But this form of contract has disappeared. In England, as early as 1888, the House of Lords investigation brought out the fact that this was true in London.[58]

The following is the testimony before the House:

Q. You just said now that the contract system was dying out.

A. Yes; that is stated from information I have received.

Q. Did you mean that there were fewer middlemen now interposed between the great employer and the sweater, or in what way is the contract system dying out?

A. The contract system is dying out in this way: that formerly a contractor would take out a very large quantity of work from the merchant and then let it out again to sweaters, but now the sweaters go direct to the merchant and obtain their work.[59]

Miss Potter says, in referring to the subcontractor:[60] "This class of middlemen was a fact of the past; with equal certainty we may assert that it is a fiction of the present." As we have heretofore pointed out, the contractor of to-day does perform a real service. The weekly income of the small contractor is, however, but little greater than that of his workmen. That the compensation of the contractor is not unduly high is shown

[58] Report of the select committee of the house of lords, 1888, XX. pp. 18, 19.

[59] The Canadian government recognizes the difference between these forms of contract, by prohibiting by statute all subcontracting. The Garment Worker. Feb., 1901, p. 14.

[60] Booth, Labour and life of the people, I. East London, p. 228.

by the fact that coöperative shops, founded for the purpose of eliminating the contractors, have not been able to pay higher wages than those paid by the contractor, and in some cases have actually paid lower wages. Joseph Lee, after a study of one of these experiments conducted in England in 1888, writes as follows: "I find that the philanthropic experiment paid rather lower wages than the average. They are paying no interest, and are showing a small profit which is not distributed." [61] Speaking of the small contractor in London, Miss Potter says: "His earnings are scanty, probably less than those of either of the skilled hands to whom he pays wages, and he works all hours of the day and night." [62] As the size of the contractor's shop increases a larger part of his income goes to pay rent, interest on capital and wages of superintendence. That the margin between the price paid the contractor by the manufacturer and that paid to the workman is not unduly high is shown by the fact that when unions demand an increase of wages from the contractor he is obliged to secure a corresponding increase from the manufacturer.[63] A case illustrating this point was brought out in the cloakmakers' strike of 1895. The demand was made for an increase of wages of from 12 per cent to 15 per cent and in order to accede to this demand the contractors asked for and finally obtained a similar advance from the manufacturers.[64] This fact is further substantiated by the organization

[61] Report of the committee on manufactures on the sweating system, 1892, p. 254.

[62] Booth, Labour and life of the people, I. East London, p. 232.

[63] Contractors association's statement in the report of the industrial commission, XV. p. 334.

[64] Ninth annual report of the New York board of mediation and arbitration, 1895, p. 162.

of the contractors and their employees into a union known as the Consolidated Board of the Cloak Industry. The purpose of this board was to provide the means whereby joint demands might be made on the manufacturer.[65] Union officials recognize this inability of the contractor to pay higher wages unless granted an increase from the manufacturer. Chas. F. Reichers, Ex-secretary of the United Garment Workers of America said in 1895:[66] "The contractor is certainly losing money. That is what makes the contractor kick so hard and that is what makes us call the contractor a fool. They ought not to blame the men; they ought not to fight the men. They should organize and go to the manufacturer and say, 'We are an organized body. For this grade of goods we want so much and for this grade we want so much.'"

The second charge made against the contractors is that the fierce competition among them forces down wages. In October 1897 the United Brotherhood of Tailors of New York issued a manifesto to the public, in which the following statement occurs: "the contractors, who, because of the competition between themselves, lower the prices paid for making a garment, and in turn drive the operative into performing an inhuman task for less than a living wage . . . We hereby declare that at a given time in the year 1899, the clothing workers of this city will refuse to work for any contractor or middle man." In 1901 the United Garment Workers of America officially declared against the contractors or sweaters, "who are forced to compete mercilessly against each other, are driven to extraordinary straits in order to do the work at a minimum cost."[67] The

[65] Ibid., p. 162.
[66] Ibid., p. 236.
[67] The Garment Worker, May, 1901, p. 3.

8

Industrial Commission says:[68] "There is always a cut-throat competition among contractors."

That competition was on a low plane in the early stages of the contract system is undoubtedly true, but, as Booth has shown, this is not the result of the contract system, but of the small master system in general. Where it is easy to pass from the position of an employee to that of an employer, whatever the system, the abuse of a low form of competition is present. It happens that the tendency of the Jew to become an employer is strong, and that his entrance to this sphere is in the clothing industry through the contract system. He, like the small master, is forced to assume risks for which he is unfitted, and his business standards do not deter him from resorting to methods to which the large manufacturer would not stoop.[69] Two forces have been at work that have largely mitigated this evil. The contractor himself, through trade union agitation, state regulation, and the general advance in the clothing industry has become a person of larger responsibility, of more intellect and higher business standards. The manufacturer is assuming those responsibilities which naturally fall to him. He no longer asserts that the methods employed by his contractors toward their workmen are of no concern to him. State regulation has played an important role in eliminating the irresponsible contractor. The manufacturer is obliged to keep a list of all contractors to whom he gives work, and he will not employ those who cannot meet the demands of the law. When he becomes responsible to the trade union for the enforcement of agreements

[68] Report of the industrial commission, 1901, XV. p. 322.

[69] See also statement of Joseph Lee in report of the committee on manufactures on the sweating system, 1893, pp. 251-255.

entered into by his contractors, he will not become sponsor for those who cannot fulfil them. This growing responsibility of the manufacturer is strikingly shown by the following agreement, which was signed by 420 manufacturers in 1901.*

"The following agreement is hereby entered into between the firm of, ———— and District Council No. 1, United Garment Workers of America.

First. All contractors doing work for said firm shall employ only members in good standing of the United Garment Workers of America, and the following conditions shall be observed in all shops conducted by said contractors:

a. The working time shall be limited to fifty nine hours per week.

b. Wages of employes to be paid on the last working day of each week.

c. The union rate of wages shall be paid in said shops.

Second. The firm agrees to withhold work from any of the said contractors not observing the above mentioned conditions.

Third. The firm also agrees to be responsible for all wages that may be due the employes of said contractor at the end of each week."

This third clause of the contract calls attention to an abuse which was very common in the early stages of the contract system. The statement made that the contractors of to-day are men of larger responsibility is strikingly shown by the almost complete disappearance of this evil. Not more than fifteen or twenty cases came up under this clause, and it is not certain that in all of these the contractor intended to cheat his employees out of their wages. The amount of wages lost owing to the absconding

*Appendix D. III.

of the contractor has been greatly exaggerated. In a public address in 1897, Mr. Albert Hochstadter, who at that time was secretary of the Clothing Manufacturers' Association, a man with intimate knowledge of the clothing industry, said that during the period when the contractor was the most irresponsible, less than one per cent of the wages earned was lost in this way. Mrs. Willett, in speaking of the women home finishers, says, "that cases where women are cheated of their wages are not common. In the greatest center for the finishing work, . . . the question itself excited astonishment."[70]

This agreement was, of course, not lived up to in every detail, or in all cases, but that such an agreement was made and actually enforced in many cases shows that an advance of great importance has been made.

That the contract system, as it exists to-day, does not depress wages is shown by the fact that for the same grade of work wages are no lower in the outside than in the inside shops. The statistics which we have cited are, from necessity, largely those of the contractor's shop, and if our interpretation of them has been correct, the movement of wages has been as favorable there as in the case of cutters, for example, who are employed directly by the manufacturer. It is claimed, it is true, that the contract system has reduced wages, both in the outside and in the inside shop, hence the fact that the rates of wages are the same in both does not prove the lack of a depressing influence on the part of the contractor. The manufacturer, it is said, plays off the outside against the inside shop.[71] That there is an element of truth in the charge cannot be denied. Where

---

[70] Employment of women in the clothing trade, 1902, p. 115.
[71] Booth, Life and labour of the people in London, IV. p. 307.

two sets of workmen are engaged under different systems of work and where the conditions of the trade are not common knowledge, it is possible to shift work from one to the other. But this condition in the clothing industry is not radically different from that which is present in all industry. Manufacturers can send their work to another center to be made up; the most advanced type of industrial organization, the trust, can play a factory in one locality against one in another just as the clothing manufacturer can play one set of workmen against another under existing conditions in New York. Such abuses, if they are abuses, can be overcome only by raising the moral tone of the industry or perfecting organization on the part of the laboring class. It is evident that what is needed on the part of the workers is concerted action and that this is more easily gained between the workers under the inside and outside systems engaged in work in the same locality than between workers in centers far removed working under dissimilar conditions. In the agreement cited[72] it was stated that a definite standard of wages should be paid to workers in outside shops.[73]

[72] Supra p. 115.

[73] The secretary of the children's jacket makers' union said to the writer in a personal interview in 1902: "Operators earn eighteen dollars in the outside shop and only fourteen in the inside."

Said a tailor in 1902 in a personal interview: "In the inside shop in the busy season we earn $14, and in the dull season $12; in the contractor's shop we get $15 in the busy season, and $13 in the dull."

W. Chuck, secretary of district council no. 1, says in a recent letter: "There is a difference between the wages paid in the inside shop and in the outside shops. In the first they are in many instances lower because of the fact that they employ a larger per cent of cheap labor."

"Manufacturers pay from $2.00 to $4.00 less a week," for the

It is urged that the contract system depresses wages because the decentralized conditions make the organization of unions more difficult, and although the contractor is quick to accede to the demands of the union, and is quite ready to sign an agreement, he breaks it at the first opportunity. In another place we hope to show that notwithstanding the popular opinion to the contrary, the trade unions have flourished to a wonderful degree in the clothing industry; that of all the fictions that have grown up around that industry, the one which affirms the weakness of trade unionism is among the most misleading. Conditions favoring or discouraging trade unions are so complex that generalization is difficult, but of two industries in the same stage of development as to the industrial intelligence of its employees, that one offers most favorable opportunities to trade unionism in which there is the most intimate contact between employer and employee. The workers in the clothing industry, as well as their leaders, have been wanting in high industrial intelligence. Transfer this same labor from the contractor's shop to the large inside shop under the foreman system, and the result will be that effective trade unionism is impossible. The contractor is intimately associated with his workers and there is a mutual understanding between them as to the strength and weakness of their respective positions; the foreman on the contrary has interests in common with the manufacturer rather than with the employees, and his irresponsible position presents a great obstacle to the enforcement of union demands. Trade

same grade of work, than the contractors. Report of local union no. 95, Syracuse, N. Y. Taken from the report of the thirteenth annual convention of the united garment workers of America.

unions themselves recognize the fact that the greatest enemy of organized labor is the foreman.[75]

The clothing industry is characterized not only by decentralization of the technical processes of production, but by a highly sensitive market. Every manufacturer realizes that if a given order is not filled immediately it is lost forever, hence he is stimulated to use all efforts to fill those orders. It is the sensitiveness of the market that constitutes an important factor in counteracting the natural tendency of the decentralized methods of production toward non-organized conditions among the laborers. In the custom trade we have an example of a decentralized class of workers employed in an industry where this extreme sensitiveness does not exist, owing to the fact that the custom tailor can ordinarily secure a delay from regular customers. From the fact that the workers are scattered, in small shops in all parts of the city, and that the employers are much more independent of them than are the employers in the clothing industry, trade unionism is woefully weak. In the building trades, on the other hand, although highly decentralized, but subject to great sensitiveness of the market, we find unionism at its strongest. Merely because the contractor in the clothing industry maintains decentralized modes of work, it cannot be drawn as a logical inference that unorganized conditions exist on the part of the workers. On the contrary the greatest stimulus exists toward their organization since they recognize that the employers are, to a considerable extent,

---

[75] In the issue of the Weekly Bulletin of the clothing trade, July 29, 1904, there are twenty-five clever bits of sarcasm aimed at the foreman. The list is too long to print, but it brings out well the feelings of the average unionist towards this individual.

dependent upon them and that they are in a position to make their demands effective. Moreover, the objection to separation of the workers, which is, that knowledge of the conditions of other workers and of the trade in general is precluded, is largely removed by the spread of trade papers, weekly meetings, and other methods of disseminating information.

The contractor is subjected to the charge that he does not live up to his agreements. This charge is based on the fact that after agreeing to pay a stipulated wage, he fails to do so in the dull season. It may be that the contractor should not be so ready to sign agreements, but it must be pointed out that trade unions will have to recognize that the same conditions cannot be maintained in the clothing industry the year round. As we have seen, wages in the contractor's shop are practically identical with those paid in the inside shop in the busy season. When the dull season comes on, only the most favored inside shops continue to work, while the outside shop, owing to its greater elasticity continues to work at irregular intervals, although it is true that lower wages are paid. Thus the working season is prolonged, and the yearly income of the worker is increased above what it would have been had the inside system alone been in vogue. In the manufacturer's contract of 1901 the section that provides that the manufacturer shall maintain union wages was found to be impossible of enforcement, but in the past two years trade unions have become sufficiently powerful to force the contractors to live up to these demands during both busy and dull seasons. This has led the manufacturers to come to the rescue of the contractors, and of themselves, by issuing a manifesto declaring for the open shop. The real motive at the bottom of this movement against the closed shop is this necessity for a lower scale of wages during the dull season, for in the busy season there are no objections to the union demands as far as wages are concerned. The periodic disturbances that come with the return of every busy season grow out of the demands of the unions for a return to busy season prices, and the unions are almost universally successful.

CHAPTER IV

Systems of Wage Payment

Two systems of estimating wages exist: the time system and the piece system. Others are simply modifications of these two. The piece system is based upon a unit of product in a unit of time, and the amount received is in constant adjustment with the product turned out. Under the time system a rough estimate is made of product in a unit of time and adjustment of wages to product is supposed to conform in the long run. In both systems the basis is product in a unit of time. The difference is in power of adjustment. Under the piece system unit of product is the chief element; increase product and you increase wages for a unit of time. Under the time system, wages for a unit of time remain unchanged from day to day though there be slight changes in product. In fixing the wage scale under the time system, it is to the interest of labor during trial periods to show as much skill and speed as possible, and when the rate is established the tendency is to slacken speed. Under the piece system it is to the interest of the employer to make it appear to the worker during trial periods that he can turn out a great number of pieces a day, and hence can earn high wages at a small piece rate; on the other hand, it is to the interest of the worker to make the employer believe that his daily capacity is low, and that he should receive a high rate for each piece, in order to earn average wages. When the rate is fixed it is the tendency of the employer to add to the difficulty of the piece and thus get more labor for a dollar, while the worker strives to produce a maximum number of units a day, thus earning a maximum wage. On these facts hinge nearly all disputes as to the method of payment of wages.

The close connection between the two systems of payment is shown by the fact that it is seldom that we find either distinct from the other. In the time system a certain minimum amount of work is often set by the employers that must be performed in a specified time, while a maximum is often set by the union, above which no laborer shall go.[1] In piece work employers often set both a maximum and a minimum, a minimum because they wish their fixed capital to be worked intensively, and a maximum because they fear deterioration of product if work is carried on at too great speed. On the part of the workers a maximum regulation is also found, owing to the fear that if a certain number of pieces a day is exceeded the employer will note the high daily earnings, and cut piece rates.

Piece wages are most applicable to those classes of industry where there is regularity in the processes. Time wages are most applicable where this regularity does not exist and where the conditions existing under trial do not remain the same after the rate has been fixed. Under the piece system any change in those conditions, such as the speeding up of machinery by the employer, will not injure the worker, for as he produces more units, his wages increase proportionately.[2]

In general, employers prefer piece rates, as supervision is

[1] An example of a maximum as set by laborers is found in sections 1 to 5 of the New York City plasterers' agreement, for 1902. New York department of labor bulletin, Dec., 1902, p. 311.

[2] For a fuller consideration of this question see Webb, Sidney and Beatrice, Industrial democracy, chapter on "The standard rate."

saved and a more accurate estimate of cost for each unit of product is afforded. From the point of view of the individual highly skilled workers the piece rate is favored, as it enables them to take the greatest possible advantage of their skill. The unskilled laborer, on the other hand, prefers the time rate, for obvious reasons. The inefficient woodchopper would rather work by the day than by the cord. The most advanced trade union looks at the question from the standpoint of collective bargaining, and the system which they prefer depends upon the regularity or the irregularity of the processes performed.

As early as 1777 the question of piece work came up in connection with the outside shops in the custom trade, and although violently opposed at first by the tailors became the prevailing system. It is evident, that garments vary in style, quality of cloth and grade of workmanship, and hence apparently serious obstacles stand in the way of uniformity. To overcome these, as early as 1811 a subdivision of the processes so minute as to include 150 separate items had made its appearance, thus affording the regularity of process necessary to the successful operation of the piece rate.[3] In the clothing industry under the family system no other form of wage payment was possible, and the conditions that prevailed in the clothing industry during the first decade following the influx of the Jews also made the piece rate almost a necessity.

The clothing industry as a whole lends itself to a close subdivision and marked regularity of process, hence it is not surprising to find that in every branch the piece method of payment has been largely used. In cloak manufacture, however, it is not the regularity and the possibility of great division of

---

[3] Galton, The tailoring trade, p. 117.

processes that has brought this about, but the fact that the highly skilled laborer can earn higher wages under it. The strength of the piece rate in the cloak industry is strikingly shown by an incident in the strikes of 1894 and 1895. In 1894 a long and bitter strike was waged on the part of the union for the introduction of the time system. One of the largest firms finally acceded to the demands of the strikers, and the very next year this establishment, under threat of a strike, was forced to return to the piece system, the skilled workers having discovered that time payment meant a decided reduction in their wages.[4]

The attitude of the trade unions in the clothing industry has usually been hostile to the piece system. They have often failed to recognize the adaptability of the industry to that system, but it is only fair to add that the opposition of trade union leaders has often been due on their part of the difficulty of controlling the natural tendency of the Jew to take advantage of the opportunity offered by the system to earn high wages at the expense of increased speed or long hours, thereby destroying that uniformity among workers which the union considers essential to its existence. In spite of this position of the trade union the piece system prevails, and the best workers will insist upon its maintenance even though it disrupt the union. Though the union opposes piece wages, it has recognized the difficulty of abolishing them, and has attempted to secure effective control by working out carefully itemized piece schedules.* Such schedules make collective bargaining possible, and permit a wide range of individual income. As

[4] Ninth report of the New York board of mediation and arbitration, 1895, p. 165.
*Appendix E. I.

the Webbs point out, the wisdom of such variation will in time be recognized by all rational trade unions.[5]

Time wages have won greater favor with employers during the past few years owing to the modified position of trade unions regarding them. Previous to 1901 the unions demanded a fixed minimum and maximum so that, for example the lower grades of skill would receive sixteen dollars, and the higher eighteen dollars weekly, with no intermediate prices. The tendency of this kind of schedule was to fix the minimum too high, since it aimed to equalize incomes and it was easier for the union to gain support for a movement to raise the wages of the less skilled workers than for one to lower, to any considerable extent, those of the highly skilled. While the man who received eighteen dollars under this schedule might be worth slightly more than his wages, yet those receiving sixteen dollars were men whose earning capacity ranged, say, from ten dollars upward. The employer of this low and medium grade labor naturally opposed time wages when fixed in such a way. Since 1901, however, there has been a change in the policy of the unions in this matter. A greater variation in wages is recognized as inevitable, and instead of establishing a set maximum and minimum which are close together, only a minimum is fixed, which, since it is not bound by any relation to the maximum as under the previous policy, is low enough to enable the employer to get value received.[6] *

[5] In the scale of prices for knee pants 110 separate items are provided for. Such minute piece scales lessen but do not entirely do away with the dispute over prices. Industrial democracy, chapter on "The standard rate."

[6] This statement does not overlook the fact that the establishment of any minimum necessarily carries with it a scaling down of the

*Appendix E. II.

The prevailing system in the manufacture of cloaks, as already stated, is the piece rate, for the most skilled workers. In the work performed by women and girls we usually find the time rate. For pants, piece rates are general. For vests, both the time and piece systems are found. For children's jackets the prevailing system is time. For coats under the Boston system both systems are found, the skilled pocket-makers and seam operators working under the piece system, the less skilled under time rates. In the case of those coats manufactured under the team system and in a few other lines there exists a peculiar combination of the two systems of payment, known as the "task system." As this has excited much comment it will be necessary to consider it here in some detail.

In England as early as 1867 a system of payment known as the "day wage system" was in vogue in the custom trade. Tailors were paid a certain wage a day with the understanding that a given amount of work was to be turned out. This form of payment was opposed by the Amalgamated Society of Tailors, who favored a straight piece rate.[7] This system of daily wage payment was carried over into the clothing industry and on the introduction of the team system became associated with it. The workers in the trade demanded weekly wages, and since they were largely employed in outside shops, some method of supervision was necessary in order to guarantee to the employer a fair return for the wages paid, and the only possible way of securing such a guarantee was by specifying what output, measured by product, should constitute a day's work. The amount of work they were to do was known as the "task" and

highest wages and a levelling up of the lowest, but in the new policy of the union this tendency is not so marked. Ibid.

[7] Galton, The tailoring trade, p. 220.

the system of payment became known as the "task system." A combination of the task system with the team system introduced a little later proved to be of great advantage, as it appealed to the personal interest of the worker, and at the same time gave him his much-coveted freedom. The close association of the two has led many people to believe that they necessarily go together,[8] but that this is not true is proved by the fact that the task system exists in certain phases of the clothing and other industries which do not have the team, and the team system in others which do not have the task.

The task system was introduced into New York by Jewish contractors just previous to the year 1880. The bulk of the coats manufactured in New York until about 1895 were made up under this system of payment. It afforded a method of maintaining a fixed weekly wage during the greater part of the year, for in the dull season nearly the same wages could be secured as in the busy season by accepting an increased task.[9] In 1894-5 there arose persistent opposition by the trade unions to the system,[10] and their activity in the succeeding years has been no small factor in the decline of the system. At present

[8] Certain locals reported to the recent convention of the united garment workers of America, against the section or modified team system, on the ground that it was task work, while the general president in his report confirms the right of manufacturers to use the team system and gives no hint that it necessarily involves the task system. Proceedings of thirteenth annual convention of united garment workers of America, 1904.

[9] Twelfth report of New York board of mediation and arbitration, 1898, p. 122.

[10] The united brotherhood of tailors in its manifesto of Oct. 1897, says: "Ever since the foundation of our organization we have struggled for the abolition of what is known as the "task system," in favor of weekly work at a standard rate of wages."

less than twenty-five per cent of the workers employed in the manufacture of coats are paid in this manner.

The task system has not been confined to New York, being found to a greater or less extent in all the large clothing centers, except Boston.[11]

The task system has occupied a very prominent place, and has a somewhat unsavory reputation among most writers who have given the clothing industry any attention. It is urged on the part of those who are opposed to the system that the adjustment as to hours and product made in the dull season becomes the adjustment for the next busy season, that there is a progressive lengthening of hours with an increasing intensity of work and an actual diminution of wage for each unit of time.[12] For example, in a given busy season each member of the team is paid a wage of three dollars for each day's output of ten coats, requiring ten hours work a day for completion. When the dull season comes on the worker, in order to make three dollars a day, is compelled to make twelve coats, working twelve hours. At the beginning of the next busy season, it is said, the adjustment stands, not ten coats and ten hours for three dollars, but twelve coats and twelve hours for the same sum. At the beginning of the next dull season two more coats are added, and this task takes fourteen hours and may be carried over into the next day. At the beginning of the next

---

[11] See testimony of Henry White, in report of the industrial commission, VII. p. 194. And seventh biennial report of the bureau of labor statistics of Illinois, 1892, p. 393.

Mrs. Willett's statement that the system is not found in any other center than New York is evidently a mistake. Women in the clothing industry, p. 36.

[12] Report of the industrial commission, 1901, XV. p. 346.

busy season the last season's rates become the standard. Thus the progressive lowering goes on until hours are frightfully long, intensity terrible and the poor victim works two days and gets only one day's pay. The United Tailors' Union said in 1886, "The weekly wages paid to men is supposed to be $15, and that to women $8, but after working a full week from sixteen to eighteen hours per day, they can only accomplish four days and would receive only pay for four days."[13] The New York Commissioner of Labor in 1886 stated,[14] "Where day wages are paid it implies a stint or task which is the cause of much dissatisfaction, being usually severe on the operative." The following statement appears in the Report of the New York Board of Meditation and Arbitration, 1894,* "the tailors were obliged to work . . . in some cases . . . two and one-half days, in order to earn one day's wages." The Secretary of the United Garment Workers of America reports to the New York Bureau of Labor in 1895 in reference to basters: "We have worked for the last twenty years on the piece or contract system and the employer used to give for a day's labor so much that it took a good man sixteen or more hours to make $2.50 per day. We had to resort to a strike to compel the sweaters to give us a fair day's pay for a fair day's labor."[15] The Industrial Commission, referring to the task system says: "The wages were always reduced on the theory that they were not reduced at all, but the amount of labor increased. In this way intense speed was developed. The men who had been

[13] Fourth annual report of New York bureau of labor, 1886, p. 618.
[14] Ibid., p. 616.
*p. 261.
[15] Thirteenth annual report of the New York bureau of labor, 1895, I. p. 125.

accustomed to making 9 coats in a task would make 10, and so on up to 15, 18, and even 20, as is the customary task at the present time. The hours began to be increased, in order to make the task in a day. Within the last 3 years it is said by the men that it is only in very rare cases that a set can make a task in a day; that it is usual for these sets of 3, even when working 12 or 13 hours per day, to make only 4 1-2 or 5 tasks in a week. In previous years, they claim, men were able to make 7 and 8 tasks or days' work per week."[16] Mrs. Willett attributes the decline of the number of women in the manufacture of coats to their inability to meet the conditions of the task system. She says: "As the length of the task was increased, and the pressure upon the worker became correspondingly intensified, the women were unable to hold their positions. They were unable to keep up the pace demanded by the other members of the team and have been replaced by men."[17] A similar statement in regard to the employment of women in the trade is made by the Industrial Commission.[18]

In all these statements it is assumed that this system of payment is particularly well fitted for the exploitation of labor; that lower wages, greater intensity, and longer hours prevail under this system than would prevail under the time or piece system. Let us now examine the philosophy of these statements. Suppose that the laborer is receiving three dollars a day or eighteen dollars a week in the busy season. When the dull season comes on, if he works he must accept less, and wages fall to two dollars and a half a day, or fifteen dollars a

[16] Report, 1901, XV. p. 346.
[17] Employment of women in the clothing trade, p. 68.
[18] Report, 1901, XV. p. 346.

week, the intensity and hours remaining the same. Or let there be a task system wage of three dollars a day for ten coats, amounting to eighteen dollars a week. When the dull season arrives, one of two results must follow. The piece rate may be cut to twenty-five cents, leaving the number of coats to be put out in a day the same, or the amount of work required for three dollars may be increased by two coats. If we assume that under the time system the average day's output was ten coats, we have a cheapening in both the time and task system of five cents a garment. In the case of the time system and straight piece system this reduction appears in a decreased daily wage. The task system compels no reduction in daily wage, for the necessary saving in the cost of production may be made up by the worker increasing either his intensity or his hours. Under the task system, then, there is a lowering of the standard of conditions of work; under the time and straight piece system there is a lowering of the standard of living; in the one, greater intensity or longer hours, in the other less to eat and wear.[19]

All systems require new adjustments at the beginning of the busy season, if the average conditions of the busy season in the trade are to be maintained. Under the time or straight piece system daily wages must be raised to effect these adjustments; under the task system, the size of the task must be

[19] In a personal interview a task worker stated that in the dull season he makes one more coat for the same wage; while a piece worker stated that he accepted a reduction of two cents a coat. The frequent charge that in the dull season work has to be carried over to the next day to be finished, does not prove any peculiar evil in the task system, because, as we have seen, other workers are receiving a decreased wage also.

lessened. Is it easier to raise daily wages than to lessen speed or reduce hours by reducing the size of the task? There is but little difference. Trade unionists all testify that reduction of hours and control of speed are more easily regulated than are wages. Walter Chuck, Label-secretary of the United Garment Workers of America, in a personal interview said that "Trade unions have been much more effective in shortening hours than they have in raising wages." This statement is agreed to by Mayer Schoenfeld, Ex-secretary of the Coat Tailors' Union, and other labor leaders. If there is any difference in the ability of the laborer to raise wages or reduce hours, the advantage rests with the matter of hours. The employer, if he can prevent the return to shorter hours, can also prevent the return to higher wages. Those who have assumed the contrary assume that the employer acts in a purely arbitrary way and that the laborer is a helpless victim in his hands. If this be true the laborer is certainly as helpless under the one system as under the other.

It is doubtless true that there are cases in which very long hours are worked under the task system, but it is to be noticed that the pressure toward the lengthening of hours has come, not from the employer, but from the workers themselves, who are willing to work comparatively long hours provided they are proportionately compensated. Thus it is that we find numbers of task workers earning more weekly than the same grade of labor working under other systems. Moreover, it has not been the policy of employers to force constantly increasing tasks on the workers who do not desire them, for the small amount of capital involved offers no incentive to its constant use. In a cloak strike in 1898, for example, the strikers asked for a decrease of wages rather than an increase in task and the demand was readily granted.[20] In a large coatmakers' strike in 1891 task workers received a reduction of task at the expense of stationary wages while the straight piece workers in the same strike were given an advance of ten per cent.[21]

Great stress has been put upon the increasing size of the task. A comparison of the size of the task for different periods is difficult. In the first place, it varies from the dull to the busy season, and the task of a busy season may be compared with that of a dull one. Moreover, the personal element of error is large, since workmen who are trying to make out a case against a certain system tend to exaggerate its evils. A careful study of this much discussed question shows that the statements made regarding the size of the task are not borne out by the facts. For example, in one year ten high grade coats are found to constitute a task, and in the next year sixteen low grade coats represent the same thing. These statements without the qualification as to the grade of goods are very misleading. The Industrial Commission says:* "the task itself, instead of being 8 to 10 coats, is now 20 to 24 coats." [22] Statements of tailors in the trade, however,

[20] Twelfth report of the New York board of mediation and arbitration, 1898, p. 122.

[21] Ninth annual report of the New York bureau of labor, 1891, part i. p. 943.

*Report, 1901, XV. p. 346.

[22] In personal interviews with task workers in 1902 the size of the task is almost uniformly stated at twelve to fourteen coats, requiring ten hours work. W. Chuck, label sec'y of the united garment workers in a recent letter states that the size of the task has increased since 1885 by from two to three coats only.

do not bear this out. A tailor who was a worker in 1876 made the following verbal statement: "The task in 1876 was from eight to ten coats in the busy season for ten hours work; in 1882 after the introduction of improved machinery the task was from ten to fourteen coats; in 1885 it was from twelve to fourteen, and took twelve hours work." This statement is verified by those of numerous others who are now and were then task workers. In 1891 the agreement between the leading coatmakers unions in New York City and the manufacturers contained this clause. "It is mutually agreed that all persons furnished by the parties of the first part, and employed as operators by the party of the second part, and who, prior to the first day of February, 1891, operated nine or a less number of coats per day, shall be allowed and reduced one-half a coat, and to those persons who, prior to said date, operated any greater number than nine, shall be allowed and reduced one complete coat." [23] It is evident then that some of the operators had as their task less than nine coats, and as the range in the size of the task in different grades could not be over six coats, this minimum would imply a maximum of from fourteen to fifteen. While there has been no such great increase in the size of the task as has been claimed by many writers, it is not to be understood that there has been none. The increase, however, has not worked injury to the worker and can be explained on entirely different grounds from those generally given. None of the writers who have insisted that the size of the task has been unduly increased has called attention to the improvements that have taken place in the sewing machine since the introduction

---

[23] Ninth annual report of the New York bureau of labor, 1891, p. 943.

of the task system. The speed and ease of operation of the machine has progressively increased and the numerous appliances which have been invented in the last decade have contributed greatly to lessen the exertion of the worker. The following is the statement of a very intelligent tailor: "It took more physical exertion to make nine or ten coats per day on the old machine than it does to make fifteen coats on the new, in spite of the fact that coats to-day are better made." It is the unanimous agreement among coat operators that the improvement in the machine has been fully fifty per cent, that the operator can turn out fifteen coats of a given grade a day with no greater effort than was necessary formerly to turn out ten. A further fact is that there has been a gradual increase in the number of workers on each task. For example, twenty years ago the bulk of the work fell to three workers, operator, baster, and finisher; to-day in place of three workers we have five or six, who it is clear, can perform a larger task with the same effort than could the three men twenty years ago.

This ability to turn out a larger product in a unit of time has not all been reflected in an increase of the task, owing to the fact that there has been, as we shall show later, a marked decrease in the number of working hours.

That the above reasoning is true is borne out by even a superficial observation of actual conditions. The intensity in the task shop to-day is no greater than in the overall industry, which is considered by some writers to be carried on under almost ideal conditions. The most casual observer must admit that the speed of the overall workers, who are almost entirely women and girls, does not fall below that of the workers under the task system, if it does not surpass it. In pants, under the time system, intensity is equally as great. The pocketmaker, under the Boston system, works with a speed equal to that of his task brother. One who visits places of work of the same grade of skill, making use of similar machinery, would find it difficult, even if an expert, to determine from the mere intensity of labor under which system of payment the work is conducted.

It is unreasonable to suppose that in the same industry, in the same locality, often in the same building with the same class of workers such tremendous variations as to hours, wages, and intensity should exist, as are charged by opponents of the task system. It predicates a reign of chance in industry that experience and observation teach us is impossible.[24]

It is evident that this system is closely related to the piece system. It is everywhere referred to in early labor reports as the piece system, and is even to-day spoken of as such by workers off their guard. With the growth of trade unions and their opposition to piece work, the word "task" naturally of a sinister meaning, was used as a lever in agitation.

---

[24] The computations of the industrial commission as to comparative costs of production in various systems belie the statements that are made in the same report on the amount of work performed in a unit of time under the task system. Report 1901, XV. p. 347 et seq.

CHAPTER V

CONDITIONS OF EMPLOYMENT: HOURS AND SANITATION

During the early part of this period the length of the working day did not vary radically from that under the previous period. Under the family system hours ranged from twelve to fifteen a day, and, as the Germans felt the Jewish competition, those who remained in the industry were forced to work even longer. A witness before the Senate Committee in 1883 testified that tailors worked with their families from six in the morning until ten at night.[1] Dr. Daniel states that in 1892 hours for this class ranged from twelve to twenty, but this represents the extreme for the most helpless workers.[2] Up to about 1892 conditions prevailing among the Jews were closely analogous to those in the German family shop, and the hours of labor were not radically different. In these small home shops, hours were given by Secretary Reichers as ranging from twelve to sixteen a day; while in the better class of contractors' shops working under the task system, the average number of hours was twelve.[3] The Progressive Tailors' Union, speaking of conditions in 1884-5, says that tailors

---

[1] Report of the committee of the senate on education and labor, 1885, I. p. 750.

[2] Report of the committee on manufactures on the sweating system, 1893, p. 184.

[3] Ibid., p. 222.

work at home from twelve to eighteen hours; those working for contractors, ten to fifteen.[4] The United Brotherhood of Tailors reports that from 1885 to 1887 hours ranged from twelve to fourteen.[5]

In 1891 the Factory Inspector said: "In the sweat-shops there is no regular stipulated number of hours, though sixty-six and seventy-two per week seem to be the minimum, the lesser number in the better shops; but in all of them in busy times the hands are required to work as many more hours as exhausted nature will permit. It is not uncommon to see men and women who have worked from sixteen to nineteen hours a day for weeks in succession, and during seven days a week at that."[6] Up to 1891 in the few inside shops hours ranged from ten to twelve, but in all branches the custom of taking work home was prevalent. These long hours, it is only fair to point out, represent the range over which work extended and not continuous occupation. In the home, work was carried on usually at a leisurely rate, and there was much talking and frequent lunches. Bearing in mind these facts, the average working day was, nevertheless, excessively long.

In the early nineties there was a noticeable decline in hours. This was due to the fact that the home shops among both the Germans and Jews were rapidly disappearing. There was a general betterment of the trade, as shown by the growth of trade unions, but the activity of the unions toward the

---

[4] Seventh annual report of the New York bureau of labor, 1889, p. 489.

[5] Ibid.

[6] Sixth annual report of the New York factory inspectors, 1891, p. 36.

shortening of hours was largely nullified by the financial depression of 1893 and the early part of 1894. From the beginning of the busy season in the autumn of 1894, however, there was a general demand for shorter hours and strikes instituted to secure them were almost uniformly successful. One of the largest of these strikes involved 15,000 coatmakers and secured a reduction to a ten hour day from their former working day of from twelve to fifteen hours. Although this scheduled ten hours was not enforced during the dull season, yet the fact remains that there was a permanent and radical gain. From 1895 there was a general levelling up of hours until in 1901 all union workers, with the exception of the cutters, demanded a fifty-nine hour week. The cutters sought to secure a fifty-four hour schedule. In 1903 many of them secured an eight hour day and a forty-eight hour week. In the years 1901 and 1902 there was another marked reduction on the part of union laborers, the Bureau of Labor for the latter year giving as the average gain for 14,385 workers (cutters, coatmakers, jacketmakers, kneepants makers, pantsmakers, pressers, and tailors) two hours and forty-eight minutes a week.[7] From 1902 to 1904 there has been little demand for further reduction of hours, but there has been a better observance of the union schedule, and hence the workers have in reality been making steady gains.

The following table shows the trend of hours as far as data are available. Returns of employers made to state officials have been purposely avoided as these returns are usually stereotyped and present the matter of hours in too favor-

[7] Twentieth annual report of New York bureau of labor, 1902, p. 1148.

able a light. Statements of individual workers have also been used with great caution, being employed only where they could be verified from other sources. Much use has been made of the statements made by trade union officials to investigating committees and to various state officials. Another source of information is the demands formulated during strikes and the agreements entered into after them. Such data are of the very greatest importance and taken over a series of years give the very best possible source of information. The meagerness of the reports in certain branches is due to the fact that trade union activity in these lines is of more recent origin.

Hours a Week

Year	Cutters	Coat makers	Cloak makers	Pressers	Knee pants makers	Pants makers	Vest makers	Jacket makers
1883	55-58½		84	84				
1884	55-58½	60-90[9]	84	84				
1885	55-58½	66-96	84	84				
1886[8]	53-54[8]	72-84	84	72				
1887	53	72-84	84	72				
1888	52-53	72-84	84	72-80				
1889	52-53	78-84	84	80-84				
1890	52-53	78-84	72-78	84-96	60			
1891	54-56½	72-84	84	84-96	69-71	84-108	80	
1892	49-56½	72-84	90	84-96	69-71	66	80	
1893	49-57	72-84	96	84-96	74-81	66	80	
1894	49-57	59-70	70-78	84-96	74-81	66	59	59-60
1895	49-57	59-60	70-102	59-60	59	59-72	59	59-60
1896	54	59-60	72		59	59	59	
1897	54	59-60	60	62	59	59	59[12]	54
1898	54	54-59	60		59	90-96[11]	96[13]	
1899	54	59	60	60	59	60	60	
1900	52	59	59	59	59	59	59	59
1901	54	59	59	59	59	59	59	59
1902	52	56	59	56	56	56	56	56
1903	52	56	59	56	56	56	56	56
1904	48-52	56[10]	59	56	56	56	56	56[14]

[8] In 1886 the cutters struck for an eight hour day, but compromised on a nine hour day. Eighth annual report of the New York bureau of labor, 1890, p. 273.

[9] Home workers worked 72-108 hours a week.

[10] Local unions nos. 2, 3, 156 and 157, coatmakers of New York city, representing a membership of 5000, give the hours of labor as fifty-four a week. Proceedings of the thirteenth annual convention united garment workers of America.

[11] Relapse into old conditions. Remedied by strike of 3000 pantsmakers. Twelfth annual report of the New York board of mediation and arbitration, 1898, p. 128.

[12] In the early part of the year hours were much increased but in September 7000 of the workers went on strike and secured return to fifty-nine hours.

[13] Return to old conditions for a few months.

[14] Local union no. 10, children's jacketmakers, report fifty-six hours a week. Proceedings of the thirteenth annual convention united garment workers of America.

No fact is more significant in the clothing industry than the shortening of the working day. The influence that has brought this about has been in general that which has been at work in all industry. The clothing trade has passed through the same industrial stages as have the other great industries, though this progression has consumed much less time. In our discussion of wages we have pointed out the influences making for their increase. These same forces, it is evident, make possible a shorter working day. But with low wages such as existed in the early years of the clothing industry these improvements would be reflected in higher wages rather than shorter hours, because the laborer preferred more money to increased leisure. At a certain point, however, improvements in the industry become reflected, at least in part, in shorter hours. The two great direct forces bringing about shorter and more regular hours have been, first, improved management resulting in a more thorough understanding of the conditions of the market, thus avoiding gluts and distributing the work more evenly throughout the year; and, second, the trade union, which has had a favorable influence on its workers by urging upon them the importance of shorter hours even at a sacrifice of wages. The union has been the agency, moreover, through which demands have been made on the employer. The growth of regularity of hours and decline in their number have been greatest in those periods when trade unions have been most active. This is usually conceded by both employer and employee. The New York bureau of labor[15] says: "The tendency toward shorter hours, however, is fundamentally a product of trade unionism, save as a temporary expedient to

---

[15] Twentieth annual report, 1902, p. 1134.

cut down production in times of depression, in which case wages are cut down proportionately. No employer would think of reducing the working time of his employees until requested so to do by the entire body of workmen. It is doubtful if the social value of trade unionism appears more distinctly in any other direction." State regulation of hours has had its greatest influence on the home shops, and has almost brought about their abolition. The increasing size of the shop has made possible a better enforcement of the laws in regard to hours of women and children; but since the body of the workmen are adult males and there are no laws regulating their hours it is clear that any influence legal regulation has on their hours is indirect, and since there is a comparatively small number of women in the industry this indirect influence must of necessity be small.

Since the beginning of this period the hours of labor of the cutters have not been greatly modified. The cutters are the most intelligent and skilled part of the workmen and therefore were early enabled through trade union activity to control the conditions of their labor. During the entire period the cutters have been organized and there has been no great variation in the ability of the unions to control either the general conditions of their trade or the activity of their individual members. The cutters' union has tried from time to time to bring about an eight hour day. This was finally accomplished in 1904, when by individual agreements the majority of shops secured a forty-eight hour week.[16]

[16] The forty-eight hour week prevails in some other clothing centers. The attempt on the part of the cutters to maintain it, has during the present year (1904), resulted in very disastrous strikes. Proceedings of the thirteenth annual convention united garment workers of America.

There were attempts made to perfect organization among the coat tailors in the early eighties, but it did not become effective until about 1890. The first great strike was not waged until 1894. The unions have experienced great difficulty in enforcing agreements as to hours, and the actual time worked was longer than that stated in the agreements from which our table is made up. Since 1901, however, the hours stated in the agreements have been pretty generally enforced and are indicative of the actual number worked. The coat tailors have gained immensely by the abolition of the home shop and the practical disappearance of the custom of taking work to their homes. The hours of labor in the large contractors' shops and the inside shop are shorter than those of the smaller contractors' shop, though the difference here is not as great as it was formerly. During the busy season where larger shops work ten hours the smaller shops will work eleven and possibly twelve, though here again since 1901 the union has largely prevented such variation.

In no class of workers has the improvement in hours been more marked than in that of the pressers. The nature of their work, since their operations are not intimately connected with the others, made it possible for them to continue their work after the others had left the shop. The presser himself was of a lower order of intelligence and this fact in itself would tend toward longer hours. As the presser was the first to be at work in the morning and the last one to leave at night, he was usually given charge of the key. He and the small contractor were often found at their task at the most unseasonable hours. It is not strange, therefore, that the gain of the presser in regard to hours has been greater than that of the worker in any other branch.

In the manufacture of pants, trade unionism first began to make itself felt as an important force in the years 1890-5. The organization of the workers has been difficult, and there have been frequent relapses to unorganized conditions. It has required much agitation on the part of the unions to preserve the short working day. As late as 1898 there was a relapse in which hours returned to the high mark of ninety to ninety-six a week, but a strike involving 3000 persons was effective in again securing a sixty hour week.[17] The trade union agreements reflect actual conditions to about the same extent as do those made by the coatmakers' unions.

In vests, knee pants, and children's jackets, while the unions have maintained a fairly good organization the actual control over conditions has been more nominal than in the other branches mentioned. Therefore the number of hours stated in the agreements do not conform so closely to those actually worked, but since 1901, the unions have been able to make their demands more effective.

The movement of hours in the cloak industry is not so favorable as our table indicates, owing to the nature of the trade, and the weakness of the unions. The union has been powerless to enforce its agreements specifying a fifty-six or fifty-nine hour week. Where the stipulated hours are observed in the shop the working day is lengthened by home work, this being particularly true of the finishers. The Secretary of the Cloak Makers' Union, said: "During the busy season practically all the workers in both inside and outside shops take out work at night."[18]

[17] See footnote [11] to table, p. 142.
[18] Personal interview.

The conditions under which the workers live have a two-fold interest. In their social aspect, we are interested in the conditions surrounding the domestic life of the worker; from the standpoint of the consumer, home surroundings are important because of the intimate connection of manufacture with the home.[19] In discussing the period before 1880 attention was called to the existence of exceedingly unsanitary conditions. There was a general disregard of all those precautions which we deem so necessary to-day. The constant influx of population into the lower part of New York City was given a new impetus by the great immigration of the Jews in the early eighties. There was a growing density[20] of population and a corresponding demand for housing. Taking those wards which became the center of the clothing industry the following table[21] shows the increase in density.

Year	Seventh	Tenth	Thirteenth	Fourteenth
1870	226.4	376.6	311.8	275.4
1880	252.9	432.3	353.2	314.9
1890	289.7	523.6	473.6	292.6
1894	366.8	701.9	543.7	355.8

Beginning with 1880, laborers were housed in three types of buildings, the isolated small wooden building, usually holding one family on the first floor and one in the cellar; the remodeled private dwelling holding from two to four families; and the tenement house originally constructed for this purpose.

---

[19] The consumer has a direct personal interest, since through clothing he may contract disease.

[20] Number of persons per acre.

[21] Report of the tenement house committee, 1894, p. 256 et seq. The seventh, tenth, and thirteenth wards are occupied principally by Jews, while Italians predominate in the fourteenth.

The tenement houses were of two classes, those fronting on the street; and those erected at the rear of other tenements, known as "rear tenements." At the beginning of this period many of the small wooden buildings had already disappeared, and in the years that followed they were rapidly supplanted. They were not subject to any regulation; the owners permitted them to run down and long use had made them breeding places of disease. Their destruction was of distinct social advantage. Before the great influx of laborers the wards mentioned above were residence districts of the well-to-do classes. With the encroachment of tenements these classes began to move farther up town and their residences were sold to investors who rented them when remodeled to the incomers. While they were well suited to the purpose for which they were originally intended they could not be well adapted for tenements, and as a rule the conditions of these houses were worse than in those originally erected for tenement purposes.[22]

For a long time they escaped regulation, as the legal definition of a tenement house did not include those in which only three families lived. This defect in the law was remedied in 1887,[23] and to-day the legal definition of a tenement house is one in which three or more families live.[24] Many of these struct-

[22] Inspector Monell in speaking of these remodeled dwelling houses in 1864 said: "In cases where these old buildings have been repaired and cut up into numerous small sized and ill ventilated apartments . . . they present the very worst features of insalubrity to be found in any class." Report of the council of hygiene of the citizens' association upon sanitary condition of the city, 1865, p. 7.

"These dwellings . . . do not afford such wholesome habitations as the tenement-houses built originally for that purpose." Report of the tenement house committee, 1894, p. 20.

[23] New York state laws, 1887, chap. 84.

[24] Ibid., 1903, chap. 179.

ures still remain, but more efficient regulation has corrected many of the abuses formerly existing.

The third class of houses occupied by laborers was the large tenement house. The public was slow to grasp the importance of the housing problem and to realize the danger of permitting owners to erect buildings with the sole purpose of housing a maximum number of people on a given area without regard to sanitation. These buildings were ordinarily five or six stories in height and had usually four families to the floor, giving a total capacity of from one hundred to a hundred and fifty persons. Those erected previous to 1880 occupied a very high percentage of the available area of the lot.[25] The entrance to the tenement was by a staircase and corridor which were dark except for such light as could filter through a small skylight. Each of the four apartments on a floor had one room facing either on the street or on the court in the rear. The two or three other rooms had only as much light and air as could reach them through the front room. Some conception of the size of these rooms can be gained from the fact that the extreme width of the lots on which these houses were constructed was twenty-five feet, and that out of this space must be taken the walls, the partitions, and the corridor. The size of these

---

[25] "The law has long limited the area which should be covered, but has permitted exceptions to be made. These exceptions have become the rule, and a block was discovered in which nearly 93 per cent. of the total area is covered by buildings; others running from 80 per cent. to 86 per cent. and a total average for 34 blocks showing 78.13 of the area built upon." Report of the tenement house committee, 1894, p. 17. Eighty-eight tenement houses, or 31 per cent. of those under construction in 1900, covered more than 75 per cent. of the lot, the extreme maximum authorized by law in any case. The tenement house problem, 1903, I. p. 244.

inner rooms ranged from six and one-half to seven feet wide by eight feet long. Attempts were made to remedy the evil of these dark inside rooms by passing laws providing for the construction of transoms between the rooms or for a door connecting with the hall.[26] In the case of buildings to be constructed it was provided as early as 1867 that each room should open either directly into the outer air or into a specially devised means of ventilation known as the air shaft.[27] These air shafts were little better than chimneys and owing to the discretionary powers given to the Board of Health were often omitted. As late as 1884 the Tenement House Commission found shafts in only 21 per cent of the houses investigated, and even these were declared to be not only useless but dangerous.[28] Originally these air shafts occupied the corner of the room, but those built after 1880 extended along its entire length, thus making the habitable space still smaller. Not until 1895 were any further regulations in regard to air shafts enforced. In that year it was declared by law that air shafts must contain an area of at least twenty-five square feet in order to count as part of the unoccupied space.[29] In the same year a minimum width of twenty-eight inches for shafts was prescribed by the charter of Greater New York.[30] In 1900 it was provided that every light and air shaft for habitable rooms shall be at least twenty-five square feet in area for buildings up to five stories, and must be increased five square feet for each additional story.[31] By the law of 1903 it is provided that in all tenements

[26] New York state laws, 1867, chap. 908, sec. 2.
[27] Ibid., sec. 14.
[28] Report of the tenement house commission, 1884, p. 38.
[29] New York state laws, 1895, chap. 567, sec. 8.
[30] Ibid., chap. 378, sec. 1318.
[31] Regulations of the department of buildings, 1900.

hereafter constructed there shall be a window in each room, and that the window area of each room shall be one-tenth of the superficial area, and that no window of a living room shall open on an offset or recess less than six feet wide.[32] For old tenements it was provided that every room should have a window on the street or on a yard not less than four feet deep, or on a court or shaft not less than twenty-five square feet in area.[33] It is also provided by this law that in every new tenement erected one room in each apartment shall be one hundred and twenty square feet in area and all the rest at least seventy square feet.[34]

The great evil of the old tenement house was due to the fact that it occupied too great a percentage of the area of the lot. By the law of 1879[35] the amount of space to be occupied by the building was specifically provided for[36] and a new class of structure, known as the "dumb-bell" or "double-decker" was devised to meet these requirements. The chief innovation was the provision for an inner court. This was little better than an enlarged air shaft, and as it had no opening on street or yard, the rubbish and garbage which naturally collected in it was seldom removed, so that it became a flue for the dissemination of noisome odors. The yard of the house was placed at its extreme rear. While this form of structure was an improvement upon the old, yet it failed to supply sufficient light and ventila-

[32] New York state laws, 1903, chap. 179, secs. 6267, 6268.
[33] Ibid., sec. 79.
[34] Ibid., sec. 70.
[35] New York state laws, 1879, chap. 504, sec. 1.
[36] The closing clause of this law permitted this provision to be modified in special cases by a permit from the board of health. The exceptions became the rule. Report of the tenement house committee, 1894, p. 17.

tion, as the open space was too narrow to permit the entrance of light and air into rooms in any but the upper stories.

On those lots on which former private dwellings stood there was a large unoccupied space in the rear; on this space tenement houses were erected which had no connection with the street except through the buildings in front. It was not alone on lots occupied by remodeled dwelling houses, however, that we find this class of tenements, for they were often constructed in connection with newly erected tenement houses.[37]

The amount of space between the two buildings was so small that very little sunlight reached the lower stories. The first law regulating the distance between these buildings was passed in 1867,[38] but owing to a faulty wording which provided only for those cases in which the rear tenement was built first, it was practically without force until 1879 when a provision was made by which this defect was remedied.[39] The distances provided for in this and succeeding laws, however, are too small. The evils of this kind of tenement are recognized in a letter from the Tenth Ward Sanitary Union, written in 1894, an extract from which follows: "We believe that the rear tenements should be wholly destroyed, and the space reserved for open courts and playgrounds for the children. Even such as are not in an unsanitary condition overshadow

[37] Sanitary inspector Monell in 1864 said: "On a lot of ordinary size, 25 by 100 feet, will be erected a front house 25 by 50, and a rear house, 25 by 25, with a court 25 by 25 and frequently less, in which are usually located hydrant, cesspool, and privy." Report of the council of hygiene of the citizens association upon sanitary condition of the city, 1865, p. 7.

[38] New York state laws, 1867, chap. 908, sec. 13.

[39] New York state laws, 1879, chap. 504, sec. 1.

the lower stories of the front house and are in turn overshadowed by them, to the exclusion of light and air." [40] In spite of the protests against this form of dwelling, the rear tenement still exists. Lawrence Veiller in a recent investigation found 2124 of them in the borough of Manhattan.*

In practically all the early tenements no provision was made for water on the separate floors and all the tenants were obliged to use the same pump, or hydrant, in the yard below, but in some few cases water was provided on the first floor. In 1887, however, a law was passed making it compulsory for the landlord to furnish water in each story.[41] This law was not generally enforced until the beginning of the Low administration in 1901. The present law provides that in the houses hereafter constructed there shall be a sink with running water in each apartment.[42]

While the law of 1887 remains the same for old tenement houses the actual working out of the laws in regard to other regulations has brought it about that even in the old tenements water in each apartment is becoming the rule. In none of the tenements was provision made for water closets on the various floors and all the occupants of the building were obliged to use common closets situated in the yard. Previous to 1887 vaults were common, and even where

---

[40] Report of the tenement house committee, 1894, p. 296. The tenement house committee of 1894 had severely condemned these rear tenements and "As a result of this condemnation, the Board of Health, in 1896, condemned or had permanently vacated about a hundred of such buildings." The tenement house problem, II. p. 95.

*The tenement house problem, I. p. 296.

[41] New York state laws, 1887, chap. 84, sec. 11.

[42] Ibid., 1903, chap. 179, sec. 94.

sewers were available, connections were often not made. In that year, however, a law was passed abolishing vaults, where possible, and providing that there should be not less than one water closet for every two families.[43] The school sinks[44] which took the place of the vaults were contrivances of unspeakable filth. Despite attempts at regulation these toilets. situated in the yard have always been the foulest kind of nuisance. In 1900 a law was passed providing that closet accommodations shall be attached to each apartment of tenements hereafter erected.[45] The school sinks connected with the old buildings were made illegal and their places were supplied by water closets either in the yard or on each floor. Most of the owners who have made the changes so far have placed them on each floor, as they find this a distinct improvement to the property.[46] Until 1900 halls and corridors were so dark that they required artificial light at midday. The laws providing for this artificial light have been inadequate and have not been enforced. The constant semi-darkness, the fact that there was a divided responsibility in caring for the halls and the long distance from toilet and water accommodations caused them to be exceedingly unwholesome and often reeking in filth. Better provisions as to artificial lighting, as to outside light and ventilation, and also more definite

[43] New York state laws, 1887, chap. 84, sections 5 and 6.

[44] "The school sink is long trough sunk into the ground connecting with the street sewer and supposed to be flushed out at frequent intervals." The tenement house problem, I. p. 294.

[45] New York state laws, 1900, chap. 179, sec. 95.

[46] Charities, 1903, X. p. 431.

responsibility[47] as to care have brought about vast improvements in this particular.[48]

External surroundings have kept pace with the improvements in the tenements. The great reform wrought by Colonel Waring in the cleaning of the streets and the removal of garbage has revolutionized conditions in this respect. The rude cobble stone has been replaced by asphalt pavements which can be easily flooded and many old buildings have been torn down and the area given over to small parks. Many narrow streets have been widened and new ones opened. While the tenements of to-day are by no means ideal, yet their condition is immeasurably better than at the beginning of this period, and when the present laws are complied with, it would seem that all has been done that can be toward bettering conditions, unless the number of people occupying a given area be reduced.

It is in such homes as we have described that the bulk of the ready-made clothing was manufactured up to 1892, and it is evident that the product so manufactured was far from sanitary. Until that date there was absolutely no regulation of the conditions of manufacture in these tenement shops, and they became so notorious that not only the state authorities but those of other states into which the clothing was shipped were aroused. In 1888 the Factory Inspectors of New York said in speaking of the Jewish home workers: "They usually eat and sleep in the same room where the work is carried on, and the dinginess,

[47] The care of the buildings is usually in charge of one of the tenants. Much good has been accomplished by creating a spirit of emulation among the janitors. This work was inaugurated by the tenement house department in 1902, but the credit for the movement and its success belongs to Dr. Blaustein, of the educational alliance.

[48] New York state laws, 1900, chap. 179, secs. 72, 80, 82.

squalor and filth surrounding them is abominable."[49] In 1890 conditions are summarized as follows: "The small, badly-ventilated rooms in which they work are crowded with toiling women and children. A furnace for heating irons is generally going at full blast. If it be winter-time, the windows are closed tightly and all chance of escape for the foul air is cut off. The same atmosphere—loaded with smells and impurities at best—is breathed over and over, oftentimes fastening new diseases upon the unfortunate inmates of the work-rooms, and always hastening to the grave the sick as well as the physically sound."[50] In 1891 Dr. Geo. C. Stiebeling accompanied a commission appointed by the Governor of Massachusetts to investigate existing conditions and reported his impressions of the places visited as follows: "these compound working and dwelling places are overcrowded, ill ventilated, overheated, full of dirt, filth, vermin and stench, and that consequently they are in a most unwholesome, health destroying and disease breeding condition." The Inspector added: "It is not exaggeration to say that nine tenths of the sweatshops of New York City are the equal in squalor, wretchedness and overcrowding with the two places mentioned in Dr. Stiebeling's sworn statement, and the vile state of affairs does not improve with time, but is becoming even worse."[51] In 1892 the report of the Government Committee which investigated conditions in the clothing trade contained the statement that "Contagious diseases, which are specially prevalent among

---

[49] Third annual report, 1888, p. 27.

[50] Fifth annual report of the New York factory inspectors, 1890, p. 27.

[51] Sixth annual report of the New York factory inspectors, 1891. pp. 39, 40.

these people, thrive along with their work,"[52] which is not strange from the fact that, "In the tenement sweat shops ... unhealthy and unclean conditions are almost universal, while those of filth and contagion are common." No doubt in all these statements there is the usual exaggeration. But after due allowance is made for this, the fact remains that the conditions were such as to warrant radical interference on the part of society.

The first attempt in New York to regulate the manufacture of clothing in places outside of factories was the Board of Health Act of 1892. By this act it was provided that no room in any tenement used for eating or sleeping purposes should be used for the manufacture of clothing except by the immediate members of the family living therein, and then only after having secured a permit from the Board of Health. The articles made under such conditions were to be subject to examination, and if any of them were found to be infected with a contagious disease they were to be destroyed by the Board of Health. All clothing manufactured in the home was to bear a tag on which should be written the name of the city and state in which it was made. This tag could not be removed until the clothing had been sold to the consumer. This law was supplemented by amendments to the factory act in the same year. The same provisions in regard to family work were made, and it was further provided that before any tenement or dwelling house or building in the rear of a tenement or dwelling house could be used for the manufacture of clothing, by any person not engaged in family work, a written permit must be obtained from the Factory

---

[52] Report of the committee on manufactures on the sweating system, 1893, pp. viii, vii.

Inspector. Before the permit was granted inspection must be made. This permit could be revoked at any time when the conditions under which it was granted were not complied with. It was further provided that the permit must be posted in a conspicuous place in the room or rooms to which it related. A minimum amount of air space of two hundred and fifty cubic feet for each person employed during the day and four hundred cubic feet during the time artificial light was used in the room was provided. Exceptions might be made by the Factory Inspector.[53]

The classes of work places recognized by these acts were first; the homes where work was now restricted to immediate members of the family; second, tenement house rooms not used by families, which were known as "tenement house shops"; and third those rooms located in non-tenement buildings in the rear of tenement houses. These were classed with and subject to the same regulations as the tenement house shops.

There has been great confusion among writers as to these different classes. Some have supposed that all shops in which outside workers were employed were located in living apartments, while the fact is that since 1892 such shops have very generally employed only members of the worker's family. This confusion is very natural. Before 1892 the shops appeared exactly the same. After that date the two kinds existed in the same building and the visitor, unless very observing, failed to distinguish between them.

It is evident that when families were denied the privilege of employing outside labor an important step had been made. The conditions of the family itself were bettered and garments came into less intimate contact with domestic affairs. It was on

[53] New York state laws, 1892, chapters 655, 673.

this very point that the law was most successful, 17,147 persons employed in the clothing trade being compelled to leave the tenement in 1893.[54] Massachusetts had a law similar to that of New York governing this class of work,[55] and in order that Boston manufacturers might have their work made in New York the conditions of manufacture there had to comply with those specified in Massachusetts. The Massachusetts inspectors made frequent visits to New York for the purpose of finding out what the conditions were. That the New York law had been well complied with is shown by the statement of one of these inspectors who said in 1895: "A tour through the tailor shops on the east side of New York developed nothing in the line of tenement-made work, with one exception."[56] From his own observation of the clothing trade beginning in 1897 the writer has been unable to discover families employing outside help in their homes except in a very few cases.

The amount of work performed by the family greatly decreased from 1892 on, with the exception of the minor processes of finishing. The size of the unit engaged in manufacture at this time was larger than the family, owing to the greater division of labor, and hence when the workers were restricted to the immediate members of the family it became impossible for them to compete with the shop.

The provision of the law specifying that tenement house shops must take out a permit, coupled with the general move-

[54] Eighth annual report of the New York factory inspectors, 1893, p. 13.

[55] Laws of Massachusetts, 1892, chap. 296.

[56] Annual report of the chief of Massachusetts district police, 1895, p. 248. By tenement-made is meant work done by the family employing outside help.

ment of work from the tenement houses due to the abolition of the family shop, caused many buildings to be used exclusively for the manufacture of clothing. During the year 1893, 371 tenements were entirely cleared of tenement house shops, and 85 tenements were cleared of residents and remodeled into shop buildings.[57] This does not mean that only those tenement house shops which were able to secure a permit continued. The complete enforcement of the law regarding permits and inspection was impossible owing to lack of adequate inspecting force, and many tenement house shops continued to exist contrary to the requirements of the law.

The details of the law as to air and space for each worker, cleanliness, etc., were not usually enforced owing, partly, to inadequacy of inspecting force and partly to the conflict of authority between the Board of Health and the Inspectors.

The law of 1897 attempted to remedy the evils not reached by the law of 1892. All work now done in tenement houses except that done by immediate members of the family was prohibited. This meant the abolition of the tenement house shop.[58] Manufacturers were required to keep a list of all contractors, who in turn were to keep a list of all persons to whom work was given. Goods discovered to be unlawfully manufactured were to be tagged and were not to be sold until disinfected by the Board of Health. The owner of tenement houses was made responsible for the unlawful use of his tenements.[59]

---

[57] Eighth annual report of the New York factory inspectors, 1893, p. 13.

[58] There was no change in the law concerning work in buildings in the rear of tenements.

[59] New York state laws, 1897, chap. 415.

This law hastened the movement which had already been in progress, and from this time on tenement house work has not been an important factor in the manufacture of clothing in New York City. Evidently with the small number of inspectors and the enormous amount of work falling to them there must be cases where the law is evaded. It is these sporadic cases that the press and sensational writers are constantly exploiting. In 1898 the writer accompanied a committee whose avowed object was to prove the extensive existence of this class of work and therefore the failure of the law. After diligent search in the very worst quarters of the city only a few such shops were unearthed.

The regulations in regard to buildings in the rear of tenements still left much to be desired. They were in wretched repair, poorly lighted and filthy. It was impossible to make headway toward enforcing the law as the difficulty of inspection was so great. All work in these rear buildings ought to have been prohibited. The great gain arising from keeping a list of contractors and of places in which work was done was principally owing to the fact that, as such lists were public, manufacturers were more cautious in giving out their work. We might point out here that manufacturers as a whole have been willing to coöperate with the authorities in raising the standards of their workshops. Factory Inspectors state time and again that when the manufacturer's attention is called to the bad conditions in certain shops where his goods are made up, he has refused to permit his work to be taken to these places. The keeping of these lists, owing to the enormous number of people involved, was difficult and it is not strange that there were many lapses from the law. In so far as the law requiring tenement made goods to be tagged was enforced, it was a bar to all manufacture of this sort, as such a tag ruined the sale of the goods; but there was no way to discover whether this tag was removed contrary to law, and further the manifest unfairness of the law, since it prevented the sale of goods legally manufactured defeated its enforcement. The provision for tagging incorporated in the law of 1897, is manifestly a marked improvement over the former provision. It limits tagging to goods unlawfully manufactured. This tag could be removed only by the Board of Health, and the clothing could not be put on sale until it had been taken off. The statement on the tag, "tenement made," was a manifest absurdity as it implied that all goods made in tenements were unsanitary, while at the same time the law recognized in the case of family work the legality of such manufacture; moreover, the goods made in rear buildings were not tenement goods at all, but were classed as such on the tag. This scheme of tagging was one of the early pet schemes to remedy the evils of tenement house manufacture. Its usefulness is doubtful. The purpose of marking goods in such a way is not to pass a general condemnation upon certain forms of workplaces, but to make it impossible for goods which are in an unsanitary condition from whatever cause to be placed upon the market. Manufacturers were bitterly opposed to these early laws in regard to tagging and rightfully so.

The new provision of the law of 1897 making the owner responsible for the unlawful use of his tenement was the beginning of a very important step toward effective regulation. The provision of this law, however, was too indefinite and accomplished little.

The important processes of manufacture had practically disappeared from tenement houses by 1897. Very few shops, either inside or outside, however, had the minor processes, such as finishing done on the premises. This work was done almost exclusively by women working in their homes. These homes were located in the worst quarters and as the people were of the lowest ranks, sanitary conditions could not be otherwise than bad. Furthermore, they were entirely unregulated by law. To reach this class of work the law of 1899 was passed.[60] It permitted the employment of members outside the family in dwellings, but no work could be carried on in the home without first securing a license from the Factory Inspector. Application for license was made on a blank furnished by the department specifying the number of workers to be employed and describing the rooms or apartments. Before the granting of the license the Factory Inspector was to make an inspection of the apartments ascertaining whether they met the requirements of the law in regard to sanitary conditions, and whether the nature of the place was such that it would continue to meet them. The license provided that the air space should be sufficient to allow each worker employed during the day two hundred and fifty cubic feet, and unless specially excepted, four hundred cubic feet at night. The law of 1899 took away from the Board of Health the power of removing the tag and gave it to the Factory Inspector, who could remove it only on application of the owner of the goods. The filing of such application admitting culpability, makes it easy for the Inspector to enforce the law. In 1900 in New York City there were 1100 instances of tag-

---

[60] New York state laws, 1899, chap. 415, sec. 7.

ging.[61] In 1901 there were 332[62] and in 1902 there were 273 cases.[63] The Factory Inspectors do not mention the number of cases of tagging previous to 1900; the high numbers for this year are accounted for by the fact that the new license law enormously increased the number of places brought under regulation, and it was but natural that the number of infringements of the law should be very great during its early enforcement. Goods found in unlicensed shops were tagged, and the system of tagging was made use of to enforce the license provision. The relative unimportance of tagging is evident from the decrease in 1901 and 1902.

Some idea of the conditions surrounding home workers may be gained from a study of the granting and revocation of licenses. From December 1, 1899, to November 30, 1900, 22,601 applications for licenses were examined; 6,082 or 26.9 per cent of these were denied, owing to unlawful conditions existing about the premises. In 1901 of 11,545 applications, 1,163, or 10 per cent were refused; and in 1902 of 15,130 applications, 544 or 3.5 per cent were refused. In 1903 of 13,084 cases investigated, 804 or 6.1 per cent were refused licenses. In the first quarter of 1904 of the 2,392 applications for licenses investigated, 148 or 6.1 per cent were refused.[64] The fact that nearly 27 per cent of all applications for licenses were refused in the first year of the operation of the law would indicate that a large percentage of the homes in which some manufac-

[61] Fifteenth annual report of the New York factory inspector, 1900, p. 37.

[62] Ibid., 1901, p. 103.

[63] Ibid., 1902, p. 9.

[64] These statistics are compiled from the New York department of labor bulletins.

turing process took place was below the standard of cleanliness, which the state considered necessary. The decline in the following years in the number of applications refused is attributable partly to the fact that those asking for licenses had taken care to improve their surroundings and partly to the fact that those asking for licenses the first year included a larger percentage of the lower class of home workers. The fact is significant that there is a constant decline in the number revoked, although each year inspection has become more thorough and standards higher.[65]

The provision of the law in regard to licenses throws light upon the conditions in licensed workshops as to contagious diseases. There has been a growing coöperation between the Health Department and the Inspectors which has been productive of much good. The New York City Department of Health mails to the Department of Labor each day a list of all contagious diseases reported. The names and addresses on this list are then compared with the lists of licensed home workers and

---

[65] A comparison of the following tables showing the number of licenses revoked and the total number outstanding at the close of each year reveals the progressive decline in the percentage of licenses revoked:

LICENSES REVOKED.

Dec. 1, 1899 to Nov. 30, 1900, 2354
Nov. 30, 1900 to Sept. 30, 1901, 789
Sept. 30, 1901 to Sept. 30, 1902, 524
Sept. 30, 1902 to Sept. 30, 1903, 331.

The number of licenses outstanding during the same period was:
Dec. 31,

Year	Number
1899	1,894
1900	16,059
1901	22,387
1902	22,949
1903	24,439

Compiled from the New York department of labor bulletins.

whenever disease is located in a licensed place, notice is at once sent to the manufacturer and contractors for whom work is done at that place warning them to send no more work there. When the total number of workers is taken into account and the fact that they are among the poorest of the city's population, and that they live in the most crowded quarters, the following figures of diseases reported in licensed working places is most remarkable. The total number of cases from October, 1901, to July, 1903, were:[66] diphtheria, 142; scarlet fever, 50; small pox, 53; typhoid fever, 16.

That these figures are approximately correct is shown by the fact that they correspond very closely with those given for Boston under similar conditions.[67]

The provision of the law permitting the employment of outside workers in the home was a step backward. Inspectors, however, usually refused to permit such work on the ground that provisions in regard to air space could not be complied with. Mrs. Willett says: "The factory inspector has adopted the policy of permitting the employment of a limited number of outsiders in properly kept homes where custom clothing is made up, but he has decreed that ready-made clothing cannot be manufactured 'under clean and healthful conditions' where persons not members of the family are employed in the home."[68] She adds that this distinction seems on its face to be an arbitrary one. The distinction is an arbitrary one, and furthermore it gives undue discretionary power to the Inspector. Such

---

[66] Compiled from New York department of labor bulletins.

[67] Report of inspector Griffin, Annual report of the chief of Massachusetts district police, 1897, passim.

[68] Employment of women in the clothing trade, p. 156.

power in the hands of an administrative officer either nullifies the law or makes possible favoritism and injustice. This was recognized by the law of 1904 in which the former prohibition of the employment of others than members of the family in the home was re-established.[69]

The law of 1899 stipulated that a member of the family in which manufacture was to be carried on should apply for a license. This license referred to his immediate apartments, but it often happened that while his apartments were unobjectionable, the building in which the apartments were located, or some part of it was in such condition that the license had to be refused. Oftentimes licenses were granted for apartments located in buildings whose halls or plumbing, for example, were in a highly unsanitary condition. This provision, basing the license on the condition of the apartment, greatly increased the burden of inspection and regulation. To remedy these evils the law of 1904 made the unit of inspection the entire building. In place of the occupant of an apartment, the owner of the tenement house is to make application for the license. If, on inspection by the Commissioner of Labor, the building is found to meet the requirements of the law, a notice to this effect is posted in the public hall of the building. This does not relieve the individual apartment from inspection, and if the inspector finds any of them below the requirements of the law, he is required to placard these apartments to this effect. This law further provides that hereafter all tenements shall be inspected at least once in each six months. The great gain in this law is that it places the responsibility for those conditions which are beyond control of the tenant on the landlord who can of course be made to

---

[69] New York state laws, 1904, chap. 550, sec. 100.

remedy the defects. The law did not go into effect until October, 1904. Another provision of this law that is worthy of notice is an increased coöperation between the inspectors and the local authorities responsible for general sanitary conditions of tenement houses. Section 100 provides that the Commissioner of Labor, on receiving an application for a license shall examine the records of such local authorities and shall take no steps toward inspecting such building until such records have established the fact that no contagious or communicable disease exists within the building.

We do not wish to assert here the wisdom of permitting goods to be manufactured in the homes of the workers. Such manufacture must always be attended with certain evils, but so far as New York City is concerned it would seem that the regulations in regard to this work are such that the evils, so far as the consumer is concerned, are reduced to a minimum.

From about 1880 until 1892 numerous small contract shops were located in tenement houses. After 1892 the majority of the shops were situated in buildings in which no families resided. The dissociation of manufacture from living conditions was a great gain but otherwise these shops were very similar to those in the tenement house, and in fact, were frequently located in vacated tenement houses which were of the very poorest sort. The conditions and surroundings were unsanitary and uncleanly. Lofts over stables and similar places were also used for this purpose, and little attention was given to keeping them whitewashed and free from vermin. The rooms were overcrowded, had little chance for ventilation, and were insufferably hot in the summer. In the early years toilets were located in the back yard, and when later they were placed adjoining the workshop, they were so neglected that they were a frightful nuisance. So numerous were these shops, that with the small force of factory inspectors, proper supervision was out of the question, and the improvement which has taken place since 1897 has been due rather to better enforcement of existing laws and to the general advance of the clothing industry than to any new legislation.

The writer began his investigation of these shops in 1897. About this time the movement toward better conditions began. In 1902 a visit was made to many of the same shops and the improvement was very noticeable. Walls were whitewashed, floors were scrubbed, and freer from litter. The presser's bed, so common in the old shops, had disappeared. The improvements in regard to light, ventilation, and general surroundings were most marked. This movement toward better conditions has continued until the present time. Shops have become larger, and many are now located in well-ventilated lofts or in upper floors of warehouses and buildings primarily designed for factory purposes. It is true that the majority are still in buildings unfit for factory purposes and as long as such are used, even reasonably fair conditions as to ventilation and light are out of the question. Shops located on the narrow streets of a large city never have a good circulation of air and during the stifling weather of the summer the workers suffer an exhaustion which is entirely unnecessary and out of keeping with modern ideas of what constitutes fair conditions of labor. Many of the present day evils are directly traceable to the carelessness of the workers. Windows are not opened, owing to the fear of a draught. Closets are in such a filthy condition that they often contaminate the air of the entire workshop, and this despite the fact that the proprietor has met all the requirements of the law in providing proper accommodations. The responsibility of the workers for these evils has been pointed out time and again by factory inspectors. The employer is responsible for the unsatisfactory character of the arrangement for heating irons, which is usually a rude furnace with poor draught; but the lack of care on the part of the employee often permits gas to flow into the room where the appliances attached, if used, would carry it off. The Factory Law provides that the air space for each employee during the day shall be two hundred and fifty cubic feet, and at times when artificial light is used four hundred cubic feet. The provisions as to air space are not well enforced, but even though they were there would be little gain since ventilation depends not on the cubic capacity of the room alone, but on the circulation of the air. Lack of attention to this detail is not peculiar to contractors' shops in New York, nor to factories in general. It is characteristic of a majority of our large halls, theatres, and churches. There are very few rooms to-day in any class of buildings where a person coming in from out of doors will not feel the stifling effects of stale vitiated air. It is not strange, therefore, that these workrooms, located in such quarters, should be woefully lacking in this respect.

The evils of this lack of proper ventilation are partially offset by the shortening of the hours of labor. Formerly the laborer spent from ten to thirteen hours a day in these rooms, while to-day he is working from nine to ten hours. The ventilation of these workshops is probably better than in the homes of a majority of the workers, and conditions which strike the outsider as intolerable are endured with indifference by those who habitually live in such surroundings. Most of the clothing shops up to the year 1900 were obliged to resort always to artificial light in the morning and evening, and often through a great part of the day. The provisions for lighting were crude. Pipes and fixtures were usually put in after the erection of the building and no attempt seems to have been made to adapt them to the peculiar needs of the tailor. No shades were provided and the position of the light itself was not adjustable. Since 1900 the use of electricity has been growing, but to-day the flaring, unprotected gaslight, with its heat, is the rule and not the exception. The remedy for this evil is easily within the power of the employer, and can be effected without any greatly increased expense. The worst conditions in all these particulars are found in those shops which largely employ recently arrived immigrant labor, such as those where the Lithuanians are working at knee pants and children's jackets.

The conditions in the class of shops just discussed are in general far worse than those existing in the large contractor's shop and the inside shop. In almost every case we find better lights, better ventilation, and better accommodations of every sort. This is largely due to the fact that these shops are located in buildings primarily intended for such purposes.

CHAPTER VI

INCOME AND EXPENDITURE

The yearly income of the heads of families has a wide range. The minimum is close to $300; this represents the earnings of the very lowest class of workers in the various branches. The weekly earnings for the thirty-two weeks of actual working time average less than $10, and for the entire year the income is less than $6 a week. From the study of incomes we are convinced that among those who really belong to the clothing industry, few receive so low a wage as this. The maximum yearly income is nearly, often quite, $1000; such income is earned by the cutters and the more skilled workers in other branches. Taking cutters on the basis of ten months' work a year and a union scale of $21 a week, the yearly income is a little less than $850. This sum represents the maximum earnings of cutters more nearly than does the larger sum mentioned above. The weekly wages of the greater number of workers range from $16 to $18. From careful study the writer is convinced that this estimate is conservative.

When the income of the family falls near the minimum, earnings of wife and children are often important. In the case of Italians, earnings of others than the heads of families play a very decided role. Among the Jews, the same is true to a much larger extent than is commonly supposed. A large percentage of Jewish married women are engaged in some form of gainful occupation. They are keepers of small shops, janitresses, etc.

This is particularly true in regard to those whose husbands earn the smaller incomes.

In the following study of family expenditure, the typical family is taken as consisting of two adults and two children. The family of this size is of course, small for the class of people under consideration. It is true, however, that an increase in size of family does not necessarily mean a corresponding increase in burden, as the older members add their quota to the income. But in the case of the Jews, this statement must be made with reservation, for as a usual thing, Jewish children add little to the family income before they have passed their fourteenth year.

The following table shows the expenditure for families with a yearly income of from $500 to $600. Column I is for a garment worker's family of four in New York City. Column III is the average in the entire United States without reference to occupation.[1]

Item	I Amount	II Percent	III Percent
Rent	$135.00	24.55	15.2
Fuel and light	29.70	5.4	6.6
Clothing	66.00	12.00	15.3
Food	255.50	46.45	43.8
Miscellaneous	63.80	11.60	19.1
Total	$550.00	100.00	100.0

The rent for New York City is 24.5 per cent of the total income, and for the United States, 15.2 per cent—a very great difference. Rent is exceedingly burdensome to the East Side worker in New York. We have allowed three rooms, but

---

[1] The estimates in column I are based upon the personal investigations of the writer. Column III. Report of the United States commissioner of labor, 1890, p. 864.

whether the number drops to two or increases to four, the fact remains that the expenditure for this item is about 25 per cent of the total income. There is no evidence that the burden is becoming heavier; as has been previously shown rents have not materially advanced since the middle of the century, while a vast improvement has taken place in housing conditions. Water rates are included in these rents. The slight advance in rents which has taken place within the past few years has, in many cases, been reflected in better conditions.

With the growth of better transit facilities, there has been a large exodus of workers to Brooklyn and uptown districts. In the case of those going to the former place, the gain has been more room for less money. The difference between the rent of similar apartments in the lower East Side of New York and in the suburbs of Brooklyn is from three dollars to five dollars a week. In Brooklyn there are better surroundings, less crowded quarters, larger and better lighted rooms. However, these gains are off-set by very marked disadvantages. The worker must carry a lunch or buy it. This becomes an important item of expense, when it is remembered that the cost of the lunch will furnish a meal for an entire family. There is expended in carfare in going to and from work, a sum greater than the gain in rent. The home is away from the center of social life, and the family spends another large item for carfare on this acount. Much time is lost on the cars. This adds materially to the length of the working day and must be considered in the light of a hardship even where the normal working day is only one of nine hours.

The necessity of intimate association with the workshop is not so important as formerly, but it is still an item which cannot be left out of account. Often the worker repairs to the shop for only a few hours of work. Frequently on going to the shop no work is found. Therefore, it is not strange that the mass of the workers prefer to pay the higher rent of the East Side. Only those of the upper ranks, the small shop-keepers, etc., have moved into the less crowded districts. It is possible that the moving of factories into the suburbs, or the growth of the provincial factory, will in time remove some of the obstacles which to-day stand in the way of the escape of the clothing worker from the present heavy burden of rent.

In the items of fuel and lighting the apparently slight advantage which the garment workers in New York City enjoy is misleading. It is really much greater than it appears in that they use a high grade of fuel, usually anthracite coal, and, in general their tenement apartments are better protected than are the isolated cheap frame dwellings of the mass of industrial workers with this income. In summer, however, the advantage lies with the isolated home. The heat of the tenement is stifling during this season, and therefore gas is largely used for cooking. Gas is relatively expensive and becomes a large factor in the amount expended for fuel and lighting. Those having a smaller income use oil for purposes of lighting, and during the summer, buy much food already cooked. So, it is evident, that the garment workers could reduce the item for fuel and lighting nearly one-half without entailing any serious hardship.

In the case of clothing also, the garment worker in New York City possesses a marked advantage over those industrial workers possessing a similar income in the rest of the United States. The garment worker is not exposed to the weather and the occupation is not hard on clothing. New York is the cheapest clothing center in the country, and besides this, the garment worker knowing the business is a good buyer, and as a consequence is much better and more tastefully dressed than are others with the same income.

The amount spent for food is higher than in the country at large. Professor Atwater estimates the requisite expenditure for food for the family under consideration, where the head of the family is engaged in moderate muscular work, at $260.61,[2] five dollars above our figures. The Jew is a good liver, and from personal investigation the writer is convinced that as a whole his food is well chosen and prepared very much better, in fact, than is that of the mass of industrial workers and many of the rural class of our population. In buying the staple articles of food, with the possible exception of meats, the clothing worker possesses an advantage over the same class of workers in other centers.

The growth of the creamery industry in recent years is of great importance to the workers of the East Side. Butter of excellent quality is found in their markets. The dairy product at its usual price even to-day must be considered almost an article of luxury; placing the amount used daily at one-half pound, this means an expenditure of scarcely less than ten cents. Butter to-day is not a common article of diet among the masses of the workers. However, this item is an important one in the budget of the Jewish worker, as the Jew substitutes butter for pork products, in many foods where other workers use the latter. The almost entire lack of butter in the diet of the Italian workmen becomes at once apparent even by superficial observation. Olive oil is often found as a substitute, however, at an expense out of all proportion to its food value. Milk on the East Side is of excellent quality and costs from four to six cents a quart, and so is,

---

[2] Mayo-Smith, Statistics and economics, p. 36.

little, if any, more expensive than in the provincial towns. It forms a very large article of diet for the Jews but is comparatively little used by the Italians.

Much has been written on the bane of the buying of supplies in small quantities by the industrial worker. A part of this grows out of necessity, many workers living from hand to mouth, a part out of lack of storage facilities. It has been held that the dweller of the East Side must buy coal by the pail or bag rather than by the load or ton, because coal bins are not furnished. The more modern tenements have private coal bins, but these have not greatly changed matters because of the trouble of carrying the coal from the basement to the top floors, and the fear that neighbors will help themselves. It is probably true that a great deal of small buying is the result of habit, and is not confined to people possessing a yearly income of five or six hundred dollars. The evils of such buying have been greatly exaggerated and the advantages too often lost sight of. Vegetables, fruit, etc., deteriorate if bought in advance of daily consumption. The retailer is provided with the proper storage for such perishable articles, and it is unreasonable to expect the tenement house dweller to possess such facilities. The shopper thinks that by buying from day to day advantage can be taken of the bargains for which there is a constant lookout.

The price for small quantities is not greatly in excess of that charged for larger ones; this is particularly true in New York. Change is made in cents. If a pound of butter costs twenty cents, a quarter of a pound costs five cents, while five pounds cost one dollar. Five cents are paid for a quart of potatoes and probably very little is saved if a bushel be taken. In the case of coal the rate by the bag or pail usually amounts to about two dollars more a ton, partly owing to the fact that in this case a middleman's profit must be met. Some of this added expense however, is offset by greater economy in the use of this fuel. The greater convenience must be taken into account. In buying in small quantities, it is supposed that the purchaser is cheated in the measure. This is true in some cases, but in general social regulation prevents this, and besides the shopper of the East Side may be depended upon to see that all is got that is justly due.

It is held that much of the food consumed is stale and unfit for use. There has been exaggeration in this respect; although it is true that the market customs of the East Side are not always up to what they ought to be from the standpoint of modern sanitary ideas. Wise regulation, particularly on the part of the Jews, guards against any danger from this source. The Jewish worker is well nourished; this is not true of the Italian, not because the income is insufficient but because of lack of knowledge of how to expend it. In the case of the Italian worker, as well as in the case of other unskilled labor in our cities, beer forms too large an item of food expenditure, and this is expensive out of all proportion to its food value. The Jewish worker, on the other hand, adds variety to the diet by purchasing the more wholesome articles of the delicatessen store.

To meet what have been termed miscellaneous expenses there remains only a small portion of the income—$63.85 or 11.6 per cent as over against 19.1 per cent for the entire country. The large rent item is mainly responsible for the difference. Out of this small sum must be met such items as medical attendance, amusements, trade union dues, provision for old age, and numerous incidental expenses. It is at once evident that the amount is entirely inadequate, but we are not to infer that the worker does not have these wants supplied. Again compensation is found in the fact that the worker is a city dweller. Free hospitals and dispensaries enable the humblest worker to have without expense or at nominal cost the benefit of the most skilled physicians. Many amusements of a high order are enjoyed without drain on the pocket. Books from free libraries, music in the parks, lectures and museums are to be had for the asking. The daily paper is secured at a nominal cost. Through collective effort the laborers provide for themselves many amusements of a high order at a low cost. This is particularly true of the Jews. The Jewish theatre puts on excellent plays well acted and the admission fees are very low. In a discussion of wages and expenditure all these facts must be kept in mind.

Our attention is often called to the advantages which attract the well-to-do classes to the large cities; but these advantages are as nothing compared with those which the workers with a small income enjoy. The opportunity for self-development and pleasure of the Jewish East Side worker is as much greater than that of the inhabitants of rural France as depicted in Balzac's Les Paysans, or even of the mass of our own rural population, as is the opportunity of the modern gentleman greater than that of the feudal lord of the fifteenth century.

It is not necessary for us to discuss here whether or not free hospitals and free amusements debase the recipients. They are every day facts, just as much as are free colleges and free schools. Moreover, it can be shown that in the long run such institutions become a charge upon production, and therefore, the workers must contribute to their support. Since this is true, such institutions must in time gain in respect and standing, just as the public schools have gained, and it will be granted that those who take advantage of them do so not by charity but by right. Much that is termed philanthropy will cease to be called this, unless we choose so to name for example free education. Furthermore, as long as the various members of society are unequal in productive power the surplus thus accruing must be distributed either through voluntary acts or by compulsion of the state. It is not to be understood that the writer advocates the payment of low wages in order that large sums may be dispensed for what we now call charities; what is here insisted on is the need of a change of public opinion regarding the recipients of such charities.

It is manifestly impossible for workers with an income of from $500 to $600 to make savings for old age. There are many savings banks on the East Side with large numbers of depositors. It is extremely difficult to determine how many of these depositors represent the class of people under discussion. But from a careful investigation among the workers themselves the writer is convinced that deposits for old age are the exception rather than the rule with the rank and file. This fact does not necessarily mean that the workers have not progressed or are not progressing. Increased earnings have brought with them a higher standard of living—better food, clothing, and shelter—and more comforts in general. As we have already pointed out there is a large movement out of the clothing industry; hence it may be inferred that in many cases savings appear as investments in some small business. Finally, opportunity for saving by making use of the labor of children has been foregone and the children are fitted for the higher occupations.

The savings that appear as bank deposits are in large part withdrawn to tide over the dull season.

There is little insurance in the old line companies. Industrial insurance is not so common as among other workers earning the same or a slightly higher income in New York. The economic condition of the workers is against regular insurance. The comparatively large premium is difficult for them to meet. Inquiry shows that where such insurance has been taken out there is a marked tendency to let it lapse. There has been, however, a decided increase in old line insurance during the past two years. This is due partly to social changes and partly to improved economic conditions.

The insurance side of trade unions is to-day only in its infancy. In 1902 there was begun in practically every branch of the trade an agitation for the establishment of such features. This has been but partially successful. Peculiar social conditions, which will be pointed out later are a great obstacle in the way of such insurance. There has been a lack of centralized effort. The matter has been left to each local—entirely too small a unit. Local Union Number 55, Brooklyn, composed of operators, basters, finishers, and pressers, and comprising a total membership of over 1200, may be used as a typical example of trade union activity in this line. The age limit of members is 55 years. The dues for each member are fifty-five cents a month. The initiation fee is $5. A sick benefit of $5 a week for ten weeks is paid. Such benefits often amount to $50 or $60 a week. In 1902, there was no death benefit. Members are paid a strike benefit of one dollar a day. From August to December, 1902, $250 was paid out in such benefits. In December

1902, the union had $1,400 in its treasury.[3] The success of this union shows what can be done by the workers themselves when sufficiently large numbers coöperate.

The leading form of insurance among the clothing workers is fraternal in its nature. The bond of union is sometimes religious, the members belonging to the same congregation, sometimes local, the members coming from the same towns in Russia. In other cases the bond of union is religious and racial, and corresponds closely to such fraternal associations as the masons, oddfellows, and the like. There are a very great number of such associations, and practically every head of a family belongs to one or more. While each association has its own regulations as to membership, dues, etc., a general uniformity exists among them.

As an example of a society formed on a local bond that of Warsaw may be used. This is composed of 125 to 130 members who formerly lived in Warsaw, Poland. Each member pays a monthly due of seventy-five cents. There is a sick benefit of $7 a week for twelve weeks, and $3.50 a week for the ensuing six weeks. A $400 benefit is paid at death. This society has been in existence for seven years. In place of a fixed benefit at death, some of these societies assess each member a certain sum on the death of one of its members. For example, the society of Krakow composed of 150 members, assesses each one dollar in case of a death. Beside the usual sick benefit, free medical aid is usually furnished.

The Chomaker is a benevolent association composed of young men from twenty to thirty-five years of age. Members

[3] During a prolonged strike in 1904 the funds of this union were entirely exhausted.

must have passed a medical examination. The dues are $6 a year. This society has a sick benefit of $4 a week. The Schuetzen is a society similarly organized; it is known as a uniformed society. In 1902 it had 300 members. The dues are $1.75 a quarter; there is a $5 a week sick benefit, and medical aid is also furnished. On the death of one of its members, each member is assessed one dollar and funeral expenses are paid.

The society known as the Independent Order of Berith Abraham may be taken as an example of another class of benevolent association. This is one of the oldest and largest societies. The dues are $3.75 a quarter. There is a sick benefit of $5 a week for seven weeks, and one half this amount for the next three weeks. Free medical aid is furnished. There is a death benefit of $500 and the funeral expenses are paid. This lodge has also a children's branch.

During the past few years new societies, based upon other than religious or local bonds, have been formed among the younger men. An example of such a society is the Arbeiter Ring. The membership is limited to men under forty. They are largely socialists and the chief object is educational. It maintains its own clubrooms, has regular meetings and provides for public lectures both in Yiddish and English. Provision is also made for aiding members in the way of small loans, etc. The society is supported by monthly dues of fifty cents. The Young Men's Aid Society of Brooklyn has educational and social benefits like those of the Arbeiter Ring.

The organizations mentioned may be taken as examples of large numbers of associations. The extent to which these exist and are patronized may be illustrated from the following statement made at the time by the writer after a personal interview in December, 1902. Herman Lewis is a coat operator. He was formerly an English tailor and has been in this country seventeen years. He has always worked foot power on a medium grade of coats. When he first came to this country, he earned $15 a week working eleven hours a day. Now his working day is nine hours and one-half and he never works overtime. His present wage is $20 a week. He could make $24 a week if he wished. He prefers task work since in this he is his own boss and makes more money. He pays $12 rent for five rooms. He has six children; one boy works in a picture frame factory, four children are in school, and the sixth is a baby. He belongs to the following societies: 1. The Brooklyn City Lodge of the Independent Order of Berith Abraham of which he has been a member for five years. He pays $3.75 a quarter. He is entitled to a sick benefit of $5 a week for seven weeks and one half of this amount for the next three weeks. There is a death benefit of $500. His funeral expenses will also be paid. His children are insured in the children's branch of this lodge. Social meetings are held every two weeks. 2. The Lodge of the Independent Order of Avis to which he has belonged two years. The benefits, etc., are the same as in the Independent Order of Berith Abraham. 3. Schuetzen Lodge, to which he has belonged four months. The dues are $1.75 a quarter; the sick benefit is $5; there is a death benefit of one dollar from each member. The Lodge has 200 members. 4. Brooklyn Benevolent Society. The dues are ten cents a week. The sick benefit is $5 a week for the first twelve weeks, and one half of this amount for the ensuing twelve weeks. The death benefit is one dollar from each member; there are 150 members. 5. Local Union Number 55, Brooklyn; he pays fifty-five cents a month dues. The sick benefit is $5 a week for ten weeks; in case of a strike, the benefit is one dollar a day. Despite the fact that these lodges would furnish him medical aid, he has always preferred to engage his own doctor. In 1902 he was just getting over a severe attack of scarlet fever, and was receiving a sick benefit of $20 a week. Herman Lewis represents the more intelligent type of working man, and his penchant for belonging to lodges may be above the average. Still he is one of a very large class whose life history is very similar.

The economy, security and efficiency of such insurance as we have been describing may be open to question. The dues are not greatly in excess of regular insurance, but from the standpoint of security and efficiency the same objections can be urged as against all other fraternal insurance. It would be difficult to overestimate the good they have brought about. They have formed a basis of social life and an opportunity for coöperation, for a people in a strange country. These are the real reasons for their success. As time goes on the bonds of union on which these associations were formed will become weaker and weaker. Regular insurance and trade union benefits will then have the greatest obstacles removed from their paths.

Much has been written to the effect that the extreme individualism of the Jewish workman stands in the way of social coöperation. It is true that this is a Jewish characteristic but that it does not prevent him from coöperation with his fellows is shown by the fact that among no other class of industrial workers do we find so much coöperation and organization for mutual benefit, and among no other nationality do we find such sympathetic coöperation of the well-to-do classes in the attempt to raise those below them.

The regularity with which the laborer is employed must exert a profound influence upon his well being. The clothing industry belongs to those industries in which the irregularity is marked. Each year brings its busy season and its dull season; sometimes the work is plentiful, causing a rush, and there are times when scarcely any work is to be had. And as we have already pointed out, subsidiary employment is the exception and not the rule.

The evils of this irregularity may be put under three heads, first, it reduces the size of the yearly income; second, workmen become demoralized through idleness; and third they suffer for lack of money to tide over the dull season. How far yearly income is reduced owing to the fact that workers in a given industry are employed 200 days during the year rather than 300 days, is a difficult matter to determine. In general, such lack of employment must be charged against the industry, and, therefore, workers in it will receive a higher daily wage to compensate for this period of idleness. That is, workers in industry A which can furnish work for only 200 days in the year, tend to receive as large a yearly income as the same grade of workers in industry B which furnishes work for 300 days.[4] That this statement is true is shown by a study of comparative yearly incomes in those industries known as seasonal and in those which furnish work throughout the entire year. We do not always realize its truth, owing to the willingness of workers to capitalize the increased leisure and therefore, be content with a lower money wage. Of course, it must be assumed that such periods of idleness are constant and not sporadic in their oc-

[4] It is true of course, that the element of friction is against industry A.

currence. Sporadic and uncertain fluctuations in the amount of working time in a given industry can not be charged against the industry, but must be borne by the workers in it. So far as the clothing industry is concerned, we are convinced that if the dull season could be abolished, the yearly income of the workers would be only slightly higher than it is now. Such an increase in wages would be measured by the added producing capacity of society due to the fact that these workers were engaged a greater number of days in productive pursuits.

It is undoubtedly true that workmen of a low grade suffer demoralization on acount of idleness. However, when we are considering the working classes in general it is easy to exaggerate this evil. Such danger ought to become less as time goes on. In so far as the Jewish workman is concerned, there is no such demoralization. He uses his idle time to good advantage. Of course, this is due to the fact that the Jew possesses self-control and a high degree of intelligence. He therefore finds an outlet for his energies in social and intellectual pursuits.

To most workers the dull season is a lean time. All classes find it difficult to put aside, from money earned in the busy season enough to meet the inevitable expenses of the dull. Here again the Jewish worker is far superior to others of the same class. It would take a keen observer indeed to discover among the Jewish clothing workers in New York, any marked difference, so far as physical well-being is concerned, between the busy season and the dull. It is true the dull season often means a more limited diet, but this in itself may be no evil. That workers and their families do not suffer injury is strikingly borne out by the fact that children of the lowest workers who are in school show no effects of the dull season in attendance or otherwise. Emphasis ought to be laid rather upon distributing the income of the worker over the entire year, than upon urging the worker of small income to save for old age. The clothing workers resort to various other means than saving in order to meet the dull season. There is frequent resort to borrowing, the workers themselves having societies for this purpose. Members are loaned small sums for short periods at normal rates of interest, by getting the endorsement of other members. Not infrequently the contractor advances money which is paid back when the busy season sets in. It must also be borne in mind that the majority of the workers are enabled to get a few days' work a week throughout the dull season. The rank and file understand the importance of maintaining their credit and it is hardly ever difficult during unusual stress for them to secure credit, although the use of such credit is not extensive. Extortionate rates of interest or abuses growing out of loans form the exception and not the rule. There are undoubtedly Shylocks who take advantage of the clothing worker, but the writer is convinced that there are so few of them that they may be left out of account. The mass of clothing workers are not patrons of the pawnshop or victims of extortionate usurers. Of course, some of them are, but we are concerned with the usual and the normal, not the exceptional and the abnormal.

CHAPTER VII

REGULATION

Attention has already been called to regulation [1] on the part of the state through its factory laws and to local regulation on the part of boards of health. The conditions existing in the clothing industry previous to the year 1890 created widespread attention, and agitation was begun urging the national government to interfere, since clothing is a very large item in interstate commerce. Largely through the influence of Massachusetts, the first state to begin to regulate the manufacture of clothing in tenement houses, the National Committee was appointed in 1892 to investigate the so-called sweating system. This Committee studied conditions existing in all the large clothing centers, particularly New York, Boston and Chicago. The Committee in its final report recommended national regulation for the clothing industry. The reasons given were those upon which the Massachusetts authorities had insisted. The Committee urged that a single state, by passing laws regulating the manufacture within its own bounds was not able to protect itself against infected goods from other states. Home merchants could evade the law by having goods destined for other states

---

[1] In order to bring before us more clearly the problem of regulation, the following outline is suggested.
1. Regulation from the outside.
    a. Legislation—local, state, or national.
    b. Public opinion.
2. Regulation from the inside.
    a. Due to the development of the industry.

manufactured outside their state and shipped direct from the place of manufacture. This destroyed home industry. The Committee implied, that states would be discouraged in their attempts to eradicate the present evils in the conditions under which clothing was manufactured,[2] and recommended that a national law be passed regulating the manufacture of clothing destined for interstate commerce.

Congress, however, refused to pass such a law and the agitation for national regulation failed. The individual states were left to protect themselves from clothing manufactured in other states as best they might. Massachusetts, and later, New York, provided that all garments manufactured without the state and brought into the state for sale should be subject to inspection

[2] Report of the committee on manufactures on the sweating system, Washington, 1893, pp. xxiv, xxv, "so long as interstate commerce in this regard is left free, the stamping out of the sweating system in any particular State is of practically no effect, except to impose peculiar hardship upon the manufacturers of that State, and to encourage development elsewhere of the obnoxious conditions; while for each State to attempt to protect itself against this involves, as is the experience of Massachusetts, the necessity of keeping under the purview of its agents, not merely all places in the State, but all places outside as well, where goods are manufactured to be sold within its borders, a task which, though in the case of States willing to undertake it; it may drive to other States the manufacture of much of the goods which its own citizens are ultimately to wear, and may do somewhat to deter the dealers of its own State from traffic at home in goods thus made, is equal to the situation only in the proportion that it covers all the branches of this business in the whole area in which it is or may be done, and is therefore a hopeless one except as a palliative; while to expect that, in advance of special inducements, each State of the Union will concur in effective steps by first clearing its own skirts is even more Quixotic."

and those found to be infected should be tagged.³ The only way to discover whether such goods were made under conditions below that demanded of home merchants was to send inspectors into states in which goods were manufactured, or to examine the goods after they had arrived in the state. The former method evidently is much more effective than the latter. Inspectors from Massachusetts made frequent visits to New York, and as a consequence, the Massachusetts firms were compelled to have their goods sent to other centers to be made up, or to have them made up at home. Inspector Plunkett wrote in 1892: "The practice of sending clothing to other States, for the purpose of being manufactured . . . has greatly decreased, owing to the requirements of this section" [4] (section 3, chapter 357, Acts of 1891). Inspector Griffin's report states that the Massachusets laws of 1891 and 1892 have decreased the amount of clothing made in the New York tenements. That twenty per cent is the largest amount of clothing that any Massachusetts firm sent to New York in 1892 and that firms which formerly had their clothing manufactured in New York are having the cheaper grades made down East, and are endeavoring to have the better grades made in Massachusetts.[5]

The sending of inspectors to look into the conditions of manufacture in other states and the subsequent advertising which such states received have exerted a powerful influence toward forcing these states to take steps to remove the evils of

[3] Laws of Massachusetts, chap. 357. Acts of 1891, as amended by chap. 296, Acts of 1892, secs. 3 and 4. New York state laws, 1892, chap. 655, secs. 3 and 4.

[4] Annual report of the chief of Massachusetts district police, 1892, p. 409.

[5] Ibid., pp. 393, 394.

which the inspectors complained. New York, New Jersey and other states engaged in the manufacture of clothing have been compelled as a matter of self-protection to pass laws similar to those of Massachusetts to regulate the manufacture of clothing in tenements. Indirectly the visits of the inspectors have had a decided influence in bringing about the coöperation of state authorities and inspectors, thereby securing a greater uniformity of conditions in the various states.

In those cases where clothing is bought ready-made from merchants of another state, it is manifestly impossible to determine whether such clothing meets the conditions laid down by the state into which it is sent. Except in the most glaring cases it is impossible to tell on examination whether clothing is in a sanitary condition. There is no adequate machinery for tracing and discovering such goods after they have entered the channels of interstate commerce.[6] The only solution for this part of the problem is to improve the conditions of manufacture in the various states.

The arguments brought forward for national regulation are first, danger of infection; and second, lack of uniformity. The situation existing in the clothing industry previous to 1890 unquestionably demanded radical action on the part of the state. It is probably true that the conditions at this time were such that the health of the consumer was often jeopardized. This danger from infection has at all times been greatly exaggerated. Direct evidence of such danger is almost entirely wanting. That there was some danger is shown negatively by the fact that when home-workers were forced to take out a license it was dis-

---

[6] Report of inspector Griffin, ibid., p. 394. Also report of inspector Plunkett, ibid., p. 409.

covered that many who applied for such licenses were manufacturing clothing under filthy conditions and often at a time when contagious diseases were present in the homes. As we have already pointed out, the series of laws which have been passed by leading states engaged in the manufacture of clothing and the better control which has been gained over infectious diseases, have practically removed the danger of such contagion. At the present time those who advocate national regulation are laying stress upon the danger of consumption. The races chiefly engaged in the manufacture of clothing in New York, however, the Italian and the Jewish, are credited with having the lowest death rate from this disease, despite the unfavorable conditions in which they live. The clothing industry itself ranks low among the industries of the country as fostering this disease. The statement that is often made that consumption* is rife among the tenement dwellers in New York cannot be substantiated.[7] The tenement houses noted for being breeding places of this disease are relatively few in number and are restricted in locality.[8] The present system of licensing and inspection us-

---

*Out of fifty-three industries in which men are employed, the clothing industry ranks thirty-third. Charities, X. p. 310.

[7] "I think the statement is perfectly safe that a majority of the tenement-house dwellers in New York City have tuberculosis in some form." Statement by Dr. John H. Pryor, quoted in a pamphlet sent out by the consumers league in 1901.

[8] Dr. Tracy says concerning wards iv. and vi. that tuberculosis is chiefly confined to certain localities and to a small number of houses in these localities. In summing up the conditions in the city in general he states that "Though tuberculosis causes from 14 to 15 per cent. of the total number of deaths in the city, yet it is confined within narrow limits and to a small number of houses." Annual report of the health department of New York City, 1896, pp. 251, 253

ually prevents clothing from being manufactured in such quarters. A decided gain against danger of contagion has been brought about by confining home-work to a few of the minor processes of manufacture, as the clothing now remains in the home for a comparatively short time.

Granting that the danger of contagion from consumption and other diseases exists, it is difficult to see how the general government could in the long run stamp it out better than the state and local authorities have done. It must be noticed that the national government to-day possesses no machinery for such regulation and that the creation of this machinery would duplicate that already in existence in the states. It is true that under the general government local influence would be less, but on the other hand the system would be more inelastic and to obtain needed changes would be more difficult. Abuses are liable to exist under either form of regulation.[9] Sanitary surroundings in general have been improved through interstate action and through coöperation between local and state authorities. The Department of Buildings and the Tenement House Commission by enforcing laws, and the Board of Health by stamping out disease, have been of the greatest aid to the state factory inspectors. The movement of the future must be by fuller and closer coöperation with such institutions rather than by an appeal to the general government.

The problem of uniformity of regulation is not peculiar to the clothing industry. It is unquestionably true that much hardship has been entailed upon manufacturers in certain states

---

[9] The Chicago theatre disaster was due to dereliction of duty on the part of local authorities. The steamer Slocum disaster was due to dereliction of duty on the part of national authorities.

because they were compelled to compete with those of other states which had lower standards. Lack of uniformity has caused some disturbance in the clothing industry, but on the other hand the regulations have been of such a nature that the actual increase of cost due to them has been so slight that the decline of the clothing industry in one locality and its growth in another cannot be traced to any such causes. It might be pointed out that uniformity of laws will not secure uniformity of conditions where such laws must be applied to widely varying conditions. Any evils growing out of lack of uniformity must be solved through voluntary state coöperation and through the creation of a saner public opinion.

Conditions which at an early stage of a particular industry excite little attention, become intolerable as that industry passes beyond the marginal stage and gains in wealth and respectability. It then attracts entrepreneurs of higher business and social ideals and the plane of the industry is raised. Manufacturers voluntarily assume responsibility and establish a minimum of conditions under which their industry shall be carried on, such as in earlier years the state had found it impossible to attain through coercive action.

This statement is strikingly true of the manufacturers in the clothing industry. The clothing industry was for a long time in the hands of entrepreneurs possessing little capital and endowed with little sense of their responsibility to society and of what constitutes proper liberty in regard to their individual actions. The clothing industry itself served a class which lacked influence and possessed little power in moulding public opinion. Crude business methods, and thoughtless disregard for the rights of their employees and the public, were the rule. At present large capital is invested and the industry has reached such a state in its development that those men who were in control in its earlier years have been crowded out. Those who are now in control, occupying as they do high social positions, refuse to do violence to these by permitting conditions for which they would be held directly responsible.

A better class of worker is also employed, and the laborer has become more intelligent and has set about creating better standards of employment. These better methods and standards in the upper ranks of the clothing industry react favorably upon the lower ranks. Greater efficiency, bringing with it shorter hours and better physical surroundings, is the result. This is true whether or not the laborers organize in an institution known as the trade union. But it is evident that this awakened consciousness will find more effective expression with organization than without it, and the trade union must be counted as one of the great regulative factors in modern industry.

As we have already pointed out by establishing a minimum of conditions the trade union has kept out of the industry that labor which could not meet such conditions. It has forced entrepreneurs to assume responsibilities which in the earlier days of the industry they refused to assume, and has exercised coercive influence upon the reluctant entrepreneurs of more modern days. Owing to the peculiar methods under which the clothing industry has been carried on, it is liable to many abuses. The furnishing of various accessories of manufacture, and in general, the isolated position of the worker, were open doors for such abuses. The trade union by insisting upon the abolition of such open doors has made most of these abuses things of the past. Trade union organization by giving opportunity for discussion, has created an esprit de corps among the clothing workers and an industrial intelligence, the almost entire absence of which, has been responsible for many of the undesirable conditions.

One of the particular weapons which trade unions have used to bring about better conditions in their industry is the trade union label.* This tag or label is affixed to the product at the time of its manufacture and usually bears the legend that the goods to which it is attached are union made. The label idea originated among the workers in cigars; and the label was supposed to be a guarantee that such cigars had been manufactured under cleanly and sanitary conditions. It is evident that such a guarantee was intended to exert an influence upon the consumer by making it possible for him to shun goods where it was not forthcoming. The label must appeal to the consumer as such, as in the above case, or it must appeal to his interest and sympathies, either as a member of society concerned in the well-being of all or as a member of a class directly affected.

Obviously the label appeals to the self-interest of the consumer on the ground of cleanliness, etc., in the case of those commodities whose consumption or use implies personal contact. Cigars for example, if made up under uncleanly or unsanitary conditions would be repugnant to the consumer, and would work him absolute injury, while the conditions under which an article of furniture is manufactured could have no such direct significance to the consumer. It is evident that clothing bears such a relation to the consumer that he is vitally interested on sanitary grounds in the conditions under which it is manufactured.

The second ground on which the label bases its appeal is

*Appendix B.

interest other than that of a consumer as such. The vital point here is that the consumer must have a direct interest in the class which is agitating for the label. It is easy to overestimate such interest. As we have previously pointed out the bulk of the ready-made clothing is consumed by a class not engaged in its manufacture—by a class that has little direct interest in the trade union or its members. Most of the strength of the union label has been due to those who have had a class interest. The label is confined largely to working clothes made by women and worn by men. In the list of firms using the trade union label, published by the United Garment Workers of America, out of a total of 257 firms using the label in December, 1904, 99 firms are designated as manufacturers of clothing, 118 as manufacturers of mechanics' clothing, and 40 as manufacturers of special order clothing. Much classed as clothing really belongs in the list of mechanics' clothing. A considerable part also of the special order clothing appeals to the class interest of the consumer, because its makers belong to the same class as he does.

A superficial study of the extent to which the trade union label is used soon convinces one that this appeal to class interest is not a very powerful factor. The laborers who are most vitally interested, being engaged themselves in the manufacture of clothing, do not confine their purchases to garments bearing the label. When the label stands between the purchaser and the same grade of goods for less money, it is disregarded. This fact is brought to mind repeatedly whenever laborers are called together in convention. It would seem that the peculiar conditions under which clothing is manufactured and the widespread exploitation of such conditions would attract the consumer to

garments bearing the label. Trade unions have laid great stress upon such conditions and have repeatedly warned the consumer of the dangers to which he is liable if he buys clothing which does not bear the label. The following circular sent out by the United Garment Workers of America appeals both to the social interest of the consumer and to his selfish interests.
"Santa Claus:

Please think of the pale-faced children who struggle for bread in the Sweat-shops, then think of the happy-lit faces of those you remember. Demand the label and support American factories and American standard of living, as against Sweatshop factories and pauper standard of living. Don't buy the product of Sweat-shops! [Don't] Carry Disease Germs into your Homes. . . . Demand clothing which bears the Label of the United Garment Workers! It is a guarantee that the garment was made under healthy conditions, and was not a blanket on a sick-bed in a pest-hole!"

The consumer either does not believe these statements or refuses to act on his belief. The weakness of the appeal to social interests is further shown by the fact that the label had made little headway in cloaks up to 1902, when there was in the entire country only one firm using the label. The same is true in the case of children's clothing. It is evident that the conditions of manufacture here might affect profoundly the selfish interest of the consumer, but the appeal has fallen on deaf ears.[10]

[10] The following statement of the broom makers' unions is a good example of what we mean by an appeal to social interests: "If you desire fair treatment of those from whom you obtain your livelihood, and are not only desirous of living yourself, but are willing to let others live as well, insist upon seeing the above label, printed in black on blue paper, under the wire of the finish of the broom you buy. It

For a number of years past the garment workers in their annual convention have passed resolutions demanding that the use of the label be restricted to those firms which have inside shops and give out no work to be done in the home, and it has instructed the general officers to withdraw the label from all firms not meeting these requirements. But the number of firms manufacturing clothing under such conditions, if we leave out of account mechanics' clothing, is relatively very small. The officers responsible for the enforcement of the demands of the convention have been compelled to modify these to meet the peculiar conditions in the various clothing centers. The withdrawal of the label has been lodged with the various district councils under the guidance of the general executive board.[11] The result of this policy on the part of the general executive board is that there is a lack of uniformity not only among the various district councils but even within the district council itself. In some cases, the label has been denied to all contractors; in others, it has been granted to contractors having a minimum sized shop and using mechanical power; and in still other cases, it has been granted only to those contractors who work for one firm.

A further regulation insisted on by the convention is that the label shall not be granted to firms who do a jobbing business. Just what jobbing consists in however is not always clear. The general executive board has defined it to consist in buying

---

is a guarantee that your purchase was *NOT* made by convicts or enemies of fair labor.''

[11] Report of the quarterly meeting of the general executive board, Nov. 7, 1904. Weekly Bulletin, Nov. 18, 1904.

from a manufacturer or manufacturing for the wholesale trade.[12] One of the reasons urged by the union against jobbing, is that such work permits firms living in one clothing center to have their work made up in another to the detriment of the workers in the former center. The general president states another reason as follows: "jobbers, as a rule, on handling label goods make a leader for them, selling them cheap in order to dispose of some other goods, and in this manner creating a great deal of trouble on account of numerous complaints from other manufacturers of jobbers selling their goods too low."[13]

It is not clear why the consumer as such should be interested in any of these regulations except possibly those which refer to home-work, and it is exceedingly difficult to understand the reasons for the various distinctions which the unions have tried to establish among the various contractors' shops. Such distinctions rest upon no solid ground and are often open doors for unjust and flagrant discriminations. It came out in the last convention that the label in some instances had been granted to firms who were on the unfair list.[14] The charge was also made that certain other firms had been granted special privileges in regard to the payment for labels.[15] In another resolution it was charged that on certain occasions, the issuing of labels was withheld "out of personal satisfaction and petty malice" on the part of a label secretary.[16] The stronger firms use

[12] Weekly Bulletin, Nov. 18, 1904.

[13] Report of the general president. The Garment Worker, Aug. 1903, p. 10.

[14] Proceedings of the thirteenth annual convention of the united garment workers of America, p. 7.

[15] Ibid., p. 18.

[16] Ibid., p. 29.

the label to crush their weaker rivals. In many instances, the employers have suffered severe loss because of the withdrawal of the label owing not to any fault of theirs but to disputes arising among the unions themselves.

The unions' attitude toward jobbing cannot be defended. The regulations have nothing to do with the conditions under which manufacture is carried on and are a serious burden on industry. They are particularly oppressive to the smaller firms and those attempting to gain a foothold in the clothing industry. That the unions themselves recognize this is shown by the fact that a special appeal was made at the convention of 1904 to permit a coöperative factory run by the workers themselves to engage in jobbing and at the same time to use the label.[17] A delegate from the Pacific coast declared that the enforcement of the resolution regarding jobbing would disrupt the organization in that locality.[18] The failure of the executive officers of the union to enforce the demands of the convention regarding the use of the label, has met with much criticism from the more radical elements in the union and at the last convention it was again "*Resolved*, That no manufacturer or manufacturers shall hereafter receive one union label who has not provided shop facilities in his or their own premises for carrying on the manufacture of clothing, and that our label shall be withdrawn from all such at once; be it further *Resolved,* That no contractor, or sweat shop, shall have the use of our union label on any condition whatever, and we demand that the Resolution No. 69 as carried at our last convention be enforced at once." These

---

[17] Proceedings of the thirteenth annual convention of the united garment workers of America, p. 34.

[18] Ibid., p. 50.

resolutions were favorably reported on by the committee and were concurred in by the convention.[19] It remains to be seen how far the general officers will be willing to go in the literal carrying out of the resolution. In case they do attempt to carry it out, it is easy to predict the outcome. There will be inaugurated, on the part of the manufacturers, a general revolt which must result either in the total demoralization of the union forces or in a complete abandonment of the position in regard to the use of the label.*

The question is often asked how far the label is a guarantee of conditions. The answer is simple; the label stands for a union shop, and in general such a shop is superior to the non-union one, but this is not necessarily true. If the consumer buys an article bearing the label he has no guarantee of the conditions under which it was made up. On the other hand, if he buys an article not bearing the label, it does not at all follow that he is buying goods that will endanger his life or that he is abetting conditions that do violence to his social ideals. The label is a powerful instrument in establishing the boycott, because it brings pressure to bear on wholesale manufacturers through the small retailers. It is evident that the small retailer who has even a comparatively small demand for labeled garments will patronize a firm using the label if such firm can furnish him with goods at practically the same cost as can the firms who do not use it. The sensitiveness of the retailer's position makes itself felt on the wholesaler.

[19] Ibid., p. 38.

*The use of the label enables those opposed to the unions to establish an effective boycott by buying unlabeled goods.

The extension of the use of the label within the past few years is not to be attributed to its ability to appeal to the consumer, but to the growth of the trade union idea.[20]

The label idea is ephemeral. Consumption is an individual process and unless the consumer is convinced that he will have some direct gain he will not take the trouble to concern himself with the conditions under which his commodities are manufactured. This is the fatal weakness of all such devices as the label. The average consumer sees in it merely an instrument of trade union agitation. The consumer who is interested because he belongs to a certain class will not give the label his support unless his immediate self-interest is thereby furthered. Therefore as an instrument of regulation, its influence cannot be said to be important or enduring. The wisdom which comes with time will convince its advocates that its use as an instrument for furthering the growth of unionism is attended by so many dangers that the evils to which it may give rise offset the good which it may be able to bring about.

It is difficult to distinguish always between regulation due to the advance of an industry itself and regulation growing out of the general advance in the standards

---

[20] The recent decline in the use of the label is shown by the following: in September 1903, the total number of firms using the union label was 320; 183 of these were firms designated as clothing, 137 as mechanics clothing. Comparing this with the figures given (p. 198) for December, 1904, for the same classes of clothing, we find that there is a decline of 103 firms or 32 per cent. The decline in the number of firms manufacturing clothing was 84, or 44 per cent, while the decline in the manufacture of mechanics' clothing was 19 or 13 per cent. The greater relative decline in the use of the label by firms manufacturing clothing is just what we would expect.

of the society in which a particular industry is carried on. However, there is a difference between the two conceptions. A particular industry may raise its standards while those of society as a whole have undergone no change. In such a case it simply changes its position relatively to other industries. On the other hand the conditions in a particular industry may be improved owing to the general advance of society. Then the relative position of a given industry to other industries remains the same. A New England mill-owner setting up a factory in the South, will, other things being equal, insist upon a higher standard of conditions than will an entrepreneur who has always lived in the South, because the former represents a different type of entrepreneur. On the other hand, the New England manufacturer in his Southern mill will permit conditions that would be impossible in New England. This, not because of state regulation, but because public opinion of what constitutes proper factory conditions is higher in New England than in the South. That is, public opinion either has higher ideals or makes itself more effective.

Many of the abuses that existed in the early days of the cotton manufacture in England were due to the infancy of the industry; but it is also true that could the cotton industry begin its growth at the present time, such conditions as existed before 1830—leaving out of account all coercive action on the part of society, would be impossible. The industrial life of society, as well as the political and the social, has its frontier stages. The conditions in the clothing industry up to 1890 and even later, were those of the frontier, and to-day we may not be wholly beyond that stage. But the ideals of society at present are such that it would be an impossibility for the clothing industry to lapse into the conditions which prevailed during its earlier years. Manufacturers well understand this fact; to-day they are very careful to state that their goods are manufactured under fair and sanitary conditions, and if they think that the public have a prejudice against certain methods of manufacture, they are very careful to make it known that their products are not made up under such methods. These statements must, of course, be taken with reservations; but the exceptions are constantly growing rarer. Indirectly, the vast improvement which has taken place since 1880, along such lines as better housing conditions, cleaner streets, and a practical eradication of certain contagious diseases, has exerted a powerful influence upon the clothing industry.

In placing stress upon improved conditions due to the gradual evolution of social forces, we do not wish to underestimate the important role played by coercive action on the part of society. Such action is necessary and has had great influence, since it has brought about a needed uniformity thus protecting those with high standards against those with low standards and perhaps helping to create a healthful sentiment; but we do wish to insist that such regulation is required only for the minority and is exceptional and that all such coercion must finally rest upon ideals present in society at a given time, that is, upon public opinion.

In the discussion of regulation growing out of advance in the clothing industry, we took up, as a particular phase of regulation on the part of labor, the trade union label. We wish now to call attention to an analogous phase of regulation on the part of the public, the label of the Consumers' League. The object of this league, as its name indicates, is to create more favorable conditions in production by diverting consumption to those firms which the League thinks are carrying on their production under the best conditions. The activity of the League is, first, to bring about the enforcement of existing laws; second, to suggest new laws and agitate for their enactment; third, to investigate factories and workshops in order to establish a standard known as a "fair house" to which shall be granted the privilege of using the Consumers' League label. This label bears the following legend: "Official label of the National Consumers' League. Made under clean and healthful conditions. Use of label authorized after investigation"

Because the League deems the clothing industry to be carried on under highly unfavorable conditions and because of the consumers' intimate interest in such conditions, it has confined its efforts largely to this industry. In a pamphlet sent out by the Consumers' League of Massachusetts, the following occurs:

"3. **What special evils is the League endeavoring to correct?**" The answer is: "Grave evils exist especially in the manufacture of clothing, where the factory system is not established. By a method of contract and sub-contract wages are forced down and hours of labor are lengthened unduly. In some cases shops and homes where work is done are filthy and ill ventilated, thereby breeding disease which is easily transmitted through clothing. This method of manufacture because of well enforced anti-sweat shop laws has been driven out of our own State but is prevalent in New York City, where so much of the clothing for sale in Massachusetts is made. Because of such competition our own garment workers have lost much of their work." [21]

[21] Pamphlet no. 3. The consumers' league of Massachusetts. The pamphlet is undated.

The motives and aspiration of the Consumers' League in many respects deserve our highest commendation. In its attempts to bring about a better enforcement of present laws, and in its suggestion of and agitation for new laws, it performs a valuable service. To the intelligent activity of the League, in large measure, belongs the credit of making the license law of 1897 more effective by its suggestion that careful lists, open to the scrutiny of the public, be kept of all firms giving out work. Its influence has been important in moulding public opinion and making this effective through organized expression. But it is to be noticed that such activity is by virtue of the fact that the League is composed not of consumers having a direct personal interest, but of citizens, intelligently interested in the well-being of the more helpless members of that society of which they are a part.

It is when we turn our attention to that particular activity which has to do with influencing the demand of consumers that serious questions arise. The League virtually asks the consumer to establish a boycott against certain firms making goods under what it considers to be unfair conditions. In this connection two questions arise: first, are the conditions necessarily unfair against which the League wishes to institute such boycott? and second, is the league in a position to guarantee to the consumer that the alleged facts on which it asks the consumer to base his actions are really true? So far as the clothing industry is concerned, the answer to the first must be that the League has been given to exaggeration. In the quotation cited above, conditions in New York and Boston are compared very unfavorably to the former city. The conditions said to exist in New York do not exist and, as we have seen in a previous chapter, are denied by the two excellent inspectors of the commonwealth of Massachusetts. That all clothing manufactured off the premises of the employer is necessarily unfit for the careful consumer, is a generalization which is unwarranted. Neither does it follow that all clothing manufactured on the premises of the employer is manufactured under fair conditions. It is a serious question indeed, whether all home-work should be so sweepingly condemned, and all so-called factory work so sweepingly commended. We are very sure that in the clothing industry it is not safe to indulge in such commendation and condemnation.[22]

Is the League sure of its facts? is our second question. Taking it for granted that the generalizations in regard to particular forms of manufacture are correct, is the League in a position to inform the consumer as to what the actual conditions are? A part of the legend on its label reads, "Use of label authorized after investigation" If this means anything, it means that the League through the personal investigation of its agents keeps itself thoroughly informed as to the conditions of manufacture for all the firms which it designates as fair. Evidently an investigation at the time of granting the label is not sufficient, for what is true to-day may not be true to-morrow. Therefore, to be sure of its facts the League must keep in the field a large body of investigating agents and have a thoroughly organized machinery for prosecuting such investigation. No such organization exists. It is quite beyond the realm of prac-

---

[22] The following quotations from an article by Miss Ada Eliot should be taken to heart by us all: "In order to interest donors or to push reforms, social workers sometimes allow themselves to emphasize evils to an extent that gives an impression absolutely false. It is sociological sensationalism." The over-emphasis of evils. Charities, April 2, 1904, p. 328.

ticability to expect any such organization. But to establish a boycott upon any less thorough searching of facts is manifestly both unrighteous and unjust. The boycott is a dangerous weapon whether in the hands of employers' associations, trade unions, or a consumers' league composed of highly intelligent and well-intentioned people. Fortunately, the essential sense of justice inherent in most of us prevents any widespread influence of such methods.

The arguments urged against the trade union label apply with equal force to the Consumers' League label. Such labels cannot make their way by depending on the consumer as such. There is no good reason why the consumer should not buy where it serves his purpose best and that he will continue so to buy there can be no doubt. At any rate neither the trade union nor the Consumers' League with their respective label devices has brought forth arguments sufficiently convincing to the contrary. Entrepreneurs must be educated to a better understanding of enlightened self-interest and to a fuller appreciation of their duties to their employees. Society as a whole must be brought to a better understanding of the fact that on the welfare of its meanest members depends the well-being of its best. All this calls for agitation and education, not of consumers as such but of all citizens. In this agitation and education such organizations as the Consumers' League find splendid opportunities for work, and the particular organization under discussion has done and is doing an excellent service.

CHAPTER VIII

Trade Unions

Outside of the ranks of the cutters, there was no trade union activity in the early years of the clothing industry because of the conflicting nationalities, the systems of work, the large number of women workers, and the low state of development of the industry. Previous to the year 1890, there were many sporadic attempts at organization, but up to this date the influence of the union upon conditions in the industry was practically nil.

It is not strange that the first unions were found among the cutters. Not only did these represent the most skilled workers in the trade, but they possessed a homogeneity which was almost entirely lacking in the other branches of the industry. It is not until recently that the cutters have acted in coöperation with the other workers.[1] But they have exerted a profound influence upon the other branches and have been a powerful factor in the development of trade unions among these, for it is to them that the tailors have looked for organizers and leaders.

Trade unions have encountered the same obstacles in the clothing industry as in many others, namely, a large mass of unskilled labor and a lack of development of the industry itself. They have also had to overcome difficulties peculiar to their in-

---

[1] In 1893, the cutters assisted the progressive tailor's union, but there was no further cooperation until the general strike growing out of the open shop agitation in 1904.

dustry. Among these may be named decentralization of the workers, their attitude toward the trade union idea, the seasonal character of the industry, the furnishing of numerous accessories of manufacture by the workers, and immigration.

The extreme decentralization of the clothing industry previous to 1895, due to the large numbers of home-workers and of small contractors' shops, made it exceedingly difficult to arouse a common interest, and to give the workers the necessary knowledge of conditions. The disappearance of home-work, the increasing size of the contractors' shops, and the appearance of a labor press gradually overcame these difficulties, and as we have pointed out the contract system under these new relations fostered rather than hindered the growth of trade unions. The seasonal character of the industry demands that adjustments be made to meet the changing conditions. The trade union from its very nature is inelastic and therefore has encountered difficulties in meeting these adjustments. The demands that are made at the beginning of the busy season must be modified to meet the changed conditions of the dull. Unless the union can adapt itself to these modifications, disorganization results. These changing conditions have been most noticeable in the manufacture of women's garments. The union has been unable up to the present time to make the necessary adjustments, and as a consequence, its organization in this industry is at a low ebb.

The unions have always recognized that the furnishing by the laborers of a part of the accessories of manufacture gives rise to many abuses and is a fruitful source of misunderstanding and irritation, and it has, therefore, strenuously insisted that such accessories be furnished by the employer.

It is easy to overestimate the influence of immigration but in the early days of the clothing industry immigration was undoubtedly an important obstacle to trade union growth. The immigrants, totally unacquainted with the aims and ideals of unionism, had to be educated and assimilated. But that it is possible to effect organization even among the unskilled immigrants and that they will remain true to the union through prolonged strikes has been proved again and again. The branches most susceptible to the influence of the immigrants are those which make children's jackets, knee pants and pants. The effectiveness of the union in these is surpassed only by that in the cutters' branch, while in the case of cloaks where a high degree of skill is demanded, the union is weakest.

The peculiar attitude of the Jewish worker toward the union is well-expressed in the following: "The Jew's conception of a labor organization is that of a tradesman rather than that of a workman."[2] This attitude is attributable to the fact that the instincts of the Jewish workman for industrial pursuits became dormant, owing to the fact that trade and not industry had been his occupation for generations. He, therefore, considers his employment in the clothing industry as merely temporary. This attitude has made it extremely difficult for the union to maintain its membership during times of prosperity and peace. But what has been perhaps a greater obstacle to overcome was lack of sympathy on the part of the rank and file for the methods of trade unions. They looked to socialism rather than to unionism for an amelioration of their condition. The weaning of the workers from their desire for political agitation had to

[2] Commons, John R., Report of the industrial commission, 1901, XV. p. 327.

be accomplished before effective trade unionism was possible, this has been done only by persistent and patient effort on the part of the trade union leaders, who on every occassion have pointed out the futility and dangers of such agitation.

The clothing industry is controlled by the Jews. Jewish individualism has often been mentioned as unfavorable to trade unionism. It is always difficult to determine how far the absence of organization is due to the stage of industrial development of the people, and how far it is due to their racial characteristics. As a matter of fact, those people who are naturally individualistic have the most highly developed trade unions, and excel in other forms of coöperation. The Englishman, for example, is more individualistic than the Frenchman, and his development of trade unions is far superior. The Jew, it is true, is individualistic; but as we have pointed out above he has a penchant for coöperation. His economic position made him feel that the union was too slow a process, but as he advanced economically he outgrew this feeling. When we take into account the obstacles which they have had to overcome, the growth and efficiency of trade unions in the clothing industry is nothing less than marvelous.[3]

Factors that have materially aided the growth of the union, are homogeneity of the workers, both as to sex and nationality, a comparatively high order of intelligence on the part of the workers themselves, and as a whole, a sympathetic and fair attitude of the employers. Another favoring influence—the contract system—must not be overlooked. This system gave an

[3] Of 4,000 cutters of men's and children's garments, 3,500 were in the union; of 30,000 tailors employed in regular workshops, 25,000 were in the union, in 1904.

elasticity to the relations existing between the employer and the employee which was very essential in the early beginnings of trade union organization.

The unit of organization is the local union, composed of members engaged in a particular process, for example, cutters, pressers, basters, or finishers. In some cases the basis of the local union is wider than those engaged in a particular process; for example, Local Union, Number 55, Brooklyn, is composed of operators, basters, finishers, and pressers, all engaged in the manufacture of coats. These local unions through a system of delegates, are in turn combined in an organization comprising the various divisions of a given branch. For example, the United Brotherhood of Tailors includes all the workers, below the cutters, who are engaged in the manufacture of coats. The associated branches of the cutting trade are known as the Amalgamated Association of Cutters and Trimmers. These various organizations, through delegates, are again combined in a general body known as the District Council. Each particular city or locality has its district council. New York's District Council is known as District Council No. 1, Philadelphia's as District Council No. 2, Syracuse's as District Council No. 7, and so on. The various locals are numbered in rotation according to the date of their affiliation with the national body.

Previous to the year 1891 the locals were affiliated with the Knights of Labor but in that year was founded a new organization known as the United Garment Workers of America, and a bitter strife was waged between this organization and the Knights of Labor for control over the clothing industry. The United Garment Workers of America was signally successful, so that to-day the unions of the leading clothing centers are affiliated with it. Its executive body is known as the General Executive Board and is composed of members elected by the delegates of the local unions at their annual convention. The executive officer of the United Garment Workers of America is known as the General Secretary; his office is located permanently in New York City. This organization is affiliated with the American Federation of Labor. In the early days of the United Garment Workers of America the cloakmakers were affiliated with it but in 1894 they withdrew and formed a new organization known as the International Ladies' Garment Workers' Union. This organization is very similar in its working and organization to the United Garment Workers of America.[4]

In the early days of trade unionism, the size of the unit had to be small in order to have a sufficiently strong common interest. The small local met this requirement. The great weaknesses of the small local were that it could not bring about uniformity in the trade and that strikes and disputes were constantly arising owing to its lack of responsibility. The introduction of agreements between the minor branches and employers was really the beginning of uniformity in the industry. Agreements entered into by a local representing the basters, for example, became the basis for similar agreements for all basters in the same branch throughout the district. A further step in uniformity was gained when all the divisions of a given branch acted as a unit. In 1897, for example, the United Brotherhood of Tailors entered into an agreement with the employers. Under this arrangement, a strike was not declared by a small

---

[4] The officers of the general executive board consist of the general president, general treasurer, general auditor, three trustees and four members, and the general secretary.

local union, but by the combined local unions, namely, the United Brotherhood of Tailors.

In New York in 1901 the District Council was the party to the agreement on the part of the unions. In this year for the first time, a general strike embracing the various branches was called. The agreement in settlement of the strike was entered into on the part of the unions by the district council, the particular schedules for the various branches being appended to the general agreement. This increasing organization on the part of the workers brought with it greater power and responsibility and has finally enabled them to substitute the manufacturer for the contractor. The agreement* entered into for 1902 begins as follows: "This Agreement made and entered into this ——— day of ——— 1902, by and between ——— party of the first part, and District Council No. 1 United Garment Workers of America" The following points are covered: maximum hours of work, frequency of wage payment and rate of wages as specified in the schedules attached. Besides this general agreement each branch or local has a supplementary agreement with a contractor or manufacturer taking up the particular points in that branch. The wage schedules submitted by the particular branches or locals are to be enforced by a general strike under the supervision of the district council, which is further under control of the General Executive Board of the United Garment Workers of America.

The constitution of the United Garment Workers of America, of 1891 did not prohibit the calling of a strike by any local union, but provided that all strikes commenced by the local union without the sanction of the general executive board should be at the expense and risk of such local

*Appendix D. III, IV.

union.[5] The General Executive Board was obliged to support all strikes caused by the reduction of wages, provided first, that the executive committee of the labor union had made an investigation and had attempted settlement with the employers; and second, that in case of failure to settle, the question had been put to a secret vote of the labor union and carried by a two-thirds majority of the members. The Recording Secretary was to transmit such action in a full statement to the general secretary.[6]

Under the present constitution it is provided that: "No strike shall be considered legal or be permitted to take place which involves a conflict with a firm recognizing the Union, without the sanction of the General Executive Board being obtained. Further, no strike shall be permitted which involves more than twenty-five persons and affects more than one union, until the grievance is first submitted to the General Executive Board and the contemplated strike approved by it."[7] The same article provided that any labor union desiring assistance from the United Garment Workers of America, can not order a strike unless authorized to do so by the General Executive Board, except as provided for by section 5 of this article, section 3 provides that in case the labor union is not sustained by the General Executive Board, the labor union can appeal to the General Secretary, who shall order a referendum vote of the general membership, and if the appeal is sustained by a two-thirds majority, then the General Executive Board shall sustain the union.

[5] Art. XIII, sec. 9.
[6] Art. XIV, secs. 1, 2.
[7] Art. X, sec. 5.

The lack of centralized authority in the early years of the union was a cause for much trade disturbance and many hasty and uncalled for strikes. This coupled with the fact that strikes were often spectacular and sensational in their character has done much to injure, in the eyes of the public, the trade union movement in the clothing industry. Centralization has brought with it a very decided change. Greater uniformity and more conservative action have been secured, fewer strikes have resulted, and when strikes have been declared, they have been much more effective.

The policy of the United Garment Workers of America has been exceedingly liberal in regard to the entrance to the trade. The constitution as amended[8] provides that, "A candidate, male or female, to be admitted to membership of a L. U. attached to the U. G. W. of A., must be 16 years of age, must be employed in the manufacture of garments for men, boys and children, and working at the trade. The initiation fee shall be as follows: in L. U.'s of less than one year's existence, not less than one ($1.00) dollar; in L. U.'s existing one year, not less than three ($3.00) dollars."

In 1899 the General Secretary in his annual report recommended: "that no local be permitted to charge an initiation fee to exceed five dollars, with the exception of such locals having charged a higher fee for a period of three years." This recommendation was adopted and became a part of the constitution, but in 1903 the constitution was again modified and to-day stands as above quoted.

The constitution* also provides that no member of the

[8] Art. XIV, sec. 1. Weekly Bulletin, Dec. 2, 1903.
*Art. VIII, sec. 8.

United Garment Workers of America shall be fined or expelled by any labor union or by the General Executive Board without being properly notified of the charges against him and given a chance for a fair hearing. At a mass meeting one of the prominent trade union leaders called attention in his address to the liberal policy of the union, stating that its doors had never been closed by tyrannical regulation and high initiation fees. This represents fairly the attitude of the United Garment Workers of America; no artificial barriers have ever been set up against workers wishing to enter the trade. The only provision in regard to apprenticeship in the constitution of the United Garment Workers of America refers solely to apprenticeships in the cutting branch. This article* provides that "not more than one apprentice in three years to be allowed to every ten cutters, or majority fraction thereof, employed, and helpers not permitted." When the traditions of the industry were still those of the custom trade much stress was laid upon the regulation of apprentices. As late as 1897 the agreement of the Brotherhood of Tailors provided that there should not be more than one apprentice to three machines.[9] The unions have usually abandoned the attempt to regulate apprentices and, instead, have taken the position that no apprentices shall be allowed.*

In the agreement of this same association, 1902, it is provided that there shall be one helper to every two operators and not more than one helper to every two basters, and no appren-

*Art. XIX, sec. 8.

[9] See agreement in report of the New York board of mediation and arbitration, 1897, p. 272.

*Appendix D. IV.

tices are to be employed.[10] The knee pants' makers also do not permit apprentices.[11]

In the Sailor Jacket Makers' Union every operator is permitted to employ not more than two helpers.[12] In cloaks the only provision is that but one presser's helper shall be permitted.[13] However, the union attempts absolutely to prevent the employment of any helpers or apprentices by the workmen themselves; failing in this it limits the number.[14]

The problem of overtime has been a very difficult one in the clothing industry. While the attitude on this question has not been different in the clothing unions from that in trade unions in general, the difficulties of regulating overtime have been very much greater in the clothing industry. The first obstacle is the great irregularity in the trade and the consequent pressure to work over time during the busy season. The second obstacle is the peculiar economic position of the worker. He is anxious to advance his position and willing to sacrifice his leisure to effect this end. The union has to deal with the wishes not only of the employer, but with those of the individual worker. The third obstacle is the decentralized condition of the clothing industry which makes it exceedingly diffi-

---

[10] Agreement of the united brotherhood of tailors, 1901, art. vi.

[11] Agreement of the knee pants makers' union, Brooklyn, local number 162, 1901, art. iv.

[12] Agreement, 1901.

[13] Agreement of the cloakmakers' union No. 1, New York, 1898.

[14] The custom in some centers has been to subject any member to a fine who teaches a person the trade unless he first gets permission from the union to do so. These regulations so far as New York is concerned have never been general. Rules to be observed by members of local union, no. 25, Boston.

cult for the State to enforce its regulations in reference to hours. Even where such regulations are enforced, the tendency is very strong for employees to take work home. The establishment of factories in the lofts of large business blocks in the well-to-do parts of the city, has greatly discouraged taking work home; as we have pointed out, the division of labor in all but women's garments has been a great factor in discouraging home work. The union during its early growth, roughly marked by the period up to 1902, gained many other concessions by pursuing a liberal policy in regard to this question.

The general policy of the union has been to leave the regulation of overtime with the various locals. In those branches of the trade where the conditions are such that its regulation is difficult, overtime is absolutely prohibited. The knee pants makers,[15] the children's jacket makers,[16] and formerly the overcoat and sackcoat makers[17] did not permit overtime under any circumstances. In the early years of the union, the cloakmakers prohibited overtime, with the exception of the cutters who were permitted to work overtime at double the regular rate of pay, and with extra money for supper.[18] In 1898, the cloakmakers permitted overtime during the months of September, October and November, but in no case was work allowed

---

[15] Agreement of the knee pants makers' union, local 162, Brooklyn 1901.

[16] Agreement of the children's jacket makers' union, locals 10 and 15, 1902.

[17] Agreement of the overcoat and sackcoat makers' union, local 30, 1894.

[18] Agreement of the cloakmakers' union, New York and vicinity, 1894.

later than nine o'clock in the evening.[19] No mention is made providing for extra compensation for such time. The sailor jacket makers permit overtime on two days in the week from half-past six to half-past eight at double the rate of wages.[20] In the early agreements of the United Brotherhood of Tailors, no mention is made of overtime.[21] In 1901, overtime was not permitted under any circumstances,[22] but in the agreement of the same association for 1902, overtime was permitted and was to be paid for at the rate of time and a half.[23]

Closely associated with the problem of overtime, has been that of taking out work; where the custom of taking out work has been prevalent, the union demands its absolute abolition. In no part of trade union activity has the union been more effective than in its regulation of overtime. While as we have said above, the union has been unable in all cases to enforce the agreement about overtime, it has brought overtime under such regulation that the abuses which were so common have been eradicated. In cloak making more overtime is worked than in the other branches. The reason for this has already been pointed out.

In the early agreements, except those of the coat tailors, there was a provision requiring the employer to furnish all accessories of manufacture. The custom of the furnishing of such accessories by the workers lingered longest in the knee pants branch. The agreement of that branch, in 1898, pro-

---

[19] Ibid., 1898.
[20] Agreement of the sailor jacket makers' union, local 159, 1902.
[21] Agreements of the united brotherhood of tailors, 1895, 1897.
[22] Ibid., 1901.
[23] Ibid., 1902.

vided that the employers shall furnish machines, tools, needles, irons, coal and all other material which may be needed for performing the work, and in the agreement of 1901, it was provided that pressers shall be furnished with coal, wood, irons and all necessary tools and that operators shall not be charged for the use of steam and electric power. So far as New York is concerned, the custom for the worker not to furnish such accessories is practically universal.

In the constitution of 1891, no mention is made as to whether work shall be week work or piece work but in the amended constitution of that year, the policy of the United Garment Workers of America is declared to be, to substitute for piece or task work, a system of week work.[24] The working out of this general policy has been left to the various locals, so there has been no uniformity. Task work has been, uniformly condemned by the union, nevertheless, union men work under this system. In 1894, a long and bitter strike was waged for the establishment of the week system in cloaks; a disastrous conflict from which the cloak unions have never recovered. In the agreement of 1899, both week and piece work are recognized. The Brotherhood of Tailors in the agreement of 1897, make no mention of the form of work, but in the agreement of 1902, it is provided that the only form shall be week work. In children's jackets, week work is the prevailing type but no particular mention is made of either kind in the agreements. In knee pants, the early agreements make no mention of the form of work, but in the later agreements it is specifically provided that piece work only shall be permitted. In vests week

---

[24] Art. xix, sec. 7.

work is the usual form, while in pants piece work prevails. The cutters enforce a rigid system of week work.

The trade union has not had a consistent policy. The early conditions in the trade partially excuse the policy of the union toward piece work, as it was maintained that it was more difficult to regulate. Of late years, the union leaders have been willing to concede piece work and have even advocated it.[25]

The growing concentration of the unions brought with it more effective organization and more conservative action, together with the gradual elimination of many of the vexing questions of earlier years. It follows that there is a decided decrease in the number of disputes between employer and employee. But the peculiar nature of this industry, characterized as it is by a busy and a dull season, makes the number of strikes still large. These strikes are periodical as they grow out of the attempt to restore the busy season's schedules which have been reduced during the dull season. These periodic strikes are usually of short duration and when no unusual demands are made are almost universally won.

It has been the policy of the general union to avoid as far as possible all labor disturbances. In 1902 the attempt was

[25] The following statement is from President Larger's annual report, 1902: "The piece system prevails in Boston, thus making it possible for old men to have an opportunity to work. This condition cannot be found in any other clothing market, where the so-called week work prevails, where our cutters work hard and no old men are employed. They turn out from sixteen to sixty suits per day, and receive from twenty to twenty-four dollars per week. After all, we find ourselves working piece-work, and giving the firm all the benefit of it, and the men who do the most work have the steady positions." The Garment Worker, Aug., 1902.

made to bring about adjustments for the busy season without the usual strike. With this purpose in view, on July 2, the following letter* was sent to the manufacturers by District Council Number 1: "Our Unions are now ready with their demands for the coming year, and should you desire to comply with the same, before any action is taken, we would like you notify us, on or before July 15th, 1902." The schedule demanded by the unions at this time was identical with that of 1901 except that it called for a reduction of three hours a week in the working time. This fact may have had something to do with the failure of the manufacturers to respond to it. At any rate the letter failed in its object, and the usual strike took place.

The periodic disturbances growing out of a demand for higher wages, as they occur at the very beginning of the season, have not usually caused severe loss in the clothing industry. Strikes not confined to these demands have often proved disastrous failures so far as the union is concerned and have been expensive to the industry. The strike of the coat tailors in 1893, when an attempt was made to force the manufacturers to employ men belonging to trade organizations, the numerous strikes waged against the contract system, and the cloakmakers' strike of 1894 against the piece system, were all lost by the union. In the latter case particularly, the clothing industry was prostrated and the union itself practically disrupted. The strikes in the clothing industry often take on a spectacular and sensational form, but when the number involved is taken into account and the easy opportunity for personal strife is remembered, the freedom from intimidation and violence is remarkable. Rioting, destruction of property and similar acts of mob excesses are practically unknown.

*Appendix C.

With the formation of the United Garment Workers of America in 1891 a bitter struggle began for supremacy in the clothing industry. The feeling at this time towards those workers who belonged to the Knights of Labor was far more bitter than it was towards the workers who belonged to no organization. At the very beginning of the struggle the two organizations were nearly evenly balanced and so intimately were they connected that some of the members on the Executive Board of the United Garment Workers of America also held office under the Knights of Labor. It was not long, however, before the United Garment Workers of America were in a position to insist that such officers withdraw from the Knights of Labor, and to demand that employers exclude those workmen who were members of the Knights of Labor from the shops in which their own members worked. In 1893 the national union demanded that the clothing manufacturers of New York should employ in their cutting shops only men belonging to the union, and a strike was threatened unless this demand was complied with. On the face of the demand it would seem that the object of the United Garment Workers of America was to exclude the non-union worker, but at this time the non-union worker was lost sight of in the desire to bring about the destruction of the Knights of Labor by forcing its members to join the new association if they wished to continue work in the same shops with members of the United Garment Workers of America. The Clothing Manufacturers' Association refused this demand, declaring that they would not discriminate against any workman whether he was a union man or a non-union man. It ordered that unless the American Federation of Labor which was representing the Cutters' Union should recede from its position, a general lockout of all the employees in the manufacturing departments of the members of the Clothing Manufacturers' Association would be declared. As the union refused to withdraw its demand, the manufacturers closed their workshops March 25, 1893.[26] A long and bitter contest followed. The New York Board of Mediation and Arbitration attempted to settle the dispute. In the discussion before this Board it was clearly brought out that the crux of the whole dispute was the question of the attitude of the employer towards those employees belonging to the Knights of Labor.

The manufacturers merely agreed not to discriminate against members belonging to either labor organization, so the United Garment Workers of America were not enabled to make good its demand that only its members should be employed, yet in the final settlement of the strike, they really accomplished what they had set out to do, for from this time on the Knights of Labor were excluded from those shops in which the United Garment Workers of America were in control.

In 1894, the United Brotherhood of Tailors demanded of the Contractors' Association, that only members of their union should be employed. The other unions from time to time made similar demands. In all cases where the Knights of Labor were not involved, the matter was left largely in the hands of the local unions, and, therefore, it is not strange that the rule demanding the employment of only union labor was not generally enforced outside the cutting branch. In 1902, the agreements not only demanded that none but union men should be employed but that the employer "shall cease to employ any

[26] Seventh report of the New York board of mediation and arbitration, 1893, p. 58.

one and all those employees who are not in good standing, and who do not conform and comply with the Rules and Regulations of said party of the third part [the union] upon being notified to that effect by its duly credentialed representatives."[27]

At the time when the local union acted independently shop strikes, growing out of disputes over the question of the right of dismissal of union men, were chronic. The union at this time maintained that the right of such dismissal was vested in it. It objected to dismissal by the employer even in those cases where he applied to the union for a workman to take the place of the one whom he had dismissed.[28]

With the growing power of the central organization this unwise and unjustifiable position on the part of the union has been abandoned, and many local unions have been warned in no uncertain words against, or severely disciplined for, attempting to dictate to the employer what workmen he shall keep in his shop.

In 1903, the General Executive Board served notice on Pants Makers Union, Number 8, consisting of over 1000 members, that unless it ceased its arbitrary action toward an employer who had dismissed a notoriously inefficient workman, its charter would be taken away.[29] This sane and eminently wise position of the General Executive Board has been opposed

---

[27] Agreement between the united brotherhood of tailors of district council no. 1, sec. 5. Appendix D. IV.

[28] In 1895, the union attempted to collect damages from a contractor on the ground of breach of contract. He had dismissed a workman and asked the union to furnish another one.

[29] Weekly Bulletin, Nov. 18, 1903.

by the more radical element and had much to do with the strife which arose in the union at a later date.

We have had occasion to allude to the apparent ease with which contractors entered into agreements and their corresponding willingness to break them. In order to bring about a better enforcement of such contracts, the union has sought to hold the contractor for damages in case of a breach of it. As the contractors usually do not possess much property and therefore lack financial responsibility, the union demanded that each contractor deposit with the officers of the union a promissory note or some other form of security. This was to be forfeited as liquidated damages in case of failure on the part of the contractor to carry out the agreement. In these agreements the union contracted to furnish workmen for the employer, and the damages were for breach of employment; the damages were liquidated in view of the fact that they could not be exactly ascertained by consultation or otherwise.*

These agreements were usually violated by the employer and frequent suits arose for the forfeiture of the security which had been given by the individual contractors. The decision of the courts as to the legality of these contracts has been by ׃ means uniform, and as no case has been carried to the court of final appeal their legality has not been determined.[30]

The peculiar conditions under which these agreements were entered into caused some courts to hold that they were

[30] Dr. Isaac A. Hourvitch, who more than any one else is responsible for the form of these agreements, in a private letter to the writer, says: "While the legality of such agreements has not been finally determined, I am of the opinion that such labor agreements can be successfully contested by the employer, and that it will require a special statute in order for a labor union and an employer to make a special contract.'

*Appendix D. II.

signed under duress and were therefore void. That part of the agreement whereby any breach of the contract calls for a definite sum as liquidated damages has not been upheld in all cases. The courts have held that the damage suffered by breach of contract must in each individual case be estimated and assessed. The trial courts have often held that such contracts were binding, and in many cases a contractor has made settlement with the union, usually for a small percentage of the total amount called for in the agreement. In those cases where the union has insisted upon the forfeiture of the full amount of the security, the contractor has taken an appeal. The courts of appeal have held against the union and on account of the great expense involved it has usually abandoned the fight.

Section 5 of the agreement of 1904, between The Protective Coat Tailors and Pressers' Union, Local Number 55, United Garment Workers of America and the firm of Morris Cohen & Sons, prohibited the firm from employing labor not belonging to the local and even from employing a member of the union unless he had a card signed by the business agent of the local. A money penalty was provided and to secure its payment the firm had deposited with the President of the local a promissory note. The firm violated the agreement and action was brought before the court to collect the amount due on the note. Judgment for the union was obtained. The case was appealed in 1904 to the Appellate Division of the New York Supreme Court. The Appellate Division by a divided vote of three to two held that section 5 of the agreement was void, because contrary to public policy, since its object was "to hamper and restrict freedom of employment on the part of both the master and the servant under penalty of both loss of service and deprivation of employment, and to coerce all workingmen within the field of its operation to become and to remain members of the contracting organization." The majority of the court also held that "the fact that a contract between a workingmen's organization and an employer's association was entered into on the part of the employers with the object of avoiding disputes and conflicts with the workingmen's organization, does not legalize a plan of compelling workingmen, not in affiliation with the organization, to join it, at the peril of being deprived of their employment and of the means of making a livelihood." That the absence of the elements of falsehood and malice which appeared in the case of Curran versus Galen, (152 N. Y. 33), decided by the Court of Appeals, was immaterial since "the underlying principle which controlled the court being the necessity of preserving in a free country the utmost liberty in the pursuit of lawful occupations, without the imposition of conditions not required for the promotion of the general welfare."

The minority dissented on the ground that, malicious motives were essential to render the contract illegal, admitting that "If it were pleaded here that the sole purpose of this contract was to injure other workingmen or hamper their freedom in pursuing their lawful callings, or to coerce them to do an act injurious to themselves, a different case would be presented; but in my opinion a contract having the lawful purpose of benefiting the parties thereto by procuring for the employer the most capable workmen, and not involving the exercise of any physical force or restraint or violence, is not invalidated because of the possibility or probability that its operation may have a detrimental effect upon the interest of others."[31]

[31] Weekly Bulletin, Dec. 16, 1904.

The constitution* of the United Garment Workers of America, reads: "It shall be the policy of the U. G. W. of A. . . . to make uniform the conditions of labor in the trade and to gradually reduce the hours of labor to eight per day." The United Garment Workers of America, during the greater part of its existence, has been engaged in securing uniformity among the various branches in a given locality, but a universal agitation for uniform hours of labor has not come into prominence until very recently. The cutters in New York, Chicago, Boston and Philadelphia had all gained an eight hour working day, and demands were constantly being made by the employers in these centers that their rivals in other centers be forced to employ their cutters under the same conditions. The General Executive Board agreed to do all in its power to bring about this uniformity.

In the autumn of 1903 a strike was declared by the cutters of Rochester to secure an eight hour day. This strike received the sanction and was under the management of the General Executive Board.[32] The Rochester dispute was bitterly contested

*Art. XIX, sec. 7.

[32] "The Rochester strike, which a year ago this month began a series of important disputes in the trade, took place with the recognition and tacit assent of the manufacturers in other cities whose employes were already working under the eight hour system." The international union was dictated by a strong desire "to keep faith with the employers of the cities in which a shorter work day had gone into effect." Weekly Bulletin, Oct. 28, 1904.

The Canadian branches of the united garment workers of America have insisted from time to time that the international character of the united garment workers of America ought to be recognized by incorporating the word "International" in the official title. Therefore it sometimes happens that the united garment workers of America is referred to as the "international union."

during the autumn of 1903 and winter of 1903-4 and the attention of all the clothing centers in the country was attracted. The manufacturers attempted to secure men from other cities to take the place of striking workmen, but so thoroughly was the union organized that but few men were secured. The United Garment Workers of America carried on an active boycott against the product of the Rochester firms, and this was so effective that much of the manufacture of clothing which had formerly been carried on in Rochester was transferred to other centers. The Clothing Manufacturers' Association of Rochester appealed to the National Clothiers Association for assistance.

During this time the National Association of Manufacturers was waging an unrelenting war upon trade unions in all parts of the country, and the press was filled with charges of trade union excesses. The unions among the clothing workers had not been entirely free from such excesses; they had been severely rebuked and some of them disciplined by the General Executive Board. The General Secretary in his annual report of August, 1903, calls attention to the rapid growth of unionism among the clothing workers and says: "So rapid has been the increase as to become a source of grave danger. The sudden introduction of so large a number of craftsmen into the ranks without any knowledge of the movement vastly increases the difficulties of management. While the growth of the organization is a source of pride it brings no strength unless the quality is especially improved. . . . I point this out in order that we may not have a false conception of our strength, and to emphasize the wisdom of proceeding slowly and cautiously."[33]

[33] Report of the general secretary to the general convention of the united garment workers of America, Aug. 1903. The Garment Worker Aug. 1903, p. 14.

The clothing industry was also less prosperous than it had been and there was a decided tendency toward lower prices in general.

That the labor leaders in the clothing industry felt that there was great danger of reaction against the union is shown by the constant note of warning sounded by the General Secretary in the official organ of the union during the autumn of 1903 and the early months of 1904. The question of the open shop had become an absorbing one and labor and capital in general throughout the country were bitterly fighting over it. In an editorial of November 4, 1903, the General Secretary calls attention to the importance which the employer justly lays upon the right to choose his own help, and says that it is inconceivable how industry could be carried on if the employer could not freely select his workmen from among either union men or men at large. He states that the function of the union is to secure a minimum rate of wages, and fair treatment for its members, and that beyond this it cannot go, without jeopardizing its position. He concludes: "Whether a union controls or not, a healthy condition of industry is only possible where individual ambition is stimulated and where every person is put upon his mettle and is rewarded according to his merits. It therefore becomes the manifest duty of the national unions, which are not governed by personal considerations or temporary advantages, to prevent local unions from committing the fatal blunder of trying to usurp the function of the employer in the hiring or discharging of workmen except within the limits indicated. The tendency of unions to do so is the gravest menace to the labor movement."[34]

[34] Weekly Bulletin, Nov. 4, 1903.

At its meeting of November 11, 1903, the General Executive Board "Resolved, That we disclaim any sympathy with attempts made by members to restrict the amount of their work, and we hereby declare that in return for a fair wage and reasonable hours of labor it is the duty of members to give their best energies to their work with due regard to their health."[35] The General Secretary in an editorial of December 9, 1903, entitled "The Impending Danger How to Avoid It," significantly said: "In many trades the unions have become so strong that the regulation of their present power is at least as important as the acquisition of more power. As the power of the unions increases so do the dangers multiply. . . . The responsibility must lie with the leaders, who are in a position to know the limitations of the union and the obstacles that beset it better than can the rank and file." He then calls attention to the abuses and the charges of excesses that are being brought against unions in other industries, and adds: "It is only necessary here to refer to some recent events in our own trade. Such occurrences enable unfriendly employers to point out the transgressions noted as a pretext for attacking the unions they have dealings with, upon the supposition that unless they are curbed or destroyed they will become just as arbitrary. . . . It is idle to pooh-pooh the organized opposition to the labor movement. It is growing with startling rapidity all over the country."[36]

In February, 1904, the Clothiers' Association of Philadelphia decided to return to a fifty-four hour week and to employ whomsoever they chose regardless of labor affiliation. The officers of the United Garment Workers of America immediately

[35] Weekly Bulletin, Nov. 11, 1903.
[36] Ibid., Dec. 9, 1903.

repaired to Philadelphia to avert the threatened lockout. In the conference between these officers and the Philadelphia Association, it was brought out that the chief grievance of the manufacturers was the restriction of output by the union schedule. The manufacturers were assured that the union did not at all desire any such restrictions. This practically settled the question, as an eight hour day was willingly conceded by the manufacturers. The question of the open or union shop was settled by leaving it alone. The clothiers practically agreed to get all their men from the union, and thus virtually recognized it, "while the union recognizes the rights of the employers to get labor elsewhere when it is impossible for the union to supply it. As the union is composed of 95 per cent of all the capable garment workers, the shop question is a small one."[37] The General Secretary, commenting upon the settlement, said: "The committee assured the manufacturers that it did not favor undue restrictions—that the manufacturer is entitled to the full capacity of the workman in return for a fair wage, and the current wages was considered fair. This assurance was the means of bringing about an understanding which was virtually a rescinding of the notice issued by the manufacturers, which was equivalent to a lockout. This creates a precedent for unions to strengthen their organization until it is so perfect that they can ignore the question of open or union shop and make it advantageous for the manufacturers and employer to employ union men without being subject to restrictions." The Press, in further commenting upon this settlement said: "Each party in yesterday's agreement agrees to nothing inimical to the interests of the other. More neither can ask, and society has a right to insist

[37] The Philadelphia Press, Feb. 18, 1904.

that any employer shall be always able to seek any man, and any man any employer. Less for either is tyranny for each." To these sentiments the General Secretary in the Weekly Bulletin heartily assented.

The agreement which was drawn up February 15 between the committee of the Clothiers' Association and the representatives of the General Executive Board was submitted for ratification at a meeting of the manufacturers on February 20. At this meeting, much to the surprise of those who had hoped for a settlement of the trouble, the agreement was rejected, and in place thereof, the manufacturers formulated the following demands: "First.—Fifty-four hours shall constitute a week's work. Second.—The wages of employes shall be regulated by the individual employer and employe. Third.—Workmen shall be employed with regard only to their efficiency and character and without discrimination because of their affiliation or non-affiliation with any organization whatever." When it is borne in mind that these firms had signed agreements which did not expire until May, 1904, and that the method of determining wages ignores the union, the radicalness of the action of the Clothiers' Association becomes apparent. The position taken is identical with that taken by the National Association of Manufacturers of which Mr. Parry is the head.

In the discussion which took place in the meeting it was brought out that the chief opposition to the settlement of February 15 came from the small manufacturers, and that it was due to their voting force in the meeting that the above resolutions were passed. These resolutions were justly considered by the union to be a virtual lockout. That such action on the part of the Philadelphia clothiers was unjustified by the general attitude of the trade unions of the clothing industry and particularly of the national officers, is evident by a study of the conditions at that time. The temper and policy of the General Executive Board, or, at any rate, of those most influential upon it, was conservative and conciliatory, even to conceding more than what would ordinarily be deemed the rights of the union. In an editorial of February 26, the General Secretary said: "The choice of our union is between suffering sometimes from such discriminations and doing what we can to protect ourselves against them, on the one hand, and allowing members, on the other, to go so far in interfering with the legitimate authority of the employer as to engender the organized antagonism of the manufacturers." This editorial from which we have quoted was called forth in answer to certain criticisms which had been made by the tailors' unions against what they considered to be a too liberal policy on the part of the general officers, and more in particular against the editorials which had been appearing from time to time in the Bulletin.

The action of February 20 of the Philadelphia Association was followed by a general lockout by the firms belonging to it. And as the Rochester trouble was still unsettled the General Executive Board had on its hands large strikes in two of the important clothing centers. The Philadelphia Association issued a circular letter to the merchants throughout the country in which they stated, "There was no desire on our part to reduce wages, nor has a single cutter been locked out. Our shops were open to them to return, but only upon consideration that we, being the parties who had furnished the means for running the business, should be entitled to conduct it." [38]

[38] Letter given in full in the Weekly Bulletin, March 25, 1904.

The extreme position taken by the Philadelphia Clothiers' Association really left no alternative but opposition by the labor union. But that those in authority appreciated the grave position in which the clothing unions were placed is shown by an editorial by the General Secretary in the Weekly Bulletin of March 18: "The open shop movement is in the nature of an employers' revolt against unionism. It has been anticipated by those who have been studying the situation. . . . . Great changes have always been succeeded by reactions because of the difficulty of adjusting new conditions to the old order of things. In this case there is, in addition to the disturbance incidental to the sudden forcing up of wages, shortening of hours and changed industrial relations, the dread that the power acquired by the working class is liable to be used destructively. . . . We notice with alarm the disposition of unionists to stake the existence of their movement, which has taken years of sacrifice and struggle to build up, in a fight with solidly organized employers, when through a little discretion they could easily keep out of the contest. This indifference to the gravity of the situation is disquieting. The movement has reached the crucial moment. . . . Never was there a time when leaders were more needed who have the courage to face the displeasure of the members and stand like a wall against the impulse to fling themselves into needless conflict. . . . To consult the rank and file is proper, but the leader in an extreme emergency who makes his judgment subject to the clamor of the membership ceases to lead and becomes a mere agent. He abandons his sacred trust, and allows his union, so fraught with possibilities, to drift on to ruin."

The disputes in Rochester and Philadelphia were still unsettled at the time of the National Clothiers' Association's meeting in April, 1904. The question of the Rochester and Philadelphia strikes became at once the most important question before the meeting. It soon became evident that the fears of the leaders of the unions were well grounded; the radical element of the association was in control and succeeded in passing the resolutions given below, virtually coming to the rescue of the members from Philadelphia and Rochester. The President of the National Clothiers' Association in his address called attention to the desirability of having some form of bureau whereby the members might seek information regarding workmen. A committee was appointed to consider this recommendation. Of the representatives on this committee, two were from New York, one from Chicago, two from Cincinnati, two from Philadelphia, two from Baltimore, two from Boston, one from St. Louis, and two from Buffalo. This Committee reported the following resolutions, as a preamble to the constitution of the proposed labor bureau:

"1. The closed shop is an un-American institution; the right of every man to sell his labor as he sees fit and the freedom of every member to hire such labor are given by the laws of the land, and may not be affected by affiliation or non-affiliation with any organization whatever.

2. The limiting of apprentices in skilled trades is not only harmful to industrial development, but deprives the intelligent American youth of a fair opportunity for advancement and tends to reduce him to the level of an unskilled laborer.

3. The arbitrary restriction of output is economically wrong, and in morals dishonest. A contract of employment is a sale of the employe's labor for the employer's money, and in-

tends an honest day's work on the one hand and a full day's pay on the other.

4. According to the spirit of our institutions the laws of the land are of general and equal application, and should be enforced, without regard to class or condition."[39]

This preamble was unanimously adopted by a rising vote. The President of the Association at the banquet the same evening showed that he was cognizant of the crisis pending by the following remarks: "Capital has in many places lost the idea of conciliation. Here and there an angry spirit of retaliation is showing itself among the employers. The situation now is such that the restraining influence which was brought to bear on labor a year ago is required to keep capital from going to extremes to-day. For it is just as wrong and unwise for capital to oppress labor now, as it was for labor to oppress capital then." [40]

It was ordered that this preamble should be struck off on placards and posted in all the shops of the association. The construction which the union placed upon this action on the part of the association is shown in the General Secretary's statement: "The manufacturers' resolutions are tantamount to a declaration of war on union labor. It is amazing that an association formed purely to deal with the credit system of the trade should come together and commit the manufacturers of the country to a policy which, if carried out, will mean a national labor conflict."[41]

The union took the position that such a policy, predicating

[39] Weekly Bulletin, April 15, 1904.
[40] Ibid.
[41] Ibid.

as it did the destruction of the union, meant a virtual return to the conditions which had formerly existed. This was expressed in general terms as a return to the sweat shop. The press throughout the country was unanimous in the opinion that there must be no return to such conditions. One part of the press held that the manufacturers did not contemplate any such return, and the other part insisted that the open shop meant a return to these evils. In many quarters the press ridiculed the statement that the closed shop was un-American, and considered that the resolutions were really, in general, evasive and insincere.[42] To allay this public sentiment, the Clothiers' Association earnestly protested that they had no desire or intention either to wage warfare on unionism or to change general conditions of employment as to wages and otherwise.[43]

In May, a committee of the National Clothiers' Association was appointed to work out the details of the labor bureau. There was a general feeling that the make-up of this committee, representing as it did some of the manufacturers who had been most favorable and conciliatory towards the union, augured well for the settlement of the dispute. One manufacturer is quoted as saying, "I hope that this labor bureau will never have occasion to act. I would feel that it was a great success even if it never acted." The Weekly Bulletin, commenting on this utterance says:[44] It "indicates a pacific spirit on the part of the committee which augurs well for an understanding." But it adds, "There can, however, be no settlement of the pending issue that does not involve the settlement of the Rochester and Philadelphia troubles and a definite understanding on the open shop question."

[42] Editorial, New York Independent, May 5, 1904.
Weekly Bulletin, May 13, 1904.
Ibid.

The Committee decided that a workman who wished to become an employee of any member of the National Clothiers' Association must make application through the National Labor Bureau, and must furnish the following information: His address, class of work for which he is an applicant, his age, whether married or not, and nationality. To this information was added that given by the bureau, as follows: Whether he had worked for any member of the association, the number of years, wages per week, quality of the work (excellent, good, fair, poor), conduct and habits (excellent, good, fair, poor), date of hiring, wages paid, hired by —— firm, in case of having left, ——cause. This information was filed with the central bureau on individual cards and duplicates of these cards were furnished to the various members of the association. This card caused deep resentment on the part of the union. It was termed a serf's card and the entire scheme was considered as a wholesale attempt at blacklisting.

The attitude of the New York Clothiers' Association is further shown by the following letter written by the secretary to its various members regarding the posting of the preamble quoted above: "I send you herewith two placards containing preamble to the constitution of the National Labor Bureau, which, pursuant to resolution of the Association, you will please post and keep in prominent places in your manufacturing department on and after this date. . . . Your attention is also called to the resolution adopted by the Association that the eight-hour workday for cutters and trimmers in the shops of our members shall be continued until further notice. It is suggested that members not later than Monday morning explain to their employes that the adoption and posting of the resolutions is done without any purpose of antagonizing or discriminating in any way against union men, and that our members have no present intention of changing the number of working hours per day or wages; in other words, your employes should be made to understand that there is no occasion for alarm on their part."[45]

The clothing cutters of New York decided not to take any action in regard to the posting of this preamble until the General Executive Board had had time to consider the matter and outline a plan of action. The tailors' unions in Philadelphia, Boston, and other centers held meetings and resolved to support the cutters in their struggle with the National Association. The Buffalo and Syracuse Clothiers' Associations decided not to cooperate with the rest of the National Association in demanding an open shop.

It is necessary at this point to explain that this action in regard to the open shop affected directly only the cutters and the trimmers, that is, those workmen employed under the direct supervision of the manufacturer, and it affected only those cutters and trimmers whose employers belonged to the National Clothiers' Association. But as we shall point out later, the action of the Clothiers' Association in regard to cutters might well be considered as of very great importance to the other branches of the trade.

All attempts to bring about a peaceable settlement of the points in dispute failed and on June 17 the General Executive Board ordered the Amalgamated Association of Cutters and Trimmers of New York and vicinity to take a referendum vote as to whether or not to strike against the open shop rule of

[45] Written by Samuel Fleischman, Weekly Bulletin, May 6, 1904.

the Clothiers' Association. The resolution to strike was carried by more than the requisite majority and on June 20 the strike was ordered in forty-two of the Clothiers' Association's houses.[46]

In this strike about 25,000 workers were involved in New York, 1500 of these being cutters. The strike was based upon no tangible reason and was utterly lacking in enthusiasm from the beginning. There was the usual spectacular demonstration but in six weeks the men went back to work and the strike was lost. The utter failure of the strike was a powerful blow to the prestige of the union. Before the strike was declared clothing manufacturers of New York had expressed no intention to force individual agreements. On July 28, the Clothiers' Association issued the following instructions to the executive committee: "1. Members must not confer with any officer, representative or member of any union, unless he be a former employee of such firm. 2. Members are not to take back former employees in a body, but only upon individual application, and only if there are vacancies. 3. Members must protect men employed since the strike and must not discharge or agree to discharge any man now working in order to make room for a former employee." The strikes called at other centers, Chicago and St. Louis, ended quite as disastrously as that of New York.

In the preceding pages we have attempted to give a brief outline of the facts in the struggle between the union and the Manufacturers' Association over the question of the open shop. In the following pages it is our purpose to submit these facts to

[46] There was dissension among the union leaders over the question of the wisdom of declaring the strike, the result of which was the resignation of the General Secretary and his ultimate expulsion from the union.

a brief analysis. The motives which impel associations as well as individuals are complex and perhaps are not always clear to the actors themselves. We have had occasion to call attention to the growing elasticity in the clothing industry due to more effective union organization. The avowed object of the trade union was to establish an eight hour day, commencing at the top with the cutters and gradually working down until it was established in all branches of the clothing industry. Each year saw the tailors' unions demanding a shorter and shorter working week. During the nineties they demanded a sixty hour working week; in 1901 a fifty-nine hour week; in 1902 the agreement called for a fifty-six hour week; the forty-eight hour week had become almost universal for the cutters. The Manufacturers' Association reasoned that at an early opportunity further reduction would be demanded in the working time of the lower branch. When it is remembered that the number of cutters compared to those working in the other branches is very small, and that it had been possible to shift a part of the burden of the shorter day enjoyed by the cutters to the shoulders of the more numerous workers in the other branches, the growing demand of these branches for shorter hours and an increasing power to make it good was viewed with increasing alarm by the employer.

The demands of the union growing out of the use of the trade union label, had forced many employers to run union shops against their will and was particularly galling to many of the Western employers and to the smaller firms struggling to gain a foothold in the industry.[47]

[47] Many have joined the unions involuntarily through the pressure of the trade union label. Annual report of the general secretary, 1903. The Garment Worker, Aug. 1902.

The arbitrary action of certain of the trade unions in reference to the dismissal of men and the tendency of certain cutters' unions to restrict output when at the same time they were enjoying an eight hour day, had driven into the ranks of the opposition many employers, formerly favorable to trade unions. The Philadelphia and Rochester strikes called attention to the effectiveness of the boycott, by which many clothing firms had been forced to suspend business, and had thus forcibly brought to the notice of the National Association the immense power which the union was acquiring. The tendency to a general depression in the clothing industry caused manufacturers to fear that they would be unable, owing to the strength of the union, to reduce cost of production should that become necessary. In general a part of the opposition could be traced to nothing more tangible than that the Clothiers' Association had caught the fever of revolt against trade unionism which was going on in so many industries. This was particularly true of the Western members and of the smaller firms, who were inclined to magnify the burden of the union and were desirous of escaping it. Finally the action of the Clothiers' Association was due in part to trade union excesses, in part to fear of excesses and perhaps in a still larger part to the influence of such associations as the National Manufacturers' under the guidance of Mr. Parry.

The suggestion for a national labor bureau, which was first broached in the spring of 1903, was a move on the part of the manufacturers to be prepared for labor disturbances which even at this time many felt were brewing. At its meeting in Philadelphia in the spring of 1904 two well defined sentiments were apparent. One was that of the larger and more respectable manufacturers, particularly those of New York City, who were really out of sympathy with the resolutions which they passed but who felt in a vague way that some attempt ought to be made to curb the trade union, though they had no desire to crush or disrupt it. The other was the more hostile sentiment of the smaller manufacturers and the manufacturers of the Western centers who were either in open conflict with the union or desirous of such conflict and whose workmen had not been so conservative and fair as those of New York. The avowed intention of this element was to crush the union; to them, the open shop meant the non-union shop.

It is also true that even the more conservative members of the association were deterred from any action which they may have contemplated by the storm of protest from the disinterested press of the country. The unions immediately made their appeal to public opinion on the ground that the open shop meant a return to the former conditions of the clothing industry, and this appeal was successful. To the public, the open shop in the clothing industry had an entirely different meaning from the open shop in other industries. How far such an interpretation is warranted is, of course, open to much dispute, but it seems to the writer that the danger of return to the so-called sweating conditions was greatly exaggerated and that the import of the open shop in the clothing industry in its present stage carries no more with it than it does in the other industries. The clothing industry has reached such a stage in its development that the conditions of manufacture existing previous to 1890 or even previous to 1900 would be wasteful and costly. The factory laws would not permit it and public opinion would not tolerate it. The argument that the conditions in the clothing industry are peculiarly menaced, owing to the pressure of immigrant labor, was valid at one time but is not to-day. The use of this labor in the clothing industry to-day would be non-economic and it would be fatuous on the part of the employers to try to make use of it. This is true not only in the case of the cutting branch, but also in the case of the lower branches.[48]

The open shop regulations applied directly only to the cutters, and to the other workers in inside shops. Unionism among the latter is weak owing to the fact that a large percentage of them are women workers and that the men represent a comparatively low grade of labor. Unionism is most effective in the medium sized shops of the contractors and these shops were not affected either directly or indirectly by the resolutions of the Clothiers' Association, except in so far as individual manufacturers had guaranteed the fulfilment of agreements entered into by their contractors.

At the very worst the effect of the declaration of the open shop on the tailors could have resulted only in a lengthening of the working day or a reduction of the wage rate. The working day in those shops where women were employed could not have been lengthened beyond the number of hours prescribed by the laws of the state governing the employment of women. It has been urged that the employer can meet this dilemma by increasing the amount of work done at home by women, but we have already pointed out that it is possible to-day to have only the

---

[48] In December, 1904, the children's jacket makers in New York struck because of an attempt on the part of the contractors to increase the hours of work. To quote the Weekly Bulletin: "The contractors had opened their establishments to unskilled workers from off the streets and to immigrants freshly landed. But they couldn't get their work done properly, and, like sensible men, settled with the union. Dec. 23, 1904.

minor processes carried on in the home, and this is already the custom in both inside and outside shops.

It is not clear that the immigrant threatens to lower the conditions in the clothing industry to any greater degree than the cheaper grades of labor pressing for entrance into other industries tend to lower conditions in them. The clothing industry is supposed to be threatened in New York City most intimately by the pressure of immigrant labor, for immigration touches New York City directly. Despite this fact, worse conditions in both union and other shops are found in practically all the great clothing centers of the country, for example, in Cincinnati, Philadelphia, Chicago and Baltimore. It is therefore, probably not too much to say that the manufacturers had no desire to return to earlier conditions and had they so desired economic and social pressure would have thwarted them.

This does not mean that they did not have in mind readjustments in the clothing industry. In the cutting branches the hours of labor would probably have again been made fifty-four a week. This would have worked no serious hardship and might have been justified on the grounds of trade conditions. Greater elasticity would probably have been brought about in the adjustment of wages, and employers would have taken steps to put an end to restriction of output, in so far as this existed. In many cases there would have been greater freedom for the employer in the hiring and dismissal of men and in general, in the management of his shop. Eventually, for the tailor's unions also there would have been readjustments, particularly to meet the demands of the changing conditions growing out of the dull and busy seasons. Many restrictions due to the use of the trade union label would have been abolished, but these restrictions, as we have pointed out, are often uncalled for, and unjustifiable, and the union when attempting to enforce them is standing in its own light. The preamble is made up of high sounding and meaningless phrases and ought not to have been taken too seriously. The demand that such preamble be posted in the cutters' shops could accomplish nothing and was a useless source of irritation, which wiser counsels ought to have prevented.

The demand of the Philadelphia Association for individual contracts, which meant the destruction of the union, ought to have been condemned by the National Association at its Philadelphia meeting. At a later date, the association gave assurance that it did not stand for such contracts, but the statement would have carried greater weight and borne better evidence of sincerity if it had been made earlier, as it would have made clear at once that the Association was opposing, not the union, but the abuses of the union. The fact that the Association virtually justified the action of the Philadelphia branch gave warrant to the union position that the open shop of the National Clothiers' Association meant the open shop of the Philadelphia Clothiers' Association and of the National Manufacturers' Association. Public protest brought this fact home to the conservative element, and the statement of President Josephi that no such attack on the union was intended, no doubt expressed the real attitude of the New York branch of the association and was a sincere statement of its position previous to the calling of the strike.

If the individual agreement idea had been carried out, the result would have been, not an open shop, but a closed non-union shop. Few will deny that the public as well as the workers were right in their protest against a policy which would have led to such an end. After the strike had been called and finally lost the Association did demand the individual agreements. But so far as New York is concerned no serious attempt has been made to insist on such agreements. The following statement made some weeks after the settlement of the strike by a prominent manufacturer, shows the attitude of the New York branch: "it would be poor policy and an unbusinesslike action for any clothing house or any combination of concerns to make any change whatsoever in the hours, wages or system of work enforced at the time of the settlement of the strike in each respective market. . . . . if the manufacturers should seek some reward for the inconvenience and in some cases material loss occasioned by the strikes in reduction of wages or lengthening of hours, they will be playing directly into the hands of that element in the union which continually struggles for absolute and arbitrary union domination. . . . . The union was the only source to which the individual mechanic could look for a betterment of his condition. The employer who loses his opportunity of sowing the seeds of industrial peace by maintaining hours and wages as they were will sow instead the seeds of discontent and trade disturbances." [49]

The hope of the union to-day is found in the tremendous public opinion which is back of it and the sympathetic and conservative attitude of the Clothing Manufacturers' Association of New York City. When the union shall have regained its ground under Mr. White's leadership, or that of some other capable man, the decision of such a momentous question as a general strike will be left not to the rank and file but where

[49] The Daily Trade Record, Oct. 8, 1904. From Weekly Bulletin, Oct. 14, 1904.

it belongs, in the hands of responsible leaders. The referendum vote, when serious questions are involved, is the greatest handicap under which trade unions in the clothing industry, as well as in other industries, labor.

The union, as well as the public, is inclined to overemphasize the militant side of labor organizations. While no one will deny that in some instances higher wages and shorter hours can be traced to the direct influence of the union, sooner or later it is brought home to all that hours and wages in a given industry are determined in the long run by forces so powerful and subtle that all direct attempts to influence them to any marked degree are futile. The low stage of industrial development of the clothing workers, their former traditions and their attitude in general toward industry, have forced the union to confine its activity largely to the development and education of its members. Through lectures and discussions in meetings and through the press, the union has awakened in the rank and file a self-consciousness and hopefulness which have exerted a profound influence on conditions of employment and ultimately upon productive efficiency. This activity has gained for the union the support of the employer. He has become sympathetic and helpful.

The spirit of the union is shown by the fact that it has generally taken the public into its confidence. Its deliberations have been remarkably free from that suspicious secrecy which has been so prevalent among the unions of other industries. With growth in numbers and increase in power there has been a marked tendency for the union to become more militant. Catching the infection from other unions, secrecy and all that goes with it has gradually crept in. The trade union label has been an important factor in this change of attitude. The maliciousness and the vindictiveness of the boycott which the union has established to enforce the use of its label has not been surpassed by that of any labor organization in this country. The boycott has its counterpart in the blacklisting scheme of the Clothiers' Association. The one is as unrighteous as the other, and hence contains within itself the elements of destruction which will bring about its overthrow or the overthrow of those making use of it.

Those who are guiding the policy of the union to-day are advocates of more militant activity, and every week witnesses the widening of the breach between capital and labor. As a result of such a policy a radical decline in trade union membership has set in among many of the leading industries of the country. If the present policy of the union in the clothing industry is persisted in, there will be a similar result.

The study of the work of the trade unions in the clothing industry can not but move one to admiration. The trade unions easily take rank above all the many other social forces at work on the East Side; the union has been to the father what the public school has been to the child. It has raised his standard of living, instructed him in American ideals, awakened his dormant consciousness and widened his mental horizon.

CHAPTER IX

THE SWEATING SYSTEM

In previous chapters attention has been called to some factors which have been held responsible for "sweating," but reference to such factors has been only incidental. Any study of the clothing industry which did not give sweating more than an incidental mention, would be incomplete, so intimately have sweating and the clothing industry been associated. Indeed many writers have characterized the manufacture of clothing as the "sweating system," so that a writer in a discussion of the sweating system in Chicago speaks of it as 'the so-called "sweating system," under which the manufacture of ready-made clothing is chiefly conducted.'[1] In a report of the Bureau of Industrial Statistics of Pennsylvania it is stated that "The Sweating System is a name given to the employment of persons in the ready-made clothing industry in the United States."[2] The United States government in its investigation of the sweating system confined itself to the clothing industry.[3] A writer of a recent text-book on economics speaks of the 'so-called "sweating trades,"' but confines his description of the trades to the clothing industry.[4]

[1] Seventh biennial report of the bureau of labor statistics of Illinois, 1892, p. 357.

[2] Annual report of the secretary of internal affairs of the commonwealth of Pennsylvania. Part III. Industrial statistics, XXI. 1893, p. B 1.

[3] Report of the committee on manufactures on the sweating system, 1893.

[4] Seager, Henry Rogers, Introduction to economics, p. 423.

The origin of the term sweating is veiled in obscurity. It seems to have come into general use about the middle of the last century.[1] About this time it was taken up by Charles Kingsley whose trenchant pen portrayed in vivid colors the frightful conditions existing in certain quarters of the custom clothing trade, and in the clothing industry, which was just in its infancy.[2] The conditions against which Kingsley was protesting he termed sweating, and the system under which the work was carried on he called the sweating system. The masters he called "sweaters," while their victims were said to be "sweated." Hours were frightfully long and irregular; starvation wages were paid; the places in which the worker toiled were filthy and unsanitary, and in general it was claimed that the worker was a helpless victim, exploited and oppressed by those above him. Kingsley did not look beneath the surface, and attributed the cause of these conditions to home work, the various forms of the contract system, remorseless competition, and passion for cheapness, culminating in what he termed a "cheap-and-nasty" product.

From 1850 on, the unfavorable conditions existing in certain London industries attracted increased attention on the part of the press and the public, and in 1888 a committee of the House of Lords was appointed to make an investigation into the causes of such conditions. This committee was known as the committee on sweating. Many witnesses were examined and it was soon discovered that sweating was not confined to the

[1] "Sweating has been known for fifty years." Fifth report of the select committee of the house of lords on the sweating system, 1890, XVIII. p. iv.

[2] Kingsley's Alton Locke. Also his tract entitled, Cheap clothes and nasty by Parson Lot.

clothing industry. The investigation, therefore, included all those industries where conditions coming under the purview of the committee were supposed to exist. Out of the maze of conflicting testimony taken, it is exceedingly difficult to arrive at any conclusions; but the committee itself concluded that there was no such thing as the sweating system, if by this is meant that the conditions are found only in the clothing industry or to particular methods of work or forms of industry.[1]

In the reports of the various state bureaus of labor in the United States the sweating system is usually attributed to the same causes as those laid down by Kingsley. Chief among these reports is that of Illinois.[2] The causes for the sweating system, as set forth in this report, are home work, the various forms of the contract system, the minute subdivision of labor, the demand for cheapness, and finally the competitive system in general.[3]

It remained for Charles Booth and his associates to present in a proper light the economic and social forces giving rise

[1] Report of the select committee of the house of lords on the sweating system, 1888. Mr. Joseph Lee of Massachusetts has made an excellent analysis of the report and he concludes that at best the sweating system is "an unsatisfactory question-begging bit of slang." Report of the committee on manufactures on the sweating system, 1893, p. 249 et seq.

[2] Seventh biennial report of the bureau of labor statistics of Illinois, 1892.

[3] "The minute subdivision of work in the sweaters' shops reduces the skill required to the lowest point." Ibid., p. 362. "The system [sweating] thrives upon the increasing demand for cheap, ready-made clothing, cheap cloaks, and cheap suits for children, which demand springs in turn from the rivalry of competing dealers and producers." Ibid., p. 358. "In its economical aspect it is the culmination and final fruit of the competitive system in industry." Ibid., p. 358.

to the conditions popularly spoken of as sweating. The results of his investigation are set forth in his monumental work, "Life and Labour of the People." Mr. Booth was a witness before the House of Lords committee, but he himself confesses that the testimony before this committee was based upon inadequate study of the problem.[1] In summing up the causes of sweating, Booth says: "Some of these evils may be due to one method and some to another, but many, or perhaps most of them, are not due in any way to the manner of employment. Their roots lie deep in human nature. They are, alas! not the less real because no trade or place has a monopoly of them, and must be considered as part of the general troubles of poverty."[2] Again he says: "The dissimilarity as regards well being that is constantly found to be compatible with similarity of industrial form emphasizes the fact that no system of production can rightly be regarded as good or bad in itself, either on social or economic grounds."[3]

While there is lack of agreement as to the causes of sweating, the conditions which characterize it are well defined. These are: extremely low wages—with its concomitant, a low standard of living, irregularity of employment, excessive hours of labor, unsanitary conditions, and, to a certain extent, exploitation of labor. Accepting these conditions as being characteristic of sweating, let us now attempt to discover what forces create such conditions, and to what extent society is directly responsible for them.

[1] Referring to his former definition of the sweating system, he says: 'My own, given in May, 1888, "The advantage that may be taken of unskilled and unorganized labour under the contract system," is neither complete nor correct.' Labour and life of the people, I. p. 485.

[2] Ibid., I. p. 487.

[3] Ibid., IX. p. 208.

The standard of living which should obtain among the various classes of any society is set up by that society and when a class for any reason whatever fails to come up to this standard, it becomes an object of social concern, and its condition is said to constitute a social problem. Even the superficial observer recognizes that there are classes which fail to measure up to the standard, and that this failure is not due to the same causes; these classes have, however, in common, a standard of living that does violence to existing ideals—an abnormal standard.

The classes of society, on the basis of development and adjustment, are: first, the defective—those lacking in power to maintain a normal standard of living owing to some organic defect or misfortune; second, those who are developed, but out of adjustment; third, those retarded in their development and capable of only partial adjustment; fourth, those who are developed and in adjustment and whose standard of living is normal.

The members who make up the first class are not capable of development and possess slight power of adjustment.[1] They are in general the degenerate, the delinquent, and the unfortunate. This class falls into two well defined divisions; the non-industrial—that supported directly by society and, therefore, removed from the industrial field; and the industrial—that which attempts to gain a sustenance through its own efforts. Those termed non-industrial are found in our various eleemosynary, and corrective institutions; they are the blind, the insane, the criminal, etc. The economists have no particular concern with them except in so far as industrial conditions are responsible

---

[1] By development is meant such a differentiation of functions, both as to quantity and quality, that the individual is enabled when adjusted to gain a standard of living which meets the demands of society at a given time.

for their creation, and the burden of their maintenance reacts upon the other classes. Those termed industrial are the chronic poor; those who have burdens beyond their capacity to bear; the widow left with a family; victims of accidents; those mentally, morally, or physically deficient; the coster-monger; the casual laborer; and in general that part of society which settles in the worst quarters of our large cities; the misfits and unfits, whose labor from one cause or another is so inefficient that it will not yield its owner a normal standard of living. These are the poor we have with us always. Their presence becomes more apparent in the most advanced societies through differentiation. Since they are intimately connected with industry, they are of profound concern to the economist and for other reasons to the philanthropist; and it is for these to discover the forces that tend to create this class and to determine to what extent its presence in the industrial field is unfavorable to the other classes.[1] The first division of this class is supported by society and hence is free from those conditions known as sweating. The second division furnishes all the opportunities for sweating. Incapacitated for attaining a normal standard of living, they are, nevertheless, thrown on their own resources, and their low productive power causes them to be employed only in marginal industries, and then only at a very low wage with its consequent low standard of living. For this division sweating conditions are inevitable.

The second class is characterized as being developed but out of adjustment. This class is created by the dynamic changes going on in society. It would not be present in a society in which no changes were going on. If a change in style, or in

[1] This division is in part directly supported by society through various systems of poor relief.

class of commodity destroys the demand for the labor engaged in its production, the workers may be forced to seek employment elsewhere. The shifting of industries from one locality to another results in labor being no longer needed in the decaying center. The introduction of machinery may destroy the demand for certain forms of labor. In general, this class is created by those industrial changes which destroy, for the time being, the opportunity of certain members of society for maintaining their customary standard of living.[1] The membership of this class is constantly changing; those out of adjustment to-day become adjusted to-morrow, and to-morrow brings with it new non-adjustments. It often happens that those thrown out of adjustment are not able to readjust themselves. The need for readjustment may come at a time in life when power to make new adjustment is gone, or adjustment may be so delayed that demoralization results, and as a consequence the standard of living remains permanently below the normal and they pass over into the first class. The fate of this class also appeals to the interest and sympathy of the economist and the philanthropist and it is their concern to discover the means whereby it may be tided over the period of non-adjustment without thereby creating serious disturbances in some other part of the industrial machinery and in society. The relative size of this class is small, and owing to the fact that its members are scattered throughout the industrial field the sweating conditions which prevail do not attract attention.

[1] "In a progressive society industrial changes are likely to be made with great rapidity, and the number of persons who find themselves stranded because there is no longer a market demand for the particular skill which they possess is therefore likely to be larger than in a stable community, where changes are infrequent." Devine, Edward T., The principles of relief, p. 14.

While the causes that created this class are different from those which created the first class the presence of sweating conditions are little less marked, though in the case of the first class they are permanent, while in the case of the second class they are temporary.

The third class is characterized as being retarded in development and capable of only partial adjustment. This class differs from the first class in that it possesses power of development and does develop and pass into the fourth class, but development has been retarded and the class is unable to gain a normal standard of living in its present condition. At first glance, it seems to be synonymous with the second class; but in the case of that class, development was such as to furnish a normal standard of living. Dynamic changes had for the time being thrown its members out of adjustment and had affected their productive capacity injuriously. The increased opportunity of society as a whole to expand its wants meant to the members of the second class a decrease in such opportunity, that is, dynamic changes have for the time being, at any rate, worked an injury to them. But in the case of the third class, such dynamic changes do not affect the productive capacity of its members. In the subsequent readjustment of the classes growing out of dynamic changes, its members remain below the members of other classes in relative well-being because of their inability to share at once in the new opportunities, that is, they are deprived of nothing, but must be developed before they reap the benefits of improved opportunities.

Dynamic changes may take place so gradually that nonadjustments may not be pronounced. The increased economic opportunity may come so slowly that it is shared by all the various members of society alike, and the relative changes in economic well-being are slight. Under such conditions society moves forward slowly and its vertical movement, that is, the movement from class to class, may be so slow that little disturbance results. On the other hand, dynamic changes may be so radical as to be revolutionary in their character. When such changes take place, readjustments on a far-reaching scale become necessary, and the undeveloped classes of society must for some time put up with a standard of living relatively below that of the developed classes, because in their stage of development they lack the power of ready adjustment possessed by those classes above them. The great inventions making possible capitalistic production brought about a shifting of population from the country to the city. The opening up of vast tracts of fertile land, resulting in emigration to such lands, and a consequent disturbance in some other part of society, necessitates the taking up of new occupations. Thus the opening up for settlement of the fertile lands of the Mississippi Valley forced the New England farmer to abandon his farm and emigrate to these new lands, or to become a factory worker in the mill towns of New England. The opening of these lands also stimulated emigration from Europe. The cheap corn brought about a depression in European agriculture and set in motion a further movement from the country to the city.

Such changes eventually cause an enormous expansion of wants for the masses, but in the meantime they give rise to many serious evils. The problems growing out of such changes are well illustrated by the conditions prevailing in England during the eighteenth and the early part of the nineteenth centuries—changes in occupations, changes from rural to urban life, changes from being master to being servant, changes from the open air to the closed factory, changes in housing, changes in the social environment—changes in which society was confronted with problems a solution of which could not be found in experience; institutions had to be created to meet these problems; new relations between the various classes were set up, employers, lacking in enlightened self interest, obstinately stood for certain things which they deemed to be to their economic advantage when the opposite was the case; labor was placed in strange environments and was subject to new temptations, the changed surroundings from country to city life were radical, and new adjustments in habits and customs became necessary, the worker took with him the individualism of the rural community which was not adapted to the social conditions of the city, heretofore he had been individualistic, then he had to be socialistic; facilities for carrying on new industry were wanting, and time and experience were needed to furnish them; housing facilities and proper sanitation was entirely inadequate; and society itself had to undergo a process of development before it realized the necessity for interference on its part—changes which brought immense opportunities to the masses of the English people. During this transition period many grave abuses existed; factories were unsanitary, women and children were not adequately protected in their employment, wages were low, hours were long, the workers were exploited, their environment in general was intolerable—all the conditions favorable to sweating existed. This state of affairs was only overcome by a long series of experiments, and the consequent development of the workers as well as of the social institutions.

The close relation existing between capacity for ready adjustment and sweating is well illustrated by the industrial history of New England. When the girls from New England villages and rural districts went into the mills of Lowell their development was such that they possessed marked capacity for adjustment and speedily grasped the better opportunities thus afforded them. As a consequence no serious problems arose from their employment. These problems appeared, however, when the English, Scotch, Irish, and French Canadians began to work in the New England mills. Here lack of development on the part of the workers was the immediate cause for sweating, and the problems were intensified in proportion to such lack of development.

When shifting of population takes place across national boundaries, the variety of the problems increases and the conditions which make sweating possible are intensified. This is particularly true where emigration takes place from a society of low economic development to one of higher economic development. The standard of living of the immigrants will be below that demanded by the more highly developed society. The ideas of the immigrants of what constitute proper sanitary conditions while quite normal in their former environment, may be repugnant to the new society. Because of strange language and customs and strange ways of doing things, the immigrants possess low productive efficiency. Despite the increased economic opportunity, their lack of power of immediate adjustment may be such that their ability to satisfy wants may be actually below that formerly possessed. While in some respects the condition of the immigrants may be improved, in others, it may be impaired, for example, they may have better opportunities to educate their children, to increase the variety of their food, and to develop their social life; but worse housing conditions and conditions surrounding their work. The desire to raise their standard of living to the level of that demanded by their new environment may result in an undue intensity of labor, and their ignorance, coupled with the strangeness of their surroundings, may make it possible and cause them to be exploited.

When emigration is due to political reasons rather than to the allurements of greater economic opportunities sweating becomes even more pronounced, and the conditions making it possible more persistent, since it may happen that the emigrant must wait for economic opportunities to be created by dynamic changes. Again when emigration is due to political reasons and the emigrant has been denied the opportunity of industrial development at home he may be forced to take up an occupation far removed from that in which he was formerly engaged, and readjustment is a long and difficult process. In such environment he easily becomes a victim of the worst sweating conditions.

With the rapid expansion of wants, made possible by revolutionary changes, the movement from class to class becomes very pronounced. The lower ranks of industry are being constantly vacated by those who pass upward and their places are taken by those less developed and possessing a lower standard of living. These in turn are transformed and in their turn pass upward. Thus society may be likened to a huge mill which to-day receives a mass of raw material which it no sooner transforms than a new supply is in waiting. As long as this supply lasts, there must necessarily be classes, whose standard of living is below that which ought to exist.

Those industries subject to this constant transition seem to have chronically bad conditions, but if the forward movement of society be stopped in time, such conditions will pass away. We do not mean to say that in a highly dynamic society, absolute conditions will be worse; the very opposite may be the case, but relative conditions will be. In the United States for example, very few sons are engaged in the same occupation as their fathers, and many workmen in their middle age are in an industry more highly developed than that in which they worked as young men. In France on the other hand, this vertical movement has been very slight indeed, and the absolute condition of the French working man is much lower than in the United States. Relatively, however, his position is such that in France it attracts little attention. Hours of labor, sanitary surroundings and the real wages of the French working man, if transferred to the United States would immediately attract wide attention.

It so happens that in the United States, the recruiting from below has come from immigration. The mass who compose the third class are largely immigrants, and it is not strange, therefore, that among these we find abnormally long hours, abnormally low wages, abnormal sanitary conditions, and to a certain extent exploitation—conditions known as sweating.

But such conditions may exist without the presence of immigration. If all immigration should come to an end and dynamic changes went on rapidly enough, the same phenomena would be present, though the relative size of the various classes would be somewhat different. Take, for example, York, England,[1] and New York, United States of America. The former receives very little population from outside, while the other is recruited each year by thousands from the outside. Both possess a large population which has a standard of living which falls below the normal, but in the case of York a relatively large number will be found in the first class, a relatively small number in the second class, and many of these, owing

[1] Rowntree, B. Seebohm, Poverty a study of town life, 1902, passim.

to peculiar conditions, are dropping into the first class. The third class will be relatively small, because the lack of economic opportunity in this city is so small that those who ordinarily would be found in it have been attracted to other fields. In New York the differentiation that is constantly going on will inevitably bring about an increase in the size of the first class. The rapid dynamic movement will tend to create the second class, but the same movement will permit of its rapid absoption. The third class will be relatively very large; for the bulk of immigrants will find themselves in this class. These are gradually and surely being assimilated and transformed and the total number of the developed and adjusted is constantly increasing. If all movement from one economic zone to another should come to an end this differentiation and readjustment would still go on if society as a whole progressed.

We wish now to apply this analysis to the clothing industry. If the undeveloped members of society are to be given an opportunity to expand their wants, some industry must furnish them with employment. Other things being equal, they will find employment in those industries which, owing to their peculiar nature, can so adjust production as to make use of them. These industries may be just coming into existence, may be still in a low stage of development, and not, therefore, in a position to make effective use of higher grades of labor. In the early days of the clothing industry, the volume of immigrants whose development would force them to take up this line of work was not large, and the mass of workers were secured from the first class. They were the dissipated and the degenerate journeymen of the custom trade; widows and women of small earning capacity. It was just this class of whom Kingsley wrote and to whose condition we owe the modern use of the term sweating.

Previous to 1880, large numbers of such workers [1] were found in the clothing industry in New York City. The lowest grade of immigrants arriving in New York in those days were the Germans, who, while working side by side with this class, were not of it. The conditions under which they worked, however, were similar. These conditions had not had time to improve before the wave of Jewish immigration set in. In a former chapter attention has been called to the reasons for the low productive efficiency of these immigrants.[2] They arrived in great numbers and New York was utterly unable to cope with the problems directly traceable to their coming. Forced to seek economic opportunity in fields utterly strange to them, with productive efficiency which absolutely precluded them from a normal standard of living, they gained on the one hand, they lost on the other. Opportunity was given for mental growth and expansion, for the education of their children; and for greater variety of food; but inadequate housing facilities,[3] unsanitary conditions under which their work was carried on, long hours of labor, growing out of their intense desire to better their material condition, and in general the low level of the clothing industry, irregular employment, and exploitation, were factors that tended to make their condition a problem of grave social concern, such that the term sweating can be applied to it without exaggeration.

No better example of the third class than the Jewish immigrant can be found. His initial power of adjustment is slight, but his immense capacity for development is only equaled by his intense desire for such development; it is not strange, therefore, that the struggle of such a class to advance its condition

[1] Supra, p. 41 et seq.
[2] Part ii. chap. i.
[3] Supra, pp. 139, 147.

should become a veritable battle, and that many unequal to the conflict should be pushed down. The stage of the industry during these early years made it still possible for many of the members of the first class to hang on, but with the progressive development that set in, some time after the coming of the Jew, these were gradually forced to abandon the industry. From 1880 to 1890 the state of labor in the clothing industry was frightful, and there were present practically all the conditions to which the term sweating is applied. After the latter date, however, the movement toward better conditions becomes apparent even to the superficial observer. The constant influx of Jewish immigration and the entrance of the Italians, representing, as they do, a lower stage of development than the Jews, have had a tendency to retard this progressive movement. But the growing power of society to cope with the problems and the development of the industry itself, precluding the use of the lowest grades of labor, have forever removed the possibility of a return to the conditions that existed previous to 1890.

In the foregoing the writer has attempted to indicate what seems to him to be the underlying causes for sweating conditions in industry in general and in the clothing industry in particular. He wishes now to raise the question whether society may be said to be directly responsible for such unfavorable conditions by permitting unwise systems of production and employment.

Many writers,[1] have urged that society is very largely responsible for sweating, because it has not insisted upon modern methods of production. Such writers have found a panacea for sweating in the factory system.[2]

[1] Supra, p. 207.
[2] Supra, p. 102.

In former chapters attention has been called to the conditions in the clothing industry which tend to create sweating. The industry is of such a nature that it can make use of cheap labor and its seasonal character makes for irregularity and long hours. Attention has also been called to the immense good accomplished by regulation on the part of society[1] and also how the effectiveness of such regulation is conditioned by the stage of development of the various factors involved in industry and upon the stage of development of society itself. Attention was also called to the part played by the system of production and of employment and how they must be considered in connection with other factors.[2] In the following pages the writer wishes to take for granted these factors, and assuming other things equal, to examine to what extent systems of production and employment are responsible for sweating conditions either through directly creating such unfavorable conditions or through hindering the development of the workers.

The characteristic features of modern industry may be briefly summarized as follows: first, a world market, in which prices are fixed by competition; second, capitalistic production, under which human labor is aided by an extensive use of machinery; third, centralized direction of industry, under which both commercial and technical processes are under the control of a single head known as the entrepreneur who assumes the risk and determines the form which production shall take; fourth, an industrial class giving rise to the industrial community, separated from the soil and entirely dependent upon industry.

[1] Supra, pp. 155, 169.
[2] Supra, p. 195.

Not all of these characteristics are peculiar to modern industry. The world market, for example, was present under the domestic system, but its present perfection waited upon the development of transportation, the invention of the telegraph and the telephone, and the establishment of those institutions which make possible mobility of labor and capital. Under the domestic system capitalistic production was often found, but the extensive use of capital in industry was not possible until the great inventions and the application of steam as a source of power.[1] That form of industrial organization in which labor assumes no risk and has no voice in the direction of production was present before the beginning of modern industry,[2] but the necessity for such organization did not become pressing until there was a widely extended market and vast sums of industrial capital. The large amount of capital involved and the problems arising on account of the world market are manifestly beyond the reach of the average workman. Under such conditions industry requires a unity and responsibility which can be secured only through the services of the entrepreneur. The entrepreneur had been developed to some extent under the domestic system, but it was not until modern times that the need of such a factor became imperative.[3] It is true that there are many instances

[1] "in the eighteenth century, labour was the chief factor in the production of wealth." Cunningham, W., The growth of english industry and commerce. II. p. 348.

[2] "Guest put the date at 1740 when the merchant, besides being the giver out of yarns, began to get the sale effected by the use of pattern books and commercial travelers, . . . then social change began." Schultze-Gävernitz, Der grossbetrieb, p. 20.

[3] "the defeat of a number of small trades, artisan work and domestic industries, came through their being incapable of organizing the *sale* of their produce . . . and not from the *production* itself." Kropotkin, P., Fields, factories and workshops, p. 206.

where workmen of much the same class as the modern industrial worker were totally dependent upon industry, but the fact remains that it was not until modern times that the mass of industrial workers became totally separated from the soil. Under the domestic system in England a very large percentage of those engaged in industry turned their attention, when work was not otherwise to be had, to some form of agriculture, and a considerable portion of their income was gained directly from the soil.[1] A purely industrial class giving rise to the industrial community only became possible when the factors mentioned above were present.

When industry is carried on under the conditions outlined above the factory system prevails. To these characteristics of the factory system, however, other writers have added a still further limitation. They insist that the factory must be present, and they define a factory as a place set aside exclusively for the manufacture of goods—a place in which a minimum number of workers are employed, and in which there exists a well defined division of labor, central motive power, and the direct employment of workers by the entrepreneur.

Such writers have placed too narrow limits on the factory system; directly, by insisting that the factory is one of its essential characteristics, and indirectly, by placing too narrow limits on the term factory. The factory is not necessarily an inherent feature of the factory system, since all the characteristics which distinguish it from other systems may be present without it. A part, or all, of the processes may be carried on in the home. Division of labor may be minute or it may be simple. There may or may not be a central motive power, and workers may or may not form a productive chain. The directing head, or en-

[1] Gaskell, Artisans and machinery, London, 1836, passim.

trepreneur, may superintend the technical processes through his foreman, or he may turn them over to the contractor. The most prominent of the characteristics of the factory system—the industrial community—is not at all dependent upon the presence of the factory.

A factory may be defined as a place given over solely to the manufacture of goods. From this definition it is clear that the factory existed long before the appearance of the factory system. The large establishments which existed in France under Louis XIV.,[1] and the establishment of "Jack of Newbury,"[2] were factories, but we should hardly say that the type of industry was that of the factory system.

Let us now look at the clothing industry. As carried on to-day, the direction and control of the industry is in the hands of the wholesale manufacturer, or entrepreneur.[3] He buys the raw material, determines its ultimate form, assumes the risks of the business, and places the finished product on the market. In some few cases, the technical processes of manufacture are carried on by him under the direction of his foremen. His establishment may be large, as in the case of the manufacture of men's clothing, or it may be relatively small as in the case of the manufacture of women's cloaks. In either case we do not hesitate to call the establishment a factory, and the type of industry, the factory system. In the majority of cases, however, the entrepreneur places the goods, in a certain stage of manufacture, in the hands of the contractor who employs labor, and, in his own workshop, carries on the technical processes of production. The contractor's establishment may be similar as to

---

[1] Martin, G., La grande industrie, passim.
[2] Taylor, Whately Cooke, The modern factory system, p. 48 et seq.
[3] Supra, p. 61.

size, motive power, division of labor, etc., to that of the wholesale manufacturer, yet certain writers deny to this establishment the name factory, and insist that such an industry is not carried on under the factory system. It is common for workmen to repair to the workshop of either the manufacturer or the contractor and receive the garments which they carry to their homes and there complete certain processes of manufacture. In certain of the clothing shops, the division of labor is simple, the team system being used; while in others, under the Boston system, division of labor is exceedingly minute. This latter has been termed the factory system, while the former has been spoken of as the transition system.[1] Unless it can be shown that the contract system and the custom of taking work to the home, under the conditions outlined above, bring about a marked change in the attitude of the workers toward industry, it cannot be held that such methods of manufacture are essentially different from those under the factory system.

In the case of the contractor it is necessary to note that he knows nothing, and need know nothing, of the market. He has no voice or interest as to what form the product shall take. It is not necessary that he should assume any large risks as it is a mere matter of calculation for him to determine whether he can afford to take the work at the price offered. Like the manufacturer he may employ labor in his own workshop, with his own machinery, under his own foreman, or he may give it out to workmen to be made up in their homes. Organization as to inside details is different from what we ordinarily think of as being characteristic of the factory system, but the essentials are the same. Evidently, this too must be called the fac-

---

[1] Willett, Mabel Hurd, The employment of women in the clothing trade, p. 35.

tory system, and the place given over to manufacture is a factory in exactly the same sense and to the same degree, whether it is run by the contractor, who hires and dismisses his labor, or by a superintendent, or foreman, acting under the authority of the wholesale manufacturer.

But when the workers repair to the warehouse or to the factory, receive the goods, take them to their homes, where the technical processes are performed, what then is the system? The workers are not collected together under one roof, yet we still have the factory system, since no change has taken place in either the social or economic status of the workers. There is still the world market, capitalistic production, the laborer assumes no risk and has no voice as to what form the product shall take, and finally, we have the industrial community totally dependent upon industry. To insist that the factory system is present where the factory does not exist may seem to be anomalous, but to say that we have a new form of industry is to invite confusion.[1]

The great characteristic of modern industry, from the social point of view, is the presence of the industrial community; for only under such conditions does socialization of industry become possible. Labor comes under the influence of progress and development is hastened. The isolation of the domestic worker was largely responsible for his unprogressiveness.[2]

[1] It is unfortunate that there is no term to describe the conditions under which modern industry is carried on in which the word *factory* does not appear. This term fitted fairly well its earlier and narrower use, but it is quite inapplicable to modern conditions.

[2] "The Domestic System tends to make trades hereditary. Burnett is of the opinion that the machine-made nail trade might have taken root in the hand-nail district, and absorbed the displaced labour if the hand-made trade had been carried on in factories ready to adopt new

He was the heathen of the industrial world. It is only in the industrial community, that society is enabled to consciously affect conditions surrounding labor by enforcing certain regulations. Mutual cooperation among the workers themselves for their uplifting through such organizations as the trade union only becomes possible under such circumstances. It is only in the industrial community that such uplifting forces as the church, the school, free libraries, etc., become effective. If the factory system, by creating the industrial community, has given rise to serious problems, and threatened the welfare of the individual, it has also created the forces that make possible the solution of such problems and also make it possible to carry the individual further forward.

It is evident that the peculiar systems of production and employment under the factory system may hinder or further the working of social forces. Where people are brought together in comparatively large work shops,[1] inspection and regulation on the part of society are much more effective, and sweating conditions much less likely to be present. The physical surroundings will usually be better. The building will be better adapted to the purpose for which it is used, machinery will be used more extensively and more effectively. The employer under such conditions will be superior to his workmen. He will be better capable of handling the problems of production. Unlike the employer in the small factory his income does not directly fluctuate with the activity of his workmen, and, therefore, he is not tempted to drive his men to overexertion, or to resort to petty means of extortion, such as "nibbling" at wages,

mechanical ideas." Smith, H. Llewellyn, Modern changes in the mobility of labor, especially between trade and trade, p. 9.

[1] Supra, p. 171.

fining, etc., to increase his income. But whatever the system of production, where the employer is on the same level as the employee, grave abuses are always present. The extreme example of this is to be found where laborers become the employers of other laborers. This custom was common in the early days of the factory system in England.[1] And as we have noticed[2] is found to-day to some extent, in the cloak industry, under factory conditions, but it thrives best under isolated conditions of production. The conditions of factory employment demand system and regularity, and there is an orderly routine which shuts out many abuses. This reacts favorably upon labor and is a powerful factor in raising its standards.[3]

The factory has mitigated the employment of women and children and when they are employed in the factory such employment is accompanied by fewer evils than under other conditions.[4]

The factory worker assumes the minimum risk and responsibility; he usually furnishes none of the accessories of manufac-

[1] "The Report of the Commission of 1833 contains a table showing that in seventy mills in Lancashire about half the number of workers under eighteen were employed by operatives instead of directly by factory occupiers." Hutchins and Harrison, A history of factory legislation, p. 37.

[2] Supra, p. 74.

[3] "My observation leads me to conclude that men who work in the master's shop will be more moral and more generally respectable in their general appearance and manner." Galton, The tailoring trade, p. 127.

[4] Le Play mentions that during the busy season the women of Westphalia carry daily on foot, two hundred and ten kilograms (462 pounds) a distance of one kilometer (.62 miles). Besides this they do the family sewing, do the chores, and cook four meals a day, the last one at 8:00 p. m. Le Play, Ouvriers européens, III. p. 134.

ture, and is not even the keeper of his own time. Where the workers furnish the accessories of manufacture the chances are that this will work disadvantageously to them. It is true, of course, that competition tends to equalize this burden, but the element of friction is against the worker. These accessories are furnished to a greater extent outside of the factory. Mayhew quotes the Morning Chronicle to the effect that Nicoll, the great custom tailor of London, said in an interview that when the workers took the work into their homes they escaped the crowded workshops, but worked longer hours, and, since they were paid by the piece, they earned more money. But Mayhew goes on to say that formerly Nicoll furnished the trimmings while since the men have begun to do the work in their homes, the trimmings are furnished by the men themselves. This meant a saving of £1,500 annually to Nicoll.[1] A speaker before the Reichstag, said that the burdens for rent, light and sewing appliances, which are imposed upon the seamstresses of Berlin often consume thirty-six per cent of their niggardly wage.[2] Making due allowance for exaggeration in these statements they, nevertheless, illustrate the point under discussion, namely, that labor is much less liable to be taken advantage of where the contract between employers and employees is simple, and where their respective functions are clearly defined. The larger interests involved and the better organization which comes with the large establishment guarantee greater regularity of employment.[3] The bringing together of a large number of people

[1] Speech of Henry Mayhew, Esq., London, 1850. Pamphlet, pp. 22, 23.

[2] Vorwärts, Feb. 13, 1896.

[3] "The smaller the capital involved and the less the permanent fixed charge of working a business, the better suited is it for irregular em-

under one roof makes possible the realization of many schemes for the amelioration of the condition of the workers of which the smaller unit does not permit. Such institutions as restrooms, bathrooms, lunchrooms, etc., have a powerful influence in maintaining the present level of labor, and in raising it to still higher levels. If the larger manufacturing unit does not raise competition to a higher level it steadies it by removing the ease with which new competitors may come into the field. Furthermore, the entrepreneur will reduce prices by improving his methods of production, rather than by oppressing his laborers. This the small employer is less able to do.

Let us now take up those systems of work performed outside of the factory. When the home worker is engaged in making a product that is also being manufactured under a superior system of production, his condition will be deplorable. Such workers as the nail and chainmakers of Cradley Heath, the handloom weavers of various countries, the cabinetmakers of East London, and the isolated home workers [1] of the early days of the clothing industry belong to this class. They are painfully and slowly producing by hand what, with the aid of machinery, could be produced with rapidity and ease, or they are assuming risks far beyond their capacity, and their isolation causes them to continue the unequal conflict. Over against this type of home worker must be placed the home worker

---

ployment. High organization makes for regularity: low organization lends itself to the opposite. A large factory cannot stop at all without serious loss; a full-sized workshop will make great efforts to keep going; but the man who employs only two or three others in his own house can, if work fails, send them all adrift to pick up a living as best they can." Booth, Labour and life of the people, I. p. 488.

[1] Supra, p. 29.

under the factory system, who is not competing with the factory system, but is of it. Under this class of home workers certain distinctions must be made. The physical surroundings of the home workers in industrial centers are liable to be more unsatisfactory than the conditions surrounding those who live in the rural community or village, since, the latter live in less crowded surroundings and will usually have more house room. Again where home work is a primary source of income, the opportunity for abuses is greater than where it is only a secondary source. The home partakes less of the nature of a factory and family life is less broken into where the work is for three or four hours a day than where it is for ten or twelve hours. In such secondary work women make use of a part of their leisure time, and the money thus earned is an important item in the family budget. Under such conditions the weekly earnings are not usually large, but such work does not generally create unfavorable conditions. Closely allied with the above form of home work is that where members outside the family are introduced. Such a practice is an open door to abuses. Such home work has many characteristics of the form pointed out above where the home worker was competing with a more advanced type of production. It has, therefore, no economic justification and ought not to be permitted. As we have pointed out the bulk of the home work in the clothing industry of New York City is that of the factory system and closely associated with the factory. It is confined largely to people who make it a secondary source of income and workers are not introduced from outside.

In the preceding chapters, the writer has pointed out the economic justification of the contractor,[1] but as we have seen

[1] Supra, pp. 51, 116.

at his door are laid many of the abuses summed up in the word sweating.[1] In the clothing industry the contractor has charge of the technical processes of production and is an employer of labor. Since the amount of capital necessary to become a contractor is small and the risks unimportant, it is comparatively easy for one to reach this position, that is, in those industries where the contract system prevails the small employer is likely to flourish and it is in this respect that he is most open to the charge of sweating. This is not on account of the fact that he is a contractor, but because he is a small employer with all the small employer's faults and weaknesses.[2] The small contractor engaged in the manufacture of men's garments possesses the same characteristics as the small cloak manufacturer, who controls both the technical and commercial processes of production; the weaknesses of the one are the weaknesses of the other. As the contractor becomes a man of larger affairs he partakes more and more of the nature of the entrepreneur, and it is entirely possible for him to possess all the characteristics necessary to make him an enlightened and responsible employer of labor.

Many writers have held that a fruitful cause of sweating is the passion for cheapness. It is inferred that commodities put on the market at a low price are produced at the expense of the well-being of the worker. Lecky says: "The horrible

---

[1] Supra, p. 110.

[2] "There exists in the industries liable to sweating a sum of conditions which determine the existence of an abnormal type of master, whom we call the penniless employer. The master with whom we are concerned is a master who cannot turn his trade to profit in the ordinary way. He has not the necessary means; he is a penniless employer." Rousiers, The labor question in Britain, p. 106.

grinding of the poor that takes place under the name of sweating is not for the benefit of the rich. They buy their clothes or shirts at a price which should amply allow for the proper payment of labour. It is in the struggle to provide clothes of extreme cheapness for the very poor that these evils chiefly arise."[1] A little thought must convince the most skeptical of the fallacy of this position. That there is no necessary connection between the price for which a commodity is sold and the conditions under which it is produced is shown by the fact that in those cases in which primitive methods of production are used, because of some whim of the consumer, wages are often a mere pittance and other conditions of employment intolerable. The hand weavers of priceless laces, the handsewers on expensive gowns, the handloom weavers of Irish linen handkerchiefs all make high priced products which are consumed by the rich yet these industries furnish their workers a wretched standard of living.

It is a fact that the great mass of products are placed on the market at a relatively low price. Their consumption depends upon cheapness. This cheapness is not obtained, however, by oppressing the workers, but by the introduction of the most improved methods of manufacture. Machinery is used as extensively as possible and division of labor is carried to such a point as to guarantee the utmost efficiency. In industries where such conditions prevail the well-being of the laborer reaches its highest point. This statement is strikingly borne out by the conditions existing in the various branches of the clothing manufacture. The worst conditions are to be found among the ladies' custom tailors, who are engaged in making

[1] Lecky, Democracy and liberty, II. p. 419.

garments for the very rich. Such garments cost from seventy-five dollars upwards. The workers are highly skilled artisans and the work is carried on in their homes often for incredibly long hours with intervals of idleness. Every attempt to better conditions by organization has failed and they are quite beyond the reach of any regulation on the part of society. The classic example of the danger of contagion from clothing made up under sweating conditions is drawn from just this class of work. We refer to the case of the daughter of Sir Robert Peel, who is supposed to have contracted a serious disease from a riding habit made up by a custom tailor. The skilled cloakmaker, who makes the entire garment for the high grade ready-made cloak trade is some what better off than the ladies' tailor since he is less subject to the frightfully long hours and irregularity of employment, but he is much worse off than the less skilled factory worker engaged in making cloaks for the masses.

The unfavorable conditions under which men's custom tailoring is carried on is notorious,[1] and the condition of the workers seems to defy improvement. Effective organization of the workers has not been possible and regulation on the part of society up to the present time has practically been futile. On the other hand there may be found on the same street firms engaged in the manufacture of ready-made garments, which retail at from eight to fifteen dollars a suit, where the condition of the workers, as compared with those under which the custom clothing is manufactured, may be said to be ideal. To-day,

[1] "It is a fact of which the public has remained curiously ignorant, that the worst forms of danger to the wearers of garments are found in heavier proportion in the manufacture of expensive custom-made clothing than in the ready-made clothing trade." Kelley, Florence, The sweating system, in Hull-House maps and papers, p. 42.

so far as New York City is concerned, the production of garments for the well-to-do is conducted under conditions which most nearly approach those known as sweating and that the great improvement in the standard of living of the workers has been most marked among those engaged in the manufacture of clothing for the masses.

The general advance in society's standard of living creates sweating by bringing about differences in relative well-being; The working of those forces which may be called cosmic are constantly bringing about disturbances, which demand new readjustments. Such changes inevitably bring sweating in their train.

A peculiar system of production is not entirely responsible for sweating, such a system merely reflects conditions that escape ordinary observation.

Society can if it wishes reduce the total amount of sweating by insisting that a minimum of conditions shall be maintained. It can for example insist that all workers shall be employed for a definite number of hours a day at wages that will permit the workers to enjoy a normal standard of living, but in so doing we must not blind our eyes to the fact that enormous numbers will be excluded from industry and that the numbers of the unemployed will be greatly increased and these must be supported with a diminished income. And what is still more important, society is engaged in the labor of Sysiphus, for such restrictions are merely palliative and do not touch the root of the problem.

The world spread of education and enlightenment will mitigate the evil but so long as undeveloped and retarded classes exist it is difficult to see how sweating conditions are to be avoided for unfortunately it is a necessary stage through which such classes must pass to higher things and that many have passed and are passing to higher things, the history of sweating in the clothing industry conclusively proves.

CHAPTER X

Conclusion

It is not always easy to trace the forces, which bring about the rise and constant growth of an industry in one center and its gradual decay in others. But in the case of the clothing industry, it is not difficult to indicate the chief forces, which have been instrumental in placing New York City in the van of all other centers. The growth of the industry depends upon its ability to keep abreast with the fashions and the style of custom clothing. New York City is becoming more and more the center of fashion, and what is there considered to be proper is becoming more and more the standard for the rest of the country. What London is to England, New York City is to the United States. It is not only the port of entry for a large part of our immigrants, but it is also the port of entry for returning tourists, who bring with them the new ideas and latest styles of Europe. The manufacturer of ready-made clothing is ever alive to his opportunity, and adopts these new styles quite as quickly as does the Fifth Avenue custom tailor. In getting hold of the latest styles his designers possess an opportunity which is not to be had by those in the other centers. While these remarks apply to the manufacture of men's garments, they apply with still greater force to the manufacture of women's, since style, in women's cloaks, for example, is even more essential for their successful sale than it is for men's overcoats.

New York City possesses an immense advantage over other centers in its ability to secure labor. This does not mean that the manufacturers of that city pay lower wages than do those of other clothing centers, because they actually pay higher wages. But labor is more highly skilled and is present in such quantities that it is always possible to secure it in its various grades at any time it is needed.[1] The large centers are usually freer from the demands of labor organizations. The large body of laborers always at hand to be drawn on, enables the employer to escape those demands, which, if granted, would place him at a marked disadvantage with his rivals. A great many instances might be cited where industries have been moved to the city to escape the domination of trade organizations. New York has been particularly free from those labor struggles which prostrate and ruin industry, while other large centers, particularly Boston and in later years, Rochester, can trace their decline in the clothing industry to such disputes.

Again New York City is an important port of entry for the raw material used in the manufacture of clothing, cloth, trimmings, etc. These can be bought at a better advantage, both as to price and quantity needed, than is possible in other centers.

---

[1] In this respect New York approaches London. In commenting upon the advantages which London possesses in this regard, Charles Booth writes: "Labour also of every kind can be easily hired. One has usually but to hold up the finger to secure whatever men are needed, and although much of London labour is unskilled and degraded, much of it is of the greatest excellence, and is being constantly recruited from among the best workmen that the country can produce." Life and labour of the people in London, IX. p. 181.

New York City is also a great manufacturing center and a depot for vast quantities of various kinds of merchandise. The city grows by its own momentum. Purchasers who come to the city to buy in other lines, at the same time make their purchases of clothing and gradually acquire the habit of patronizing the New York manufacturers.

The great disadvantage under which the city labors is in the item of rent. Available space, on which to rear modern factories, is not to be had, and in most cases manufacturers have had to depend upon buildings designed for other purposes. The nature of the clothing industry is such, however, that this difficulty has been partially overcome by keeping the size of the manufacturing unit small. The newer buildings have been erected with a view of using their top stories for factory purposes, and many excellent clothing factories are now to be found in such buildings. The importance of having the factory in close proximity to the laborers is shown by the fact that in the suburbs of Brooklyn, many buildings which had been erected for factory purposes have been abandoned, owing to the inability of such factories to attract the requisite labor to the locality. In late years there has been much agitation, and some serious attempts to remove the clothing industry, from the city to less crowded districts. While there has been considerable progress in this direction, such a movement has had little appreciable influence, if the size of the industry be taken into account. The problems involved in a general movement of manufacture from the cities are so many and are so complex that their solution must be considered as being far removed from the present.

Previous to 1900 large amounts of clothing were manufactured in the rural districts, particularly in New England. The amount of clothing manufactured in such districts since that date has steadily declined. This decline, so far as New England is concerned, was noticeable in 1898. Chief Wade in commenting upon the decline of the clothing manufacture in New England villages says that the bulk of it has been transferred to New York.[1] The causes for this decline are in general, the changed conditions of manufacture in regard to a more minute division of labor, and the inability of the workers in a village to turn out as well made garments as the workers in the city. Another cause has been the growing demands of the labor unions that such work be discontinued. With the expansion of the clothing industry many of the smaller towns have become important centers of manufacture, but they are usually engaged in the manufacture of the cheaper grades of clothing and of mechanic's clothing. While New York still continues to manufacture large amounts of the cheaper grades, it is becoming more and more the center for the manufacture of the better. For the reasons already pointed out, it is difficult to see how the provincial factory can compete with it in the making of such clothing. But in the manufacture of the cheaper grades it will not be surprising if New York suffers a relative decline, since the conditions which have given it the advantage in the manufacture of such grades are gradually disappearing.

In style and general make-up American clothing is radically different from that of Europe, but every year these differences become less pronounced. In 1903 it was reported that an English firm had sent its agent to New York City to study styles and processes of manufacture. The same report further says

[1] Annual report of the chief of Massachusetts district police, 1898, p. 10.

that at no very distant date American made clothing will be found in London shops.[1]

While there has been little foreign competition in men's clothing, in the case of cloaks the difference between foreign goods and our own is much less marked, and foreign competition has been important. Previous to 1890 large numbers of women's cloaks were imported; since that date, however, there has been a steady decline in such importation.[2] During the strike of 1894 the New York manufacturers threatened to import their cloaks and in some cases certain firms did so. In the manufacture of cloaks New York has no rival. The growth of this industry has not only increased absolutely, but it has also increased relatively over that of other cities.[3]

The high degree of perfection to which ready-made clothing has attained has brought it into direct competition with the custom trade, and this branch has been forced to adopt the same methods of manufacture as its younger rival. This in turn has reacted upon the clothing industry and the consumer has the choice between high grade ready-made clothing, and a suit made to order from his own measure, at practically little more cost. It is, therefore, not at all improbable that the wholesale manufacturer will give more attention to the custom order trade and employ the same methods of manufacture that are used in the manufacture of ready-made clothing. While such clothing would possess little superiority over that ready-made, the fact that the consumer may have a choice in the goods and have them

[1] Weekly Bulletin, Oct. 14, 1903.

[2] A speaker in an address before the Reichstag states that in 1891 Germany exported to the United States 12,000,000 marks worth of clothing, but owing to a change in the tariff laws of the United States exportation had fallen to 2,000,000 marks in 1894. Vorwärts, Feb. 13, 1896.

[3] Appendix A.

made up to his measure appeals to him strongly. The growing intimacy between the lower branch of the custom trade and the upper branch of the clothing industry has brought about a conflict among the workers in the two branches, and in 1903 an attempt was made by the unions to map out the respective fields of each.[1] The retail branch of the industry is becoming divided into general store clothing and men's furnishing house clothing. The better grades are usually found in the latter establishments, which are passing more and more into the hands of the Jews. There is nothing in the nature of the manufacturing processes that appeals particularly to the Jews. At the time they entered the clothing industry they were the lowest grade of immigrants and their peculiar circumstances and conditions were powerful factors in causing them to go into this industry.

To the Jews more than to any other people belong the credit for the magnificent development which the clothing industry has attained.

To-day they control both the commercial and technical processes of production. The commercial processes present problems worthy of the mettle of this race and it is not improbable that this branch of the industry will continue in their hands. In recent years, however, still lower grades of immigrants have come in and these have been gradually displacing the Jews in the technical processes. More centralized production, bringing with it an increased subdivision of labor, is gradually bringing an increase in the employment of women. But despite these tendencies there is every indication that for some time to come the controlling force in the technical processes will be the Jew-

[1] Report of the thirteenth annual convention of the united garment workers of America, 1904.

ish worker. But should Jewish immigration come to an end it would only be a question of time when the race would disappear from the lower ranks of the industry, as few American Jews enter them.

The conditions which have existed in the clothing industry in New York City have been far from ideal. When account is taken of the material with which the industry has had to work and the magnitude of the problems growing out of its environment the unfavorable conditions become explicable. There is reason for congratulation and hope in the fact that a wonderful transforming process has been going on and that at the same time conditions have progressively improved. No industry has, in the same length of time, wrought so much good in the lives of those directly dependent upon it, and no single industry has done so much to administer to the happiness and well-being of the masses; for it has furnished, at a cost within the reach of all, an abundance of one of the prime necessities of life.

BIBLIOGRAPHY OF THE SOURCES CITED.

Books

Bishop. A history of American manufactures from 1608 to 1860. By J. Leander Bishop. Philadelphia: Edward Young & co., 1864. 2 vols.

Booth. Labour and life of the people. Edited by Charles Booth. London: Williams and Norgate, 1891. 3 vols. [I-III].

Life and labour of the people in London. Edited by Charles Booth. London: Macmillan and co., 1893-7. 6 vols. [IV-IX].

Cunningham. The growth of English industry and commerce in modern times. By W. Cunningham. Cambridge: At the University press, 1892. 2 vols.

DeForest and Veiller. The tenement house problem. Edited by Robert W. DeForest and Lawrence Veiller. New York: The Macmillan co., 1903. 2 vols.

Devine. The principles of relief. By Edward T. Devine. New York: The Macmillan co., 1904.

Galton. Select documents illustrating the history of trade unionism. I. The tailoring trade. Edited with an introduction by F. W. Galton, with a preface by Sidney Webb. London: Longmans, 1896.

Gaskell. Artisans and machinery. By P. Gaskell. London: 1836.

Griscom. The sanitary condition of the laboring population of New York, a discourse delivered 30 Dec. 1844, by John H. Griscom. New York: 1845.

Kingsley. Alton Locke. By Charles Kingsley. London and New York: Macmillan and co., 1889.

Kropotkin. Fields, factories and workshops. By P. Kropotkin. Boston: Houghton, Mifflin & co., 1899.

Lecky. Democracy and liberty. By William Edward Hartpole Lecky. New York: Longmans, Green and co., 1896. 2 vols.

Le Play. Les ouvriers européens. By F. Le Play. Paris: Tours, 1855. 2 Ed., 6 vols.

Martin. Le grande industrie sous le régne de Louis XIV. Par Germain Martin. Paris: Arthur Rousseau, 1898.

Mayo-Smith. Emigration and immigration, By Richmond Mayo-Smith. New York. Charles Scribner's sons, 1901.

Statistics and economics. By Richmond Mayo-Smith. New York: The Macmillan co., 1899.

Residents of Hull-House. Hull-house maps and papers. By Residents of Hull-house. New York: Thomas Y. Crowell & co. [1895.]

Rousiers. The labor question in Britain. By Paul de Rousiers. Translated by F. L. D. Herbertson. London and New York: The Macmillan co., 1896.

Rowntree. Poverty a study of town life. By R. Seebohm Rowntree. New York: The Macmillan co., 1902.

Schulze-Gaevernitz. Der grossbetrieb. Von Gerhart von Schulze-Gaevernitz. Leipzig: Duncker und Humblot, 1892.

Seager. Introduction to economics. By Henry Rogers Seager. New York: Henry Holt and company, 1904.

Senior, Political economy. By Nassau William Senior. London: John Joseph Griffin & co., 1850.

Smith. Modern changes in the mobility of labor, especially between trade and trade. By H. Llewellyn Smith. London: Frowde, 1891.

Taylor. The modern factory system. By R. Whately Cooke Taylor. London: Kegan, Paul, Trench, Trübner & co., 1891.

Webb. Industrial democracy. By Sidney and Beatrice Webb. London: Longmans, Green & co., 1897. 2 vols.

Willett. The employment of women in the clothing trade. By Mabel Hurd Willett. New York: 1902.

STATE AND GOVERNMENT REPORTS

Connecticut. First annual report of the bureau of labor statistics of the state of Connecticut, 1885. Hartford, 1885.

Illinois. Seventh biennial report of the bureau of labor statistics of Illinois, 1892. Part II. The sweating system in Chicago. Springfield. 1893.

Massachusetts. Annual report of the bureau of statistics of labor. Boston. Third, 1872; tenth, 1879; twenty-eighth 1897; thirty-third, 1902.

Report of the chief of the Massachusetts district police. Boston. Reports for the years 1891, 1892, 1895, and 1897.

New York. Annual report of the bureau of statistics of labor of the state of New York. Albany and New York. Third, 1885; fourth, 1886; sixth, 1888; eighth, 1890; ninth, 1891; twelfth, 1894; thirteenth, 1895.

Annual report of the factory inspectors* of the state of New York. Albany. Third, 1888; fifth, 1890; sixth, 1891; eighth, 1893; twelfth, 1897; fifteenth, 1900; seventeenth, 1902.

Annual report of the board of mediation and arbitration of the state of New York. Albany. Seventh, 1893; eighth, 1894; ninth, 1895; twelfth, 1898.

Report of the select committee appointed to examine into the condition of the tenement houses of New York and Brooklyn, March 9, 1857. Assembly document No. 205.

Report of the tenement house commission of the state of New York, February 17, 1885. Senate document No. 36.

Report of the tenement house committee, as authorized by chapter 479 of the laws of 1894. Assembly document No. 37. Albany. 1895.

Report of the tenement house commission, appointed under the authority of chapter 279 of the laws of 1900. Albany. 1901.

Report of the council of hygiene and public health of the citizen's association of New York upon the sanitary condition of the city. D. Appleton & co. 1865.

New York labor bulletin. Published quarterly by the state department of labor. 1899-1904. Albany.

Ohio. Nineteenth annual report of the bureau of labor statistics, for the year 1895. Columbus, 1896.

---

*From 1896 the reports are entitled, "Annual report of the factory inspector of the state of New York."

Pennsylvania. Annual report of the secretary of internal affairs of the commonwealth of Pennsylvania. Part III. Industrial statistics. Vol. XXI. 1893.

United States. Annual report of the commissioner of labor. Washington. Sixth, 1890; thirteenth, 1898. Vol. I. Hand and machine labor.

Bulletin of the bureau of labor. Issued every other month. Washington.

Treasury department. Tables showing arrivals of alien passengers and immigrants in the United States from 1820 to 1888. Prepared by the bureau of statistics. Washington. 1889.

Consular reports.

State of labor in Europe, 1878. 46th congress, 1st session. House executive document no. 5. Washington, 1879. Labor in Europe. 48th congress, 2d session. House executive document no. 54, part I. Washington, 1885.

Wholesale prices, wages and transportation. Report by Mr. Aldrich, from the committee on finance, March 3, 1893. 52d congress, 2d session. Senate report no. 1394. In four parts. Washington, 1893.

Report of the committee on manufactures on the sweating system. 52d congress, 2d session. House report No. 2309. Washington, 1893.

Report of the committee of the senate (on education and labor) upon the relations between labor and capital. Washington, 1885. 5 vols.

Report of the industrial commission.

On the relations and conditions of capital and labor employed in manufactures and general business. Vol. VII. Washington: Government printing office, 1901. On immigration and on education. Vol. XV. Washington: Government printing office, 1901.

Census reports.

Manufactures of the United States in 1860; compiled from the original returns of the eighth census. Washington: Government printing office, 1865.

The statistics of manufactures. Ninth census, 1870. Vol. III. Washington: Government printing office, 1872.

Report on the manufactures of the United States at the tenth census, 1880. Washington: Government printing office, 1883.

Report on manufacturing industries in the United States at the eleventh census, 1890. Part I. Washington, D. C.: Government printing office, 1895.

Twelfth census, 1900. Vol. IX. Manufactures, part III. Washington: United States census office, 1902.

Occupations at the twelfth census [1900]. Washington: Government printing office, 1904.

France. Ministère du commerce, de l'industrie et des colonies. Exposition universelle internationale de 1889 à Paris. Rapport général par Alfred Picard. Paris, 1891-92. 10 vols.

Great Britain. Reports from the select committee of the house of lords on the sweating system. H. L., 1888, XX. and XXI. H. L., 1889, XIII and XIV. London.

PERIODICALS AND MISCELLANEOUS DOCUMENTS

Beilage zum "Vorwärts" Berliner Volksblatt. [Berlin.]
New York Herald. [New York.]
Popular Science Monthly. [New York.]
Proceedings of the annual conventions of the united garment workers of America. [New York.]
The Daily Trade Record. [New York.]
The Garment Worker. [New York.]
The Independent. [New York.]
The Jefferson Inquirer. [Jefferson City, Mo.]
Weekly Bulletin of the Clothing Trades. Official organ of the united garment workers of America. [New York.]

APPENDIXES

APPENDIX A

The following statistics compiled from the census reports show the immense strides which New York City has made during the past half century in the manufacture of clothing. The shortcomings of these statistics, are those that are common to statistics taken from the census reports. The element of error is increased, by the fact that custom clothing and ready-made clothing have not always been separated, and because of the difficulty of collecting statistics in the clothing industry. But taking into account these shortcomings, the tables below give a fairly accurate statement of the growth of the clothing industry.

Production of Mens' Factory Product in Leading Centers[1]
TABLE I

	1860	1870	1880	1890	1900
New York	$17,011,370	$34,456,884	$60,798,697	$68,798,697	$103,220,201
Baltimore	3,124,342	5,574,342	19,446,793	15,032,924	17,290,825
Boston	4,567,749	17,578,057	16,157,892	19,640,779	8,601,431
Chicago	540,709[2]	5,669,990	17,342,207	32,517,226	36,094,310
Philadelphia	9,962,800	16,429,067	18,506,748	24,490,213	18,802,637

Production of Women's Factory Product in Leading Centers
TABLE II

	1860	1870	1880	1890	1900
New York	$2,699,467	$3,824,882	$18,930,553	$42,121,271	$102,711,604
Baltimore	49,035	121,640	469,718	870,681	2,506,654
Boston	472,460	1,268,214	1,808,520	1,506,212	3,258,483
Chicago		799,600	1,585,990	6,422,431	9,208,454
Philadelphia	695,310	974,265	2,466,410	3,335,746	9,452,259

Number of Workers Engaged in Men's Factory Product
TABLE III

	1860	1870	1880	1890	1900
New York	21,568	17,084	47,416	34,040	30,272
Baltimore	5,811	7,033	11,099	12,656	9,097
Boston	4,017	7,569	9,090	5,621	2,615
Chicago	399[2]	4,796	8,102	15,016	13,085
Philadelphia	14,203	13,073	17,565	4,684	6,298

Number of Workers Engaged in Women's Factory Product
TABLE IV

	1860	1870	1880	1890	1900
New York	2,119	3,663	12,319	23,030	44,450
Baltimore	52	116	504	472	1,838
Boston	305	672	1,969	943	1,732
Chicago		491	1,560	2,511	3,942
Philadelphia	579	746	2,608	2,238	6,170

[1] These tables are compiled from the census reports of the dates given. The figures for 1860, 1870 and 1880 include custom work. In 1860 and 1870 the figures are for New York City and county; Baltimore, city and county; Boston and Suffolk county; Chicago and Cook county; Philadelphia, city and county.
[2] All clothing.

APPENDIX B[1]

Representative Circulars Sent Out by Trade Unions to Arouse Public Opinion.

TO THE PUBLIC.

Attention,

What assurance have you that the ready-made garments you wear were not made in disease-infected tenement house sweat shops, and that you are not liable to be stricken with disease through the germs which lurk in such goods?

It is well-known that a large proportion of clothing is still made under such conditions. Repeated exposures have been made in the daily papers of the extent to which clothing is manufactured in prison under unhealthy conditions and for the benefit of private contractors to the detriment of free labor.

The organized garment workers have issued an official label to be attached to Clothing, Cloaks, Shirts and Overalls, as a guarantee of being made by fair labor in clean shops.

Reduced Size.

Fac-simile  of Label.

By giving your preference for goods so labeled you will be protecting your own health and encouraging a more humane system of labor.

The leading labor and reform organizations of the United States and Canada have endorsed this label and a number of large manufacturers in various cities have already adopted it.

Demand this Label from the Retailer.
Don't Wait for others to Act First.
Use your Patronage for a Good Cause.

N. B.—You will find this linen label attached by the machine stitching to the inside of the breast pocket of the coat, the inside of the buckle strap of the vest and on the lining waist band of the pants. On overalls the labels are printed on Gummed Paper and are Consecutively Numbered.

---

[1] The appendixes B, C, D, E are verbatim, literatim, et punctatim.

Attitude Toward Contractors

Office of United Brotherhood of Tailors of the United Garment Workers of America 104 Orchard Street.

NEW YORK, October, 1897.

TO ALL CLOTHING MANUFACTURERS OF NEW YORK.
GENTLEMEN:—

In behalf of the Coat Tailors of this city, I am urged to address you as follows:

During the past four years the trade has been disturbed by periodical strikes and which although under the circumstances, beneficial to labor have injured the trade materially while such disputes were in progress.

Our experience has shown that such troubles cannot be avoided as long as the present method of manufacturing continues. The clothing industry being one of the largest and wealthiest in the country can surely afford at least humane conditions of labor, and there is no occasion for the irresponsible, petty contract system which has made the infamous sweat shop possible. We realize the difficulty in the way of any firm while the present methods continue, however good the intentions to dispense with the services of the contractor, who, because of the competition between themselves, lower the prices paid for making a garment, and in turn drive the operative into performing an inhuman task for less than a living wage and amid the poorest and unhealthy surroundings. As if to add to such distress even the slender earnings of a sweat shop victim is often denied him because of the inability of the contractor to pay the wages due, or because of the manner in which the contractor frequently decamps with the small pittance earned after so many hours of excessive toil.

Ever since the foundation of our organization we have struggled for the abolition of what is known as the "task system," in favor of weekly work at a standard rate of wages. On four occasions, after an heroic struggle, we forced the contractors to grant the ten hour work day and minimum wage scale. We even induced them to give security for the faithful performance of the agreements entered into. Although successful in each contest, the terms of the agreements were ignored as soon as the busy season was over and the old conditions again restored. This summer we again made the issue and won, and although the condition of the tailors has been much improved in consequence, we have every reason to fear a recurrence of the experiences already described.

We have therefore, after mature thought and considering the obstacles to be contended with, come to the unanimous conclusion that the time has arrived to take such steps as would abolish entirely the system of contract work.

We hereby declare that at a given time in the year 1899, the clothing workers of this city will refuse to work for any contractor or middle man. We make this announcement two years in advance in order to give the manufacturers ample time to consider our purpose and gradually pave the way for this wholesome change by opening clean, ventilated shops operated under their own management, just as the clothing cutters are now employed. If this great reform is accomplished in this city, the great clothing manufacturing center of the country, we are certain that it will be followed in the other clothing markets.

This declaration is issued in all earnestness and should not be construed either as a threat or means of gaining notoriety. The organization has proven its ability and courage to undertake any movement determined upon. In this supreme issue we feel that we will again have the hearty support and sympathy of an appreciating public, and all friends of human progress; and we have reason to hope that the last year of this century will be marked by the abolition of that great blot upon our civilization—the sweating system.

With the hope that your firm will become interested in this cause and assuring you of our willingness at all times to meet your representatives for a friendly discussion of the subject, we remain, Yours truly,

Joint Executive Board, of the United Brotherhood of Tailors, of New York, U. G. W. of A.

MAYER SHOENFELD,
Business Manager.

APPENDIX C

Miscellaneous

I. Communication sent with a view to prevent the usual strike.

District Council No. 1 of the United Garment Workers of America A. F. of L.

W. Chuck, Secretary

Office
99 Norfolk St

New York, July 7th 1902

Gentlemen :—

Our Unions are now ready with their demands for the coming year, and should you desire to comply with same, before any action is taken, we would like you notify us, on or before July 15th, 1902.

Respectfully yours,
W. Chuck, Sec'y
District Council No. 1.

P. S.—Our representative will be present at Room 116, Bible House Building, 8th Street, to furnish you with all the necessary information.

II. Shop Rules

NOTICE.

Rules and Regulations of the Pants Makers' Union No. 8, United Garment Workers of America.

1   Every workingman in this shop shall be a good standing member of this union.

2   No workingman shall be admitted to work unless he has a card from the business agent.

3   Every member in the shop must see that his work is made satisfactorily and in the event that the employer, or, the foreman finds fault with this work, the grievance shall be re-

ferred to the Executive Board of the Organization, and if the latter body and the employer find that the employee has neglected his duty, the former has the right to discharge said employee.

4 The shop-chairman is hereby instructed to enforce the above rules. He should act as arbitrator in any controversy and if he cannot effect a settlement, same shall be referred to the business agent of the local; but, he shall not have the authority to stop work unless endorsed by the local Executive Board.

5 The employer shall not be permitted to stop the operation of the shop during the day unless approved by the local Executive Board and the employer.

6 All members shall treat the foreman and employer with respect and the same treatment is likewise expected from the foreman and the employer.

By order of the Executive Board of the Pants Makers' Union No. 8.

APPENDIX D

Agreements

I. Agreement between a manufacturer and the United Garment Workers of America.

Boston February 8th 1893

In consideration that it will be to the interest and mutual welfare of all parties concerned, this agreement is entered into by and between Rhodes, Ripley & Co. as party of the first part and the United Garment Workers of America A. F. of L. as parties of the second part.

First All contracting tailors in the cities of New York and Boston doing mens' and youths' work for the party of the first part shall during the term of this agreement employ only good standing members of the parties of the second part. In country towns this clause shall be lived up to as near as possible for the present. . . . (This excludes the cutters and trimmers who are at present considered union men of a recognized labor orfanization.

Second All mens and youths garments manufactured in said cities during the term of this agreement shall bear the official label of the United Garment Workers' of America, in accord with the official rules governing the use of the same (appended to this agreement). Work sent into the country to be made shall be left to the discretion of the party of the first part, for the present, or until such time as . . . they—the employes—are thoroughly organized, which period shall not cover more than two (2) months.

This agreement can be declared null and void upon ninety (90) days written notice being served by one party to the other.

This agreement to go into effect on the date first written above and to terminate one year from date.

Signed.
For the firm. For the United Garment Workers
RHODES RIPLEY & Co   CHAS F REICHERS
Genl. Secty U. G. W. of A.

II. Agreement between a contractor and the United Brotherhood of Cloakmakers.

Memoranda of Agreement made by and between ———— of the Borough of ————, New York City, part— of the first part and the United Brotherhood of Cloakmakers No. 1 of New York and Vicinity, party of the second part, to wit:

Whereas the said part— of the first part ———— cloak contractor— and want— to secure for ———— orders the help and services of skilled and competent mechanics and,

Whereas the said party of the second part is a Co-operative Corporation composed of skilled cloakmakers, and undertakes to render to the said part— of the first part such services,

Now therefore in consideration of the premises and of the mutual covenants and promises hereinafter more particularly set forth, it is hereby agreed by and between the said parties:

That the said part— of the first part hereby engage— the said party of the second part to perform all the work required to be done on the orders of the firm of ———— or any other firm or firms where orders now are or may hereafter be filled in the shop of the part— of the first part occupying the premises known as No. ———— in the City of New York, Borough of ——————— for the term commencing on the date of these presents and ending on the — day of ——— 1899; and that the said party of the second part does hereby agree to do all said work or to employ its members to do the same and to keep the said part— of the first part at all times fully supplied with help required to do the work of said firm or firms, provided always a separate agreement to that effect shall have been entered by and between every such firm and the said party of the second part.

That no part of the said work required to be done in said shop shall during the continuance of this agreement be given away by the part—of the first part to any person or persons but to the said party of the second part or its members employed by it to do the said work.

That the party of the second part does hereby agree to and with the said part— of the first part that at all times whenever a sign or bill reading "Help Wanted" or substantially the like shall be posted by the said part— of the first part at the outer door of said shop, as many of the members of the party of the second part as may not at such times be otherwise engaged shall and will without any further notice call at the shop of the part— of the first part to do ——— work.

That during the continuance of this agreement the said part— of the first part shall pay to the said party of the second part by the piece in accordance with the schedules of prices which have been or may hereafter been agreed upon between the said party of the second part and the firm of ——————— or other respective firm or firms whose [schedules] will hereafter be filled by said part— of the first part, which said schedules are hereby made part of this agreement, it being understood and agreed that prices on new styles or numbers of garments not therein included shall be determined by the said part— of the first part with the concurrence of a committee of the operators and tailors employed in said shop, reference being had to similar garments in said schedules contained.

That every person supplied by the said party of the second part to the part— of the first part, as aforesaid, shall be furnished with a book wherein the said part— of the first part shall make an entry of all work, together with the prices thereof, assigned by ——— to the holder of such book, such entry to be made at the time the work is assigned, and that as soon as the same is delivered it shall likewise be checked off in the said book by the part— of the first part.

That the party of the second part shall be credited with all the work performed by its several members at the shop of the said part— of the first part, and shall likewise be charged with all the moneys paid by the part— of the first part to such members of the party of the second part on account of the work performed by them, and that the part— of the first part may account directly with each said member for the work so done by him or her and pay to him or her the amount due therefor in accordance with the prices aforesaid; such payment to be accepted as payment to the party of the second part.

That the part— of the first part shall pay to the party of the second part on ———— of each and every week for the work performed during the week ending on the previous Friday.

That no hands supplied by the party of the second part to the part— of the first part shall be laid off by him before the expiration of the term of these presents except at such times during which there is no work for any one in the said shop, it being understood and agreed that in case there shall not [be] enough work to keep all hands employed full time all the work on hand shall be distributed among the said hands equally.

That the fees of counsel retained by the said party of the second part to draw this agreement shall be paid by both parties equally.

And Furthermore This Agreement Witnesseth: *Whereas* it is understood and agreed by and between the said parties that in the event of a breach of this agreement by the part— of the first part, the said party of the second would suffer great losses and damages, the amount whereof is incapable of exact ascertainment by computation or otherwise,

Now, therefore, it is further agreed by and between the said parties that in the event of a breach of any of the covenants, conditions or provisions of this agreement by the said part— of the first part—he—shall pay to the said party of the second part the sum of ———————— dollars ($————) as liquidated damages.

That the faithful performance of this agreement by the part— of the first part shall be secured by a bond with sufficient sureties or other security of the sum of ———————— dollars ($————).

In Witness Whereof the Said Part—of the First Part ha— hereunto set —— hand— and seal— and the party of the second part has caused these presents to be signed by one of their officers and its corporate seal to be affixed hereto, this day of ——— 1898.

In the presence of ———

III. Agreement between a manufacturer and District Council No. 1, United Garment Workers of America.

THIS AGREEMENT made and entered into this — day of ——— 1902, by and between ——————— party of the first part, and District Council No. 1 United Garment Workers of America a voluntary association, party of the second part.

Witnesseth as follows:—

That in consideration of One (1) Dollar lawful money of the United States of America each party to the other in hand paid, and in consideration of their promises mutually interchanged, and of these presents, it is hereby mutually agreed by and between the parties hereto:

I. That all garments of any kind and description manufactured by them are to be made by persons affiliated with the party of the second part and no others, and that all the contractors doing work for said party of the first part shall employ only members in good standing of the party of the second part, and the following conditions shall be observed in all shops conducted by the said contractors to-wit:

A. The hours of work in any one week shall not exceed 56.

B. The wages of the employees to be paid on the last working day of each week.

C. The rate of wages shall be according to the schedules hereto attached, and made part of this agreement.

II. The party of the first part is to withdraw any work from any contractor, not observing the conditions and covenants hereinbefore set forth, and also to withhold any and all work from them.

III. The party of the first part hereby undertakes and guarantees to become liable and to pay any and all wages that may be due the employees of the contractor whom they employ on such work as performed on garments of the party of the first part. Said guarantee to be limited to one week's wages, providing the party of the first part is notified of any default of such contractor on the day following the ending of the week's work.

IV. The party of the second part is to furnish any and all help that they may have on their Application Books to the contractor employed by the party of the first part as well as to the party of the first part directly. Such furnishing of help to be without any compensation to the party of the second part.

This agreement is to be binding upon the parties hereto for the period of one (1) year from date hereof.

In witness whereof the parties hereto have set their hands and seals the day and year first above written.

(L. S.)
District Council No. 1
United Garment Workers of America.
By
Sec'y (L. S.)

IV. Agreement between a contractor and the United Brotherhood of Tailors.

ARTICLES OF AGREEMENT, made and entered into this ——— day of ——— 1902, by and between ——— party of the first part and ——— by ——— their representative and attorney in fact, parties of the second part, and the United Brotherhood of Tailors District Council No. 1 of the United Garment Workers of America, a duly organized voluntary association parties of the third part, all of the said parties being of the Borough of ——— City, and State of New York.

Whereas, the party of the first part is carrying on and conducting the business of tailoring and making up men's coats, and it being greatly beneficial for the said party of the first part to employ the parties of the second part, and,

Whereas, the parties of the second part possess great skill and ability in the art of making said coats, and,

Whereas, the party of the third part is an association duly organized by the parties of the second part, for the protection of their rights and interests in and about the carrying on the aforesaid work, and desire to work only with those who are affiliated with the party of the third part, and further desire to be guided and regulated by the Rules and Regulations of the said party of the third part of which association they are all members of.

Now Witnesseth:—

That in consideration of the sum of One Dollar, lawful money of the United States of America, each party to the other in hand paid, the receipt whereof is hereby acknowledged, and their several promises by each party with the other mutually interchanged, and in consideration of these premises, it is hereby mutually covenanted and agreed by the parties hereto as follows:—

I. That the party of the first part is to employ the parties of the second part as operators, baisters, finishers, pressers, fitters, bushlers and buttonhole makers, each in his own capacity, and for no other work than that he was engaged for, in ——— shop or shops situated at No. ——— ——— Street, Borough of ——— City of New York, for the period of One (1) year from the date of these presents, at the salary and remuneration as hereinafter set forth.

II. That the system of work in and about the said business, shall consist of that known as week work only, and that the employees are to be engaged to work only by the week.

III. That the total number of hours which shall make up and compose a week's work shall not exceed 56 in number in any one week, which shall be divided as follows.—For the five days at nine and one-half ($9\frac{1}{2}$) hours per day, and on the last working day of the week, eight and one-half ($8\frac{1}{2}$) hours. Under no circumstances or consideration shall work be carried on by the parties of the first and second part, at any other hours than herein specified without a written consent of the party of the third part, executed by its duly authorized officer, and under no consideration shall overtime be allowed on the last day of the week. When any work shall be carried on at any other hours than hereinabove specified with the aforementioned consent, it shall be paid for, and counted as one and one-half time. The hours of labor for any working day shall not begin earlier than seven o'clock in the forenoon, and the day's labor to end not later than half past five ($5\frac{1}{2}$) in the afternoon, excepting the last working day of the week, when the day's labor shall end not later than half past four ($4\frac{1}{2}$) o'clock in the afternoon. The said last day's work shall not exceed eight and one-half hours (8½). The hour from twelve, noon, to one o'clock in the afternoon, of each and every day, no work shall be carried on, the noon hour is to be devoted for recess.

IV. That the wages of each and every week's work shall be paid to the employees on the last working day of the week, and not later than 4-30 o'clock in the afternoon of that day. The week's work to begin according to the consent of the parties of the first and second part.

V. That the party of the first part, shall not employ any help whatsoever other than those belonging to, and who are members of the party of the third part, and in good standing, and who conform to the Rules and Regulations of the said party of the third part, and the said party of the first part shall cease to employ any one and all those employees who are not in good standing, and who do not conform and comply with the Rules and Regulations of said party of the third part, upon being notified to that effect by its duly credentialed representatives. The party of the first part hereby agrees to abide by the Rules and Regulations of the party of the third part, as known in the trade, and to permit and allow representatives of said party of the third part to enter in ——— shop or shops at any and all hours of the day and night, for the purpose of inspection and enforcement of the terms of this contract, as well as all the Rules and Regulations herein referred to. That the party of the first part shall not engage any help whatsoever even those who are members of the party of the third part, without their first having produced a pass card duly executed and signed by the authorized Business Agent of the party of the third part; said card to show that the bearer thereof is a member in good standing of the party of the third part, and has complied with the Rules and Regulations thereof in force at that time. In the event of the party of the first part removing his or their shop or shops, he or they as the case may be, must notify the party of the third part within three days after such removal, the place where he or they moved to.

VI. The party of the first part shall not employ more than one helper to every two operators, or one helper to every two baisters, and under no consideration to employ any apprentices.

VII. That the parties of the second part are to devote all their time attention, skill and diligence in the performance of the work hereinbefore described, during the hours hereinabove stated for the entire period of this agreement, and to accept the remuneration hereinafter mentioned. Also not to employ any apprentices; and to abide by the Rules and Regulations of the party of the third part. In the event of any one of the parties of the second part not remaining, and for the entire period of this contract be in good standing, and who does not in all respects conform with the Rules and Regulations of the party of the third part, that then the party of the first part shall cease to employ such employees whoever he or she may be, and that such employee who so violates the Rules and Regulations of the party of the third part, or any one of them, hereby waives all rights, claims and benefits under this contract; and that such violation of the agreement on the part of any of the parties of the second part shall in no way affect the validity of this agreement, which shall continue in full effect and force, as to the remaining parties thereof.

VIII. That the party of the third part is to furnish any and all help that they may have on their application books, which books they are to keep for the benefit of the parties of the first and second part, and that it is to furnish to the party of the first part any and all help whenever so requested, without charging any fees or receiving any remuneration for such services, nor are they to charge any fee or accept any remuneration, or fee for like services from the parties of the second part.

IX. That the party of the second part may quit work during a so called "Sympathy Strike" providing no new demands are made by them, and that such quitting of work on their part shall in no way affect the validity of this agreement, or suspend its operation.

X. The following is the minimum Scale of wages to be paid to the parties of the second part by the party of the first part, and to any one that is employed by ——— and also to each one of them, for the entire period of this agreement, viz:—

Operators Eighteen (18) Dollars per week and upwards.

First Assistant Operator Sixteen (16) Dollars per week and upwards.

Second Assistant Operator Ten (10) Dollars per week and upwards.

Baisters Seventeen (17) Dollars per week and upwards.

Assistant Baisters Thirteen (13) Dollars per week and upwards.
Finishers Fourteen (14) Dollars per week and upwards.
Assistant Finisher Twelve (12) Dollars per week and upwards.
Pressers 1st grade Eighteen (18) Dollars per week and upwards.
Pressers 2d grade Fifteen (15) Dollars per week and upwards.
Edge Pressers Twelve (12) Dollars per week and upwards.
Under Pressers Nine (9) Dollars per week and upwards.
Fitters Twelve (12) Dollars per week and upwards.
Bushlers Eleven (11) Dollars per week and upwards.

XI. The party of first part hereby agrees to deposit and hereby does deposit with the party of the third part, a promissory note in the sum of —— Dollars; said note to be deposited as security for the faithful performance by the party of the first part, of all the covenants and conditions herein contained. The security hereby deposited to be deemed as liquidated, and ascertained damages upon the commission of any breach, or violation of any of the covenants hereinabove set forth on the part of the party of the first part, and said security shall also to be applied to the payment of any wages that may be due and owing to the party of the second part, or any one of them, and also of any other help that he may hereafter engage, who shall be members of the party of the third part.

This agreement to be binding upon all the parties hereto and their legal representatives, during the period of One (1) year from date hereof.

In Witness Whereof the parties hereto have severally and duly set their hands and seals the day and year above named.

(L. S.)

as attorney in fact for the parties of the second part.

United Brotherhood of Tailors District Council No. 1 of the United Garment Workers of America.

By

Secretary (L. S.)

State of New York City and County of New York Borough of Manhattan ss:—

On the —— day of ——, 1902, before me personally appeared ——————— to me known and known to me to be the individuals described herein and ———— who is known to me to be the Secretary of the within named Association, who stated to me that he is familiar with the seal of the above named Association, and who duly and severally acknowledge to me that they executed the foregoing instrument.

APPENDIX E

SCALE OF PRICES

I. Piece Prices.

SCALE OF PRICES—KNEE PANTS MAKERS UNION, LOCAL 19 UNITED GARMENT WORKERS OF AMERICA [1902.]

OPERATORS.

Cotton without tape and Stripes........ Doz.	30
" with tape and straps	35
Satinetes without	34
Cotton with back pockets	50
Satinetes and Union goods, common made	40
Satinetes and Union goods, with back pockets	55
Cotton Flannel without tape straps	40
" " with " "	45
Hip pockets	58
Chordroy, common make, without back pockets	45
" " " with " "	60
Pocket waisting	3
Chordroy, better make, with back pockets	65
All these lines, with back pockets, better make	65
Tricot coks and diagnol worsted chevoit serge and cashmir, with back pockets	75
Cotton Jersey	60
Closed Jersey	80
Jerseys	75

Trimmings.

Double stitch band	Doz.	5
Overlaps of sides		2
Clams		5
Crotch pieces		3
Front lined		8
Whole lined		15
Black in the pockets		3
Tapped from band to band		10
Kreitz taped		5
Knee piece		5
Double stitched pockets		5
Patent Rubber bands		5
Hooks		6
Pockets stitch, large or small		8
Legs sewen twice		5
With cord		12
Raise the pockets outside		3
Sew piece for tape from the back to the front		4
Corner pockets		18
Legs taped		18
Buckle straps		18
Double seat and knee binding		18
Double seat and knee binding when it comes to the clothes		24
Curtain		10
Legs with tape		2
Seat pieces		15
Knee pieces, bent and closed with tape		5
Closed with tape		18
Sweats on the back		3
Sweats back and front		6
Seat pieces sewed with rubber at back		3
Seat pieces sewed on back		3
Extra rubber		6
Lap seam		18
Bent tape		3
Pocket facing from goods		6
Front tape		3
Facing turned over		6
Loops in Knee pants		18

Front belts .... each 5
Tops piped 3
Linen coveting .... Doz. 18
Cloths coveting 24
Bloomer pants extra .... each 2
Band crotch pieces .... Doz. 5
Loops bent 24
Double stick closed 12
Extra straps in Bloomer 2
Loops taped 24
Slits 18
Rubber made 6
Ready made 10
Legs taped in double needle machine 6

FANCY GOODS.

Common linen .... Doz. 40
Common linen with legs bound...................... 45
Common linen with cord 65
Bearder in linen 24
White goods with cord 75
Duck pants in white goods 75
String Shutash 12
Bound half and half 36
Flat bound 32
Ribbon 18
Buckle straps by the legs 12
Velvet white serge and stout pants 1 20
Ribbon and velvet 36
Binding 80
String Shutash 18
Buchr[a]m under hands 5
Back pockets common 12
    "   " better ones 15

Extra Work Extra Pay

II. Weekly Wage Prices.

CHILDREN JACKET MAKERS—SCALE OF PRICES—UNIONS LOCAL 10 & 155—UNITED GARMENT WORKERS OF AMERICA
[1902]

Baisted Work

Operators, Seventeen (17) Dollars per week and upwards
Baisters, Sixteen (16) Dollars per week and upwards
Baisters Helpers, Twelve (12) Dollars per week and upwards
Fitters, Sixteen (16) Dollars per week and upwards
Lining Makers, Thirteen (13) Dollars per week and upwards
Bushlers, Thirteen (13) Dollars per week and upwards
Pressers, Fourteen (14) Dollars per week and upwards
Assistant Pressers, Eleven (11) Dollars per week and upwards
Under Pressers, Eleven (11) Dollars per week and upwards

Unbaisted Work

Operators, Seventeen (17) Dollars per week and upwards
Pocket Tackers, Fourteen (14) Dollars per week and upwards
Lining Makers Eleven (11) Dollars per week and upwards
Coat Stitchers, Thirteen (13) Dollars per week and upwards
Trimming Makers, Eleven (11) Dollars per week and upwards
Sleeve Makers, Eight (8) Dollars per week and upwards
Pressers, Fourteen (14) Dollars per week and upwards
Assistant Pressers, Eleven (11) Dollars per week and upwards
Under Pressers, Eleven (11) Dollars per week and upwards

INDEX

Accessories of manufacture, 279, 280; causes of abuses, 196, 212; furnished, by employers, 223, by workers, 29-31

Acts, Board of Health, provisions of, 157; Tenement House, 67

Advertisements, for ready-made clothing, 12; for labor, 30; for second-hand clothing, 7 (note)

Agent, business, issues pass card, 315

Agreements, 145, 146, 223, 224; individual, 144, 246, 252, 253; trade union, 216, 217, 228, 230, 308, 309, 312, 313; as a source of wage statistics, 83-85, 89; not kept by contractors, 114, 120; strike, 141

Agriculture, European, depression in, 264; Jews not fitted for, 49

Air shaft, 150

Aldrich Report, 36, 81, 82, 90

Alexander II, Czar, assassination of, excuse for persecution, 46

Alliance, Educational, 150 (note)

Apprentices, 74, 220, 221, 241, 315

Apprenticeship, 8, 12, 18, 227; under team system, 66

Associations, Clothiers', National, 234, 243-250, 252, 253, 255, address of president of, 241; of Buffalo, 245; of New York City, 116, 227, 228, 244, 253; of Philadelphia, 236, 237, 240, 252, declares a lockout, 239, demands of, 238; of Rochester, 234; of Syracuse, 245; Contractors', 228; credit, 109; Manufacturers, National, 234, 238, 248, 252

Atwater, Professor, on cost of food, 176

Baldwin Locomotive Works, contract with foremen, 63 (note)

Baltimore, represented in committee, 241; condition of workshops in, 251; statistics, 303

Balzac, alluded to, 179

Banks, savings in, 181

Bargaining, collective, 125

Basters, 24, 66-68, 70 (note,) 75, 136, 215, 216, 220, 316, 321; unions among, 67 (note), 181, 215; wages of, 32, 33, 34, 35, 36, 37, 79, 80, 87, 89, 95, 99, 316, 321

Basting, 28, 67; eliminated under Boston system, 73

Benefits, death, 181-183; sick, 181, 182, 184; strike, 181

Berlin, strike in, 51 (note), 52 (note); seamstresses of, 280

Blacklisting, 244, 255

Blaustein, Dr., care of buildings, 155 (note)

Board, Consolidated, of the Cloak Industry, 113; of health, 150, 151 (note), 153 (note), 157, 160, 162, 189, 194, coöperation with Factory Inspectors, 165; of Mediation and Arbitration, 85, 130, 228

Bobbins, self-winding, 76

Booth, Charles, 114, 259, 289 (note)

Boston, 28, 33, 41, 45, 70, 129, 159, 166, 189, 208, 225 (note), 233, 241, 245, 289, 303

Boycott, 203 (note), 208, 210, 234, 248, 255; label used for establishing, 203

Brooklyn, 28, 53, 55, 59 (note), 174, 290; rent in, 38

Buffalo, represented in committee, 241; association against open shop, 245

Building, increased cost of, 95 (note)

Buildings, in rear, used for manufacture, 160 (note)

Bulletin of labor, United States, 90, 92

Bundles, 29, 50, 51

Bureau, Labor, of the National Clothiers' Association, 241, 243, 244, 248

Bureau of Labor, National, 140; Illinois, 256; Massachusetts, 32, 33, 36, 79, 92; New York, 85, 91, 143; Ohio, 110; Pennsylvania, 256

Bureaus, statistics collected by, 83-85

Bushelers, 71 (note); unions among, 67 (note); wages of, 80, 87, 89, 317

Button-hole machine, 75, 78; making, 26, 28, 75

Button sewing machine, 75, 78

Buying in small quantities, 177, 178

Cabinetmakers, 281

Canadian government, prohibits subcontracting, 111 (note)

Canadians, French, in New England mills, 266

Capital, 14, 19, 49, 50, 62, 108, 112, 123, 133, 195, 196, 242, 272, 273; furnished by contractor, 61; furnished by manufacturer, 14; Jewish lack of, 48; organization of, makes for regularity, 103

Card, serf's, 244

Carl, S., testimony of, quoted, 83

Cellars, dwellers in, 42, 147

Changes, 262 (note); dynamic, 261, 263, 267; in society, giving rise to sweating, 265; revolutionary, influence of, 264, 267

Charities, need for a new conception of, 180

Charter of Greater New York, referred to, 150

Cheapness, passion for, 257, 283

Chicago, 189, 194 (note), 233, 241, 246, 251, 256

Child labor, 13, 82, 144, 156, 172, 173, 199, 279; small amount of, 29, 30 (note), 58-60, 180

Children, see Child Labor

Christians, persecution of Jews by, 46

Chuck, Walter, 117 (note), 133, 134 (note), 307

Cigars, early use of label on, 197

Cincinnati, represented in committee, 241; conditions in workshops in, 251

Civil War, American, 6, 9, 25, 31, 33, 79

Classes, influence of, on spread of clothing, 2, 3; necessity for, 267; of society, on basis of development, 260; spread of clothing to capitalistic and professional, 3

Clerks, many Jews become, 106

Cloakmaking, 27, 28, 34, 57, 58, 64, 73, 74, 104, 124, 125, 127, 133, 146, 199, 224, 275, 288, 292

Cloaks, chief work on, 25; imported from France, 17; makers, 54 (note); wages of, 80 (note), 89, 90, 97, 98, 101, 102, 142, 311; unions of, 54 (note), 113, 213, 216, 221, 222

Cloak trade, 17, 54 (note), 146; Consolidated Board of the Cloak Industry, 113

Clothing, children's, label on, 199; expenditure for, 173, 175, 176, 180; laborers', 2 (note), 9, 10; mechanics', 200; label on, 198; sailors', 5, 10; second-hand, traffic in, 5-8, 10, 45, 47; servants', 5; soldiers', 5

Clothing industry, definition of, 2 (note); statistics, 303; growth of, 44, 53 (note), 106

Coat, "balloon," 71; makers, 80 (note), 140, 142, overcoat and sackcoat, unions among, 222, unions of, 109, 135, 146, 215, wages of, 86, 87, 95-99, 100, 101; making, 13 (note), 15, 16, 17, 18, 21, 22, 24, 26, 31, 32, 45, 53, 56 (note), 57, 58, 66, 68 (note), 69-71, 73, 74, 77, 95, 127-129, 131; stitchers, 75; tailors, 99, strike of, 145

Commerce, interstate, clothing an article of, 190

Commission, Industrial, 98, 107, 114, 130, 131, 134, 137 (note); Tenement House, 93, 150, 194

Commissioner of labor, New York, 135, 167, 168

Committee, investigation, as a source of wage statistics, 83; National on Sweating, 57 (note), 59, 60, 156, 189, recommends national regulation law, 190 (note); National Clothiers' Association, 241, 243, 244; New York Clothiers' Association, instructions to executive, 246; New York Tenement House, 93; Philadelphia Clothiers' Association, 238; Select, on Tenement Houses, 38; Senate, on Education and Labor, 39, 80, 89, 138; United Garment Workers of America, 203, 237

Commons, John R., on the wage movement, 98; quoted 213

Community, industrial, 272, 274, 277; rural, 265

Competition, 58, 65, 106, 138, 207, 258 (note), 280; among contractors, 113, 114; between female and Jewish labor, 56; foreign, 292

Conditions, housing, 265; sanitary, 265; unsanitary, 259

Consumer, 210; directly interested in conditions of manufacture, 147 (note); interests of, appealed to, 197; tasteless, 103

Consumption, and production, close adjustment between, 108; not materially affected by label, 204

Consumption, see Tuberculosis

Contagion, danger from, 147 (note), 157, 192-194; see also Tagging

Contract, signed under duress, 31

Contractors, 13, 18, 19, 29, 52, 56, 57, 61, 67, 70, 72 (note), 75, 107, 110-116, 118-120, 128, 139, 160, 161, 166, 202, 217, 229 (note), 231, 250 (note), 275, 276, 282, 283, 309, 313; failure to keep agreements, 230; loan money to workers, 188; Association, 228, opposed by consumers' League, 207

Convention, United Garment Workers of America, 55; attempts to enforce use of label, 198, 200

Coöperation, 192; among the Jews, 185; among tailors, 15, 20 (note); among workers, 278; between cutters and tailors, 211 (note); between state Board of Health and Factory Inspectors, 165, 168, 194

Cost of living, 34, 38, 92

Costermonger, alluded to, 261

Country, objection of Jews to, 48

Courts, Appellate Division of New York Supreme, 131; pass upon legality of contracts, 230, 231

Cradley Heath, nail and chainmakers of, 281

Currency, depreciation, effect of, on wages, 81; disturbance of, by Civil War, 31; inflation of, 31; during Civil War, 79

Custom trade, 5, 20, 21, 43, 44, 119, 124, 127, 166, 257, 303; attempts to supply demand for ready-made clothing, 10-13; causes of irregularity in, 40; division of labor in, 21-23; long hours in, 39; nationalities in, 27; sex in, 28; short season in, 34, 35

Customs, opposed to female labor, 56; religious, 49, 50, social, 52

Cutters, 17 (note), 22, 27, 104, 142, 144, 214 (note), 222, 233, 244, 247, 250-252; become foremen, 27; early trade union activity confined to, 211; special, for orders, 12; unions among, 144, 213, 215, 225, 227, 228, 245, 248; wages of, 32, 79, 80, 85, 86, 95, 100, 101, 116, 172

Cutting, 61; done on premises, 14, 23; under control of Irish, 27
Cutting machinery, 22 (note), 25, 26, 77
Damages liquidated, 230, 231, 311, 317
Daniel, Dr. Annie S., quoted, 46 (note), 59, 138
Day wage system, 127
Day, eight hour, 237, 244, 246-248; agitation for, 142 (note), 243; working, 146, 184; forces bring about shorter, 143
Death-rate, among Jews, among Italians, 48 (note)
Decentralization, 51, 64 (note), 212, 221; effect on trade unions, 118, 119
Demoralization, due to lack of adjustment, 262
Density, for various wards, 147
Department of Buildings, 194
Department of Labor, growing coöperation with Inspectors, 165
Deposit, from isolated worker, 19
Depots, for distribution of second-hand clothing, 6
Depression, financial, 140
Designer, of clothing, 288
Designing, 61 (note); done by cutter, 22
Development, 260 (note), 265; capacity for, on the part of the Jew, 270; certain classes retarded in, 263
Diphtheria, number of cases of, 166
Disease, 54, 147 (note), 148, 166, 285; contagious, 156, 157, 165, 168, 193, 194, 199; eradicated through general advance of society, 206; Jewish immunity from, 48 (note); of the eye, common among home workers, 42; transmission of, through clothing, 207
Dismissal of men, Unions' attitude towards, 229
Displacement, 52, ibid. (note), 53
Dissension, among union leaders, 246 (note)
District councils, Number 1 (New York), 117 (note), 307, 312, agreement with manufacturers, 115, party to agreement, 217, sends letter to manufacturers, 226; of different cities, 215; various, 200
Districts, tenement house, 48 (note); uptown, movement to, 174
Division of labor, 11, 104, 110, 124, 159, 222, 274, 276, 284; see also Team system and Boston system; accentuated by invention of sewing machine, 15; eliminates skilled tailor, 69; in the various branches, 73-75; minute, 258 (note), required where cheap labor is employed, 8, 54, under Boston system, 70 (note); under contract system, 65; varied forms of, 21-25
Double-decker tenements, 151

Dumb-bell tenements, 151
Dwellings, private, remodeled for tenement purposes, 152
Dyche, J. A., quoted, 54 (note), 64 (note), 65 (note)

Education, 210, 254, 270, 286; lack of, among Jews, 47
Eliot, Miss Ada, quoted, 209 (note)
Emigrant, sweating of, 267
Emigration, for political reasons, 267
Employers, 242, 265, 278, 279, see also Manufacturers; attitude of, towards unions, 214, 221; penniless, 283 (note); responsibility of, for conditions, 170, 171; right of, to dismiss workmen, 235; Western, attitude of, towards unions, 247, 249
Employment, irregularity of, 221, 259, 285; causes for, 103; evils of, 186, 187; seasonal, 84; subsidiary, 97
England, 10, 25, 45, 46, 69, 76, 111, 112, 127, 205, 264, 274, 279, 288
English, 27, 214; influence on men's garments, 17; in New England mills, 266; to study American styles, 291
Entrepreneurs, 108, 195, 196, 205, 210, 272, 273, 275, 281, 283
Europe, persecution of Jews in, alluded to, 46
Expenditure, 34, 38, 92, discussion of, 173-179, 181-185, table of, 173; marginal, 102
Experiment, philanthropic, to raise wages of workers, 112

Factories, 69 (note), 222, 265, 275, 276, 277; coöperative, of workers, asks permission to do jobbing, 202; definition of, 274, 275; government, 8; in Russia, Jews employed in, 51; women engaged in, 17
Factory methods, 8, 10
Fair house, of the Consumers' League, 207
Federation of Labor, American, 216, 227
Fee, local union initiation, 219
Felling, 28, 66
Female labor, see Women
Finishers, 24, 25, 54, 66-68, 74, 75, 116, 136, 146; unions among, 67 (note), 181, 215; wages of, 32, 33, 34, 35, 36, 37, 70 (note), 79, 80, 87, 90, 317
Finishing, 23, 29, 69, 159, 163; by Italians in homes, 53
Fitters, 70 (note); unions among, 67 (note); wages, 317, 321
Food, expenditure for, 173-178, 180; products, decline in price of, 37
Foremen, 15, 22, 27, 29, 62, 63, 65, 119 (note), 275; favoritism of, 40; opposition to, on part of the unions, 118
France, 9, 17, 179, 268, 275

French, individualism, 214; influence on women's garments, 17

Fuel, expenditure for, 173, 175, 177, 178; for heating irons, 30, 224

Gauges in stitching, 76

General Executive Board, of the United Garment Workers of America, 200, 216-218, 220, 227, 229, 233, 234, 236, 238, 239; officers of, 216 (note); orders referendum vote, 245

Germans, 27, 28, 42, 46, 47 (note), 52, 53, 56, 58, 93, 138, 139; in family system, 24

Germany, export of clothing affected by tariff, 292 (note)

Gould, E. R. S., quoted, 94

Graham, Robert, quoted, 93

Griffin, Inspector, report of, 191

Hands, work to be distributed among, 311

Hearn, George A., advertisement, 17 (note)

Heat, in summer, exhaustion due to, 169, 175

Helpers, 75, 220, 221, 315; employed on cloaks, 74; wages of, 79

Hirsch, Baron de, donation of, 48 (note)

Hochstadter, Albert, testimony of, 51 (note); address of, 116

Homes, of workers, 41, 42

Homogeneity, favors trade unions, 214; lack of, among tailors, 211

Hood, Thomas, quoted, 29

Hospitals, referred to, 179

Hours of labor, 29, 38, 40, 41, 81-83, 99, 103, 112, 115, 125, 129-133, 135-146, table 142, 170, 174, 207, 217, 222, 226, 233-236, 238, 240, 245, 247, 250, 253, 254, 259, 268, 270, 312; in custom trade, 39; under the sweating system, 257

Hourvitch, Dr. Isaac A., quoted, 230 (note)

House of Lords, Investigation before, 111, 257, 258

Immigrants, 6, 8, 42, 47, 48, 49, 50-52, 55, 56, 106, 107, 109, 110, 250 (note), 266, 268, 269

Immigration, 27, 82, 108, 147, 212, 213, 251, 268; Jewish, 270, 294, magnitude of, 46; statistics of, for New York, 105

Income, of consumers of clothing, same as of manual laborers, 3; of workers, 282, influence of irregularity on, 186, in outside shops, 32; of heads of families, 172, 173; of small contractors, 111; piece system permits wide range in, 125; small proportion of, for miscellaneous expenses, 178; yearly, tables, cutters', pressers', basters', operators', finishers', 35, 83, 89 (note), 10, 120, 173, 174, 176-180, 186-188

Industries, certain seem to have bad conditions, 267; marginal, 261; modern, 273, characteristic features of, 272

Inspection, 58, 190, 193, 278; see also Tenement houses

Inspectors, 52 (note), 53, 57, 139, 155, 161, 163-165, 191, 192, 194, 209; discretionary power of, 166

Institutions, eleemosynary and corrective, 260

Insurance agents, many Jews become, 106

Insurance, fraternal, 182-185; industrial, 181, 185; old line, 181; trade union 181, 182, 185

Intelligence, industrial, important factor in determining conditions, 118

Interest, rate of, 188

Intermediary, see Middlemen

Interviews, as a source of wage statistics, 83, 85

Inventions, changes caused by the great, 264, 273

Irish, 27, 42, 46, 47 (note), 52, 53, 266

Italians, 48 (note), 54, 55, 58, 93, 147 (note), 172, 176-178, 193, 271; enter industry, 53; increase of, in clothing trade, 105

Jack of Newberry, referred to, 275

Jacketmakers, 140, 142, wages of, 89, 97, 100, 101; children's, 68, 75, 127, 171, 250 (note); unions of, 109, 146, 213, 222, 224; sailor. unions of, 223

Janitors, emulation among, 155 (note)

Jewish Colonization Society, 48 (note)

Jews, 7, 27, 43, 46-55, 57, 58, 69, 72, 93, 106, 107, 114, 124, 125, 128, 138, 139, 147, 155, 172, 173, 176-179, 185, 193, 271, 293; American, 294; English, 66, German, 45, Roumanian, 47 (note), Russian, 47, 48 (note), 105; their conception of trade unions, 213; engaged in commercial pursuits, 45; individualism of, 214; middlemen, 18 (note); make good use of leisure, 187

Jobbers, 7, 14, 20, 21; opposition to, 201

Jobbing, 45, 102; definition of, 200; prohibited to firms using label, 200-202

Jones, S., advertisement, 17 (note)

Josephi, President, statement of, 252

Journeymen, 10-12, 14, 15, 18

Kenny, Geo. J. & Bro., quoted, 94

Kingsley, Charles, 18, 257, 258, 269

Knights of Labor, 215, 227, 228

Krakow, Society of, 182

Labels, Consumers' League, 206, 207, 209, 210; trade union, 197-204, 206, 210, 247 (note), 251, 254, 255, decline in use of, 204 (note), 309, facsimile of, 304, 307

Labor, exploitation of, 265, 267, 268; organized, 83, 97, influence on long hours, 103

Laborer, casual, 261

Lancashire, 279 (note)

Land, influence of opening up new, 264

Landlords, 162, 167; responsibility for conditions, 160

Language, English, 54, 183, lack of knowledge of on part of Jew, 50; Italian, 54; Yiddish, 54, 183

Larger, President, report of, 225 (note)

Laws, factory, 249, cause decrease in female labor, 57; tenement house, cause a decrease in female labor, 57; tariff, 292 (note)

League, Consumers', 208-210, objects of, 206, 207, Massachusetts, 207

Lecky, W. E. H., quoted, 283

Lee, Joseph, 112, 114 (note), 258 (note)

LePlay, F., quoted, 279 (note)

Lewis, C. and T., advertisement of, 12 (note); Herman, membership in benefit societies, 184

Libraries, alluded to, 179

License, 168, 192, 193; changed from apartments to entire building, 167; law made effective by Consumers' League, 208; number granted, 164; revocation of, 165, table, 165 (note); to be taken out by home workers, 163; from inspector, 157, 159, 160

Life, social, of workers, 179, 185, 187

Light, artificial, 42, 171; expenditure for, 173, 175, 177, 178; in daytime often inadequate in tenements, 154

Lithuanians, 55, 171

Liveries, manufacture of, alluded to, 5

Lock-out, declared by Philadelphia Association, 237, 239

Lofts, 222; shops located in, 170

London, 11, 18 (note), 72, 111, 112, 257, 280, 288, 289 (note); East, 281

Louis XIV, period of, 275

Low administration, 153

Lunches in outside shops, 41

Machinery, 25, 27, 61 (note), 62, 65 (note), 75, 77, 78, 110, 123, 135, 136, 224, 272, 281, 284; influence of, on child labor, 58; introduction of, on labor, 262; saving brought about by, 26

Management, improved, influence of, on hours, 143

Manhattan Island, Germans, disappearance of in industry on, 53

Manifesto against task system, 128 (note)

Manufacturers, 14, 19, 20, 22, 24, 27, 45, 51 (note), 61-63, 65, 72, 73, 103, 104, 107, 109-120, 128 (note), 135, 166, 190 (note), 194, 195, 198, 201-203, 217, 226-228, 233 (note), 234, 237-239, 241, 243, 245, 246, 248-251, 253, 275; appeal to the public, 206; coöperation of, with authorities, for enforcing regulation, 161; large, decline of, in cloaks, 64; must be acquainted with the demands for raw material, 4; of laborers' clothing, 10; opposed to tagging, 162; opposition of to label, 204; required to keep a list of contractors, 160; small cloak, 283

Markers, duties of, 23

Market, 20, 103, 108, 262 (note), 273, 276; influence of second-hand clothing, on, 8; small master not able to judge, 21; sensitiveness of, 119; world, 273, 277

Massachusetts, 38, 39, 156, 159, 189-193, 207, 209

Mayhew, Henry, quoted, 280

Mayo-Smith, R. on placement, 52 (note)

Middlemen, 14, 18 (note), 52, 110, see Contractors

Miscellaneous expenses of living, 178, 179, 181-185

Mobility of labor and capital, 273

Monell, Inspector, quoted, 148 (note), 152 (note)

Montreal, contract system in mill in, 63 (note)

Movement of society, vertical, 264, 268

Museums, alluded to, 179

New England, 205, 290

New Jersey, laws relative to clothing in, 192

New Orleans distributing center for the South, 12

New York City, 6, 9, 12 (note), 17, 20, 24, 27, 28, 37, 41, 43, 45, 55, 56 (note), 57, 59 (note), 64 (note), 70, 82, 92, 105-107, 117, 129 (note), 135, 147, 157, 159, 161, 173, 174, 187, 189-193, 207, 208, 221 (note), 224, 233, 241, 246, 251, 253, 268, 286, 288, 289 (note), 290, 291, 292, 294, 303; rents in, 38; system of manufacturing clothing, 50

New York Herald, early advertisements in, 7, (note), 12, 16, 17

Nibbling of wages, 278

Nicoll, London tailor, referred to, 18, 280

Occupations in which Jews are found, 106, 107 (note)

Open-work, method of manufacture, 71, 72

Operating, definition of, 15 (note), 28, 69; carried on by members of tailor's family, 23

Operators, 15 (note), 16 (note), 24, 25, 29, 54, 55, 66-70, 74-76, 135, 136; in inside and outside shops, compared, 117 (note); women overtaxed as, 43; unions among, 67 (note), 181, 215, 220, 221, 224; **wages of**, 32-37, 79, 80, 84, 86-90, 95, 96, 99, 184, 316, 321

Opportunity, economic, created by dynamic changes, 263

Opposition, growing, to unions, 236

Order trade, see Custom trade

Organization, 285; among ladies' tailors fails to better conditions, 285; brings better wage conditions, 108

Output, restriction of, 241, 248, 251

Overalls, intensity of work in, 136; workers in, 69 (note)

Overcrowding, 43, 156, 166, 168; not serious, 42

Overseers, 79, 80; see also Foremen

Over-time, 84, 104, 184, 221-223; see also Home work; policy of the unions in regard to, 98

Pants, makers, 140, wages of, 88, 96, 100, 101, unions of, 109, 213; making, 16, 18, 24, 26-28, 33, 53, 56 (note), 57, 58, 74, 127, 137, 142, 146, 225; knee——makers, 140, 142, unions of, 109, 146, 213, 221-224, knee——making, 74, 126 (note), 171

Parks, small, referred to, 155

Parrisot, M., early establishment of, for manufacture of clothing, 9

Parry, President, referred to, 238, 248

Patterns, standard, 23

Pavements, asphalt, alluded to, 155

Pawn-shops, 62 (note); patronized to only a small extent, 188

Peel, Sir Robert, sickness of daughter, 285

Period, transition, many abuses, present during, 265

Permit, see License

Persecution, of Jews, 45, 46

Philadelphia, 215, 233, 236-238, 240, 241, 243, 245, 248, 251, 252, 303

Picard, A., quoted, 9, 10

Piece-rate, 31, 104; an intermediary takes goods from warehouse at, 51; straight, 132

Placement, 52 (note), 53; prevents glut of laborers, 106

Playgrounds, alluded to, 152

Plunkett, Inspector, report of, 191

Pocket tacker, in unbasted work, 75

Poland, Russian, 48 (note), 182

Poles, 107, 108

Population, shifting of, 266

Potter, Beatrice (Mrs. Sidney Webb), quoted, 71, 72, 111, 112, 126
Poverty, alluded to, 259
Power, electric, 77; foot, 43; steam, 76
Prague, manufactures uniforms for soldiers during Civil War, 9
Premises, of manufacturers, 61; of masters, 13
Press, labor, 54, 120, 212, 254
Press, the Philadelphia, quoted, 237
Pressers, 24, 25, 54, 55, 66, 70 (note), 71 (note), 75, 140, 142, 145; unions among, 67 (note), 181, 215, 221, 224; wages of, 33-36, 79, 80, 88-90, 96, 97, 100, 317, 321
Pressing, 23, 74; unfitted for women, 43
Pressing machines, 77
Price, a fair estimate of movement of retail prices, 92; general average, 36; readjustment of prices, for busy season causes strikes, 121; wholesale 37, 82, average, 90, table, 91
Processes, commercial, 4, 5, 8, 14, 27, 61, 272, 283; technical, 4, 5, 8-10, 14, 21, 27, 45, 61, 119, 272, 275, 283
Producer, blind, example of, 21
Production, 110; and consumption, close adjustment between, 108; capitalistic, 264, 272, 277; stock, decline of, 102
Profits, of custom tailor, 11
Pryor, Dr. John H., quoted, 193 (note)
Public opinion, 180, 189 (note), 195, 205, 206; influence of Consumers' League on, 208

Referendum vote, 218, 245, 254
Regulation, 58, 104, 144, 148-171, 178, 189-210, 222, 250, 278, 285; see also Unions and Inspections; demands for uniformity in, 194, 195; growing out of advance of society, 204, 205; influenced by various factors, 272; little attention to, on the part of the city, 42; national, 190, 192; state, eliminates irresponsible contractor, 114, shuts out low grade immigrants, 109
Reichers, Chas. F., quoted, 57 (note), 59, 113, 138
Reichstag, mentioned, 280, 292 (note)
Religion, as bond of unions, 182, 183
Rent, 38, 39, 83, 173-175, 178, 184, 290; movement of, 92-95
Resolutions of the National Clothiers' Association, 250; preamble, 241, 242, 244, 252
Revolution, industrial, made possible raw material, 4
Risks, 273, 275, 276, 277, 279, 281
Rochester, 56 (note), 233, 234, 239-241, 243, 248, 289
Routine in factory, prevents abuses, 279

Rules, shop, 307
Russia, 46, 47, 51, 182
Russian immigrants, 46, 47
Sanitary Union, Tenth Ward, 152
Sanitation, 149-171; little attention to, on the part of the city, 42
Savings for old age, 180, 188
Scarlet Fever, number of cases of, 166
Schoenfeld, Mayer, quoted, 133; address of, 305
Scotch, in New England mills, 266
Season, busy, 32, 41, 64, 84, 98-102, 104, 117 (note), 121, 128, 129, 132, 134, 135, 139, 140, 145, 146, 186-188, 212, 221, 225, 226, 251; causes long hours, 103; dull, 32, 35 (note), 65, 74, 98, 104, 117 (note), 120, 128, 129, 131, 132 (note), 134, 140, 181, 186-188, 212, 225, 251; attempts to overcome, 103; in custom trade, 11, (note); length of, 34; of mourning, influence on hours, 40; varying, 41
Secrecy not characteristic of unions in clothing industry, 254
Secretary, general, of United Garment Workers of America, 130, 216, 218, 219, 234-242, 246 (note)
Senior, N. W., quoted, 6
Serging machines, 78
Sewell, Hannah, quoted, 59 (note)
Sewing machines, 42, (note), 18, 19, 67, 70 (note), 220; division of labor accentuated by, 15-17, 23; early form of, 25; hours shortened by, 40; methods revolutionized by invention of, 12; mitigated evil of eye disease, 43 (note); modern, 75-77, 135, 136; time saved by, 26
Shopkeepers, small, many Jews become, 106
Shop chairman, duties of, 308
Shops, cloak, 64; closed 120, 241, 243, 252; contractors, 13, 15, 18, 57, 61, 62 (note), 63, 64, 66, 67, 70, 112, 117 (note), 120, 138, 148, 170, 171, 201, 212; coöperative, 112; cutters', 252; family, 138, disappearance of, 160; increased size of, brings about better enforcement of laws, 144, does away with home work, 104; inside, 13, 18, 23, 24, 27, 28, 30, 31, 41, 43, 50, 51, 55, 62, 64, 65, 69 (note), 75, 116 (note), 117, 118, 145, 146, 163, 171, 200, 250, 251, hours in, 120, 139, women in, 16, 17; non-union, 249, 252; open, 120, 211 (note), 237, 240, 243, 245, 246, 249, 250, 252, agitation over, 235; outside, 23, 24, 28, 30, 32, 56, 69 (note), 116 (note), 117, 120, 124, 127, 146, 163, 251, and piece system, 124, women in, 16; small, 62 (note), 63, 67, 119, 168, advantages of, over the large, 64, give opportunity for the employment of women and children, 57 (note); sweaters, 257; tailor, 159; tenement house, 59, 155, 158, 159, decline in number of, 160; union, 237, 251
Sikes, J. H., advertisement, 12

Slop product, referred to, 7

Small-pox, number of cases of, 166

Socialism, 213

Socialization of industry, 277

Societies, Arbeiter Ring, 183; Avis, 184; Berith Abraham, 183, 184; Chomaker, 182, 183; Krakow, 182; Schuetzen, 183, 184; Warsaw, 182; Young Men's Aid, 183

Society, 260, 268; ideals of, 205; to what extent responsible for sweating, 259

South, market for second-hand clothing, 6; conditions in, compared with New England conditions, 205

Standard, of comfort, 2; of decency, 2; of living, 3, 48, 132, 180, 199, 206, 255, 260, 268, 284, 286, of Italians, lower than of Jews, 54, 55, of Jews, low, 47

Standardization, process of, 5, 8, 9

Stiebeling, Dr. George C., report of, 156

St. Louis, 241, 246; distributing center for the West, 12

Strikes, 51 (note), 52 (note), 54, 68 (note), 102 (note), 112, 120, 133, 134, 140, 141, 142 (note), 144 (note), 145, 146, 181, 211 (note), 213, 216-218, 224, 225, 228, 233, (note), 234, 237, 239, 245, 248, 250 (note), 252, 253, 292, 307,; general, called, 246; nature of, 226; sensational character of, 224; shop, 229; sympathy, 316

Style, cause of irregularity of, 102, change in, 261; important factor, 4

Sub-contract, opposed by Consumers' League, 207

Subcontracting, referred to, 111

Subcontractors, 19, 45, 52, 111

Supervision, less need for, under piece system, 123, 124; possible under contract system, 52

Sweatshops, 199, 202, 243, 305; hours of work in, 139, 156; tenement, 157

Sweaters, 111, 113, 256

Sweating, 249, 257, 261, 262, 265, 267-271, 283 (note), 284, 286; characteristic features of, 259; origin of term, 257; system, 189, 190 (note), 257, 258, (note), 259 (note), 306

Syracuse, district council, 215

System, of payment, piece, 122-137, 225 (note), 226: task, 129-138, 184, 311, definition of, 127, 128; team, 32 (note), 65-69, 72, 74 (note), 79, 99, 127, 128, 276; modified team, 67, 69, 73-75, 128 (note), compared with Boston system, 72; of week work, 224, Boston, 69, 70, 72, 73, 137, 276; employs both piece and time systems, 127; transition, 276; competitive, 258 (note); contract, 50, 110-121, 130, 212, 214, 226, 258, 276, 305, advantages of, 62-65, brings about differentiation between commercial and technical processes, 61, elasticity of, 104, Jews best fitted for, 51, 52, in reference to wages and employment, 110; inside, 63 (note), 65 (note); determined by grade of goods, 73 (note); domestic, 273, 277 (note); factory, 271, 274-279, 282; family, 23, 24, 50, 51, 55, 56, 82, 83, 124, child labor under, 58, 59, wages, under, 79, 81; handicraft, attempt to make more elastic, 18; inside, 15, 50; outside, 15, 117

Tagging, by Board of Health, 157, 160, 162-164, 191, 197

Tailors, 3, 15, 21, 22 (note), 27, 32, 40, 69, 74, 138; coat, 99, manifesto of, 305, strike of, 145; custom, 72, 103, early employed by upper classes, 3; found in early retinue, 3 (note), 11; opposed to piece system, 124; displaced by green immigrants, 107; from England, 10, 70; Jewish, 45; journeymen, 19; ladies', 42 (note), 285; master, 11, 14, 15, 18, 21; merchant, 10; skilled, eliminated, in pants and vests, 25, present in family system, 24, 50; the small, takes up clothing industry, sells to jobbers, 20

Task, size of, 131-136; maximum, in coats, 135, minimum, 135

Team unity, see Section work

Tenement house, 39 (note), 93, 94, 149-166, 175, 177, 189, 191, see also Inspection; act, 67; area of lot, 149 (note); classes of, 148; increase overcrowding, 43; manufacture in, 192, 193; rent of, 38 (note); rear, 148, 152; to be inspected every six months, 167

Thurber, F. B., quoted, 37

Toilets, 43, 153, 154, 169

Tracy, Dr., quoted, 193 (note)

Trade, retail, 14; wholesale, 14, 23

Trades, sweating, 256

Tradition among coat tailors against the factories, 17, 18

Trimmers, 17 (note), 244, 245; wages of, 79, 80

Trimming, referred to, 23

Trimming maker, 75

Trousers 13 (note), 16 (note), 21; made largely by women, 16

Trust, power of a, referred to, 117

Tuberculosis, 193 (note), 194

Types, of individuals, 5

Typhoid fever, number of cases of, 166

Unemployed, restrictions on the part of society increase number of, 286

Unfair list, 201

Uniforms, manufacture of, influences clothing industry, 5, 8, 9

Unions, 54 (note), 57, 70, 83-85, 89, 98, 102, 103, 112-115, 118-121, 123-126, 127 (note), 128, 133, 135, 137, 139-146, 172, 174, 178, 181-185

198, 201-204, 210, 211-255; appeal to selfish interests of consumer, 199; centralization of authority of, 218; formation of, in various branches, 109, effect of, on regulation, 196, 197; influence of, on members, 254; local, 68 (note), 69 (note); obstacles to growth of, 211, 212; prevent lower grades of labor from entering industry, 108; Amalgamated Association of Cutters and Trimmers, 144, 213, 215, 225, 227, 245; Amalgamated Society of Tailors, 127; Childrens' Jacketmakers, 109, 146, 213, 222, 224; Cloakmakers, 148, 213, 221, 222; Coatmakers, 109, 146; Coat Tailors', 223; International Ladies' Garment Makers', 221; Knee Pants Makers, 109, 146, 213, 221-224; Overcoat and Sackcoat Makers', 222; Pants Makers', Number 8, 109, 146, 213, 229; Progressive Tailors', 138, 211 (note); Sailor Jacket Makers', 221, 223; The Protective Coat Tailors' and Pressers', Local Number 55, 181, 184, 215, 231; United Brotherhood of Tailors, 67 (note), 113, 139, 215-217, 220, 223, 224, 228, 239, 251; United Tailors', 130; Vest [Makers'], 221, 223

United Garment Workers of America, 68 (note), 69 (note), 113, 115, 128 (note), 130, 133, 134 (note), 198-201, 215-218, 217, 220, 224, 231, 233, 234, 236; liberal policy of, towards entrance to trade, 219; strife with Knights of Labor, 227, 228

United States, masses engaged in agriculture, 9; immigration to, 105

Utica, clothing industry in, 56 (note)

Valley, Mississippi, referred to, 264

Veiller, Lawrence, quoted, 153

Ventilation, bad, 170; of inside shops, 43; of tenement houses, 151, 169

Vest, makers unions of, 146, 224, wages of, 88, 96, 100, 101, 142; making, 16, 18, 24, 26-28, 33, 53, 56 (note), 57, 58, 74, 127, 146

Vienna, clothing made in, 9

Wade, Chief, quoted, 291

Wages, 11, 18 (note), 29, 56, 61, 62, 63 (note), 98-102, 106, 108-110, 112, 113, 117 (note), 118, 120, 121, 143, 179, 180, 184, 186, 207, 217, 226, 236-241, 243-245, 250, 251, 253, 254, 312, 316, 317, 321; average weekly, 33, 34, 38; during dull season, 104; failure of contractor to pay, 115, 116; general movement of, 105; low, 259, 268; maximum, attitude of unions, 135; minimum, attitude of unions, 135; rate of, 235; money, 30-34; 79-90; real, 31, 36, 39, 92, 95-97, decline in, 37; strike caused by reduction of, 218; systems of payment of, piece, 122-137, time, 31, 122-137, task, 127-137; union scale, 84; basters, 32-37, 79, 80, 87, 89, 95, 96, 99, 316, 321; bushelers, 80, 87, 89, 317, 321; coat stitchers, 321; cutters, 32, 79, 80, 85, 86, 95, 100, 101, 116, 172; finishers, 32-37, 70 (note), 79, 80, 87, 90, 317; fitters, 321; lining makers, 321; operators, 32-37, 79, 80, 84, 86-90, 95, 96, 99, 184, 316, 321; pocket tackers,

321; pressers, 33-36, 79, 80, 86-90, 96, 97, 100, 317, 321; sleeve makers, 321; trimming makers, 321

Waistcoats, 13 (note), 21; made largely by women, 16

Warehouses, 19, 22, 66, 277; establishment of, by manufacturer, 15; time lost in going to and from, 51

Waring, Colonel, referred to, 155

Warner, Hon. John DeWitt, quoted, 59, 60

Warsaw, Society of, 182

Water, provisions for, in tenements, 153; rates, included in rent, 174

Wearing apparel, ready-made, use of, increased by invention of sewing machine, 12

Weavers, 12, 17; hand, 284; loom, 281, 284

Webb, Sidney and Beatrice, quoted, 126

West, The, referred to, 6, 7, 12

White, Henry, testimony, 129 (note); referred to, 253

Willett, Mrs. Mabel Hurd, quoted, 58, 116, 129 (note), 131, 166

Windows, regulations concerning, 15

Women, 43, 74, 75, 78, 82, 108, 116, 127, 131, 136, 156, 163, 172, 198, 211, 250, 279, 282; hours of work for, 41, 139, 144; in custom trade, 13; in various branches, 17, 27, 28, 74; isolated, 29; Italians, 53, 54; Jewesses, 49; Jewish prejudice against, 50; percentage of, 55-59; two classes of operators, 16; under various systems, 19, 24, 28, 69, 70; wages of, 32-37, 79, 80, 87-90, 96, 97, 100, 101, 130

Women's garments, 17, 22, 28, 53 (note), 212, 222; see Cloak trade

Woolfolk, A. S., testimony of, 93

Work, basted, workers engaged in, 75; unbasted, workers engaged in, 75

Work, factory, 209; home, 20, 29, 31, 34, 40-42, 50, 51, 53-55, 57, 58, 67, 104, 116, 142 (note), 192-194, 200, 201, 209, 212, 223, 250, 251, 258, 282; in the custom trade, 13, 15, 16, 18: length of hours in, 138, 139, opposition of unions to, 222; intensity of, 98, 122, 123, 125, 129-133, 136; outside, 41; piece, 224, 225; task, 81 (note), 82, 224, see also Task and Team systems; tenement house, decline of, 161; week, 224, 225, 314

Workers, Jewish home, 155; outside, paid a piece-rate, 31, permitted, 166, prohibited, 167; outside the family, brought in, 20 (note), not permitted, 158; second, 67, 68, see also Team system, modified; task, 132 (note)

Workrooms, ill-ventilated, 41

Workshops, 275, early, 8; government, 8, factory methods in, 8; necessity that workers live near, 174

Wright, Carroll D., quoted, 38, 39

Year, working, length of, 99, 100, 101, increase of, 102

York, England, compared with New York, U. S. A., 268

THE
UNIVERSITY OF MISSOURI
STUDIES

EDITED BY
FRANK THILLY
Professor of Philosophy

VOLUME II

PUBLISHED BY THE
UNIVERSITY OF MISSOURI

Press of E. W. Stephens
COLUMBIA, MO.

CONTENTS OF VOLUME II

NUMBER		PAGE
1.	Ithaca or Leucas? by WILLIAM GWATHMEY MANLY, A. M., *Professor of Greek Language and Literature.*	1
2.	Public Relief and Private Charity in England, by CHARLES A. ELLWOOD, Ph. D., *Professor of Sociology.*	53
3.	The Process of Inductive Inference, by FRANK THILLY, Ph. D., *Professor of Philosophy.*	149
4.	Regeneration of Crayfish Appendages, by MARY ISABELLE STEELE, M. A., *Sometime Fellow in Zoology*	189
5.	The Spermatogenesis of Anax Junius, by CAROLINE MCGILL, *Fellow in Zoology*	236

Volume I   SOCIAL SCIENCE SERIES

UNIVERSITY OF MISSOURI STUDIES

THE CLOTHING INDUSTRY IN NEW YORK

BY

JESSE ELIPHALET POPE
Professor of Economics and Finance

PUBLISHED BY THE
UNIVERSITY OF MISSOURI
September 1905

PRICE, $1.25

UNIVERSITY OF MISSOURI STUDIES

VOLUME I

NUMBER 1

Contributions to a Psychological Theory of Music, by MAX MEYER, Ph. D., Professor of Experimental Psychology. pp. vi, 80. 75 cents.

NUMBER 2

Origin of the Covenant Vivien, by RAYMOND WEEKS, Ph. D., Professor of Romance Languages. pp. viii, 64. 75 cents.

NUMBER 3

The Evolution of the Northern Part of the Lowlands of Southeast Missouri, by C. F. MARBUT, A. M., Professor of Geology. pp. viii, 63. $1.25.

NUMBER 4

Eileithyia, by PAUL V. C. BAUR, Ph. D., Acting Professor of Classical Archaeology. pp. vi, 90. $1.00.

NUMBER 5

The Right of Sanctuary in England, by NORMAN MACLAREN TRENHOLME, Ph. D., Assistant Professor of History. pp. viii, 106. 75 cents.

UNIVERSITY OF MISSOURI STUDIES

VOLUME II

Number 1
Ithaca or Leucas? by William Gwathmey Manly, A. M., Professor of Greek Language and Literature. pp. vi, 52. $1.00.

Number 2
Public Relief and Private Charity in England, by Charles A. Ellwood, Ph. D., Professor of Sociology. pp. viii, 96. 75 cents.

Number 3
The Process of Inductive Inference, by Frank Thilly, Ph. D., Professor of Philosophy. pp. v, 40. 35 cents.

Number 4
Regeneration of Crayfish Appendages, by Mary I. Steele, M. A. pp. viii, 47. 75 cents.

Number 5
The Spermatogenesis of Anax Junius, by Caroline McGill. pp. viii, 15. 75 cents.

VOLUME I SCIENCE SERIES

Number 1
Topography of the Thorax and Abdomen, by Peter Potter, M. A., M. D., Associate Professor of Anatomy, St. Louis University. pp. vii, 142. $1.75.

Number 2
The Flora of Columbia and Vicinity, by Francis Rotter Daniels, Ph. D. *In the Press.*

VOLUME I SOCIAL SCIENCE SERIES

The Clothing Industry in New York, by Jesse E. Pope, Ph. D., Professor of Economics and Finance. pp. xviii, 340.

THE UNIVERSITY OF MICHIGAN
GRADUATE LIBRARY

DATE DUE

JAN 05 1998

DO NOT REMOVE
OR
MUTILATE CARD